VIETNAM
I'M GOING!

VIETNAM

I'm Going!

Letters from a Young WAC in Vietnam to her Mother

Linda S. Earls

LINDA S. EARLS

Library of Congress Control Number:		2012908228
ISBN:	Hardcover	978-1-4771-0894-9
	Softcover	978-1-4771-0893-2
	Ebook	978-1-4771-0895-6

To order additional copies of this book, contact:
Xlibris Corporation
1-888-795-4274
www.Xlibris.com
Orders@Xlibris.com
114489

Contents

This book is dedicated to my mother who gave me the freedom to be myself; to choose my career and to live the Army motto at that time: "Be all you can be". Because of her love and caring through my life and her support of my career I was able to go off into a world of adventure and be very successful.

I wish to thank my aunt, Florence Henebry for her encouragement and guidance in getting started with this book. Also thank you to my friend, Deloris Abrassart for her help in proofreading more times than we could count, helping to locate photos and constant nagging at me to get it done.

Prologue

To fully understand this book, one must have a brief overview of my background. I grew up in a household which consisted of my grandparents and mother. We lived on a farm in the country and were quite isolated from neighbors and towns. I went through the eighth grade in a two room country school about 5 miles from home. In order for me to attend high school, something no one else in my immediate family had done, my grandfather had to work a deal between two school districts. The district we lived in had no bus on our side of the river so I needed to go to the school which did run a bus near our house. He was successful and I graduated from Westville High School in Westville, Illinois in May 1964.

The Cuban Missile Crisis happened in my sophomore year in high school. Some of the teachers were in the Army Reserves and I heard them talking about it and wondering if they would be called to active duty. That was when the seed was planted for me to join the Army. My mother and I went to the post office and I found a pamphlet about the Women's Army Corps (WAC). I read that pamphlet hundreds of times and I knew that was what I wanted. In my senior year a new teacher came to the school, a retired Navy man. I was in one of his classes and he talked about his life in the Navy and encouraged me when he found out I wanted to join the Army. He brought a WAC recruiter to school to talk to me. I visited the recruiters in the local town many times. In May of my senior year my mother and I went on a train to Chicago so I could be tested and take the physical. I graduated from high school knowing I would join the WAC in the fall.

Because I lived so far from school I was unable to participate in after school activities, go to games, or do anything that prevented me from riding the bus home. My life consisted of going to school and being at home with occasional trips to town or to visit relatives. The few times I had been away from home overnight I was with relatives. I loved being at home and being outdoors. I helped with the farm chores as my age permitted. My mother and I took walks in the woods through all kinds of weather, in summer and winter. We were very close and stayed that way no matter how far from her I traveled in later years. My teachers were very surprised when I joined the Army because they saw me as a quiet shy stay-at-home girl. None of them knew what was inside; the determination to be someone special, to do exciting and new things.

I left home for the Army on 31 August, 1964 flying from Chicago to Fort McClellan, Alabama for basic training. I did well in basic and enjoyed it. My mother and cousin came to Alabama to see me graduate and I was so proud when my company marched in front of the reviewing stand. From there I went to Fort Knox, Kentucky for schooling to become a clerk typist. I went home on leave for Christmas 1964 and in January 1965 flew to El Paso, Texas for my first permanent duty station, William Beaumont General Hospital. I served my first enlistment (3 years) there. During those three years I was hearing about Vietnam and starting to want to go. I knew I was a career soldier and I felt I just had to serve in Vietnam.

I tried to re-enlist for Vietnam but couldn't because there were no openings in my military occupational specialty (MOS) at that time. So I re-enlisted for Oakland Army Base which was as close as I could get. After three months in Oakland, the minimum time required, I requested to be reassigned to Vietnam. On 12 March, 1968 I received notification that I was on orders to report for duty in the Republic of Vietnam (RVN). My report date was 1 May 1968. I was so excited to be going. I was 21, had the attitude of most that age, that nothing could hurt me, and I was doing something that was a great adventure. I went home on leave and then flew back to California to Travis Air Force Base.

The first of my "Vietnam" letters to my mother was written on the day I was told I was going. I'm able to write an account of my year in Vietnam because my mother kept all the letters I wrote to her. I wrote in great detail and quite often. I have decided to write these letters into a book because they are history and should not end with me. Hopefully someone will find something of interest whether for educational purposes or just for the story.

I called my mother by her first name, Ruby. She called me by my childhood nickname "Susie". Hence, all my letters began "Dear Ruby" and were signed "Susie". My grandmother was "Mom". Aggie was a neighbor and dear friend.

CHAPTER I

"I'm going!"

12 Mar 68

Dear Ruby,

My letter is way off schedule again but I finally have some news for you. The First Sergeant called and woke me up this morning. When I answered the phone she said, "This is 1SG Spyker. Are you packed?" I was still half asleep but that sure woke me up. Then she went on to tell me that the Sixth Army Area WAC Staff Advisor had just called her and said I have been alerted for RVN and will leave in April. The paperwork didn't come yet so there are no more details. I hope it's not long till I get my orders and port call. You wouldn't believe how happy I am. I can hardly believe it yet. Last night I dreamed again that I was over there and this morning I woke up to find that I'm going. As soon as I get the details I'll tell you. If they give me a leave, I'll take it, if not, I'll be happy to go anyway. I do hope I get a leave though. Everybody else is happy because they're getting married and look at me—on cloud nine because I finally got orders. I'll be glad when I get them on paper. Barbara and Grace aren't too happy but they wanted me to go because I want to so much. Just yesterday evening Barbara and I were at the beach in Alameda watching jets take off into the sunset and it was so beautiful. I wondered when I'd ever get to go. Just imagine, 22 hours on a big beautiful bird over 8,000 miles of ocean. I can't wait to get going. Start finding more storage space because almost everything I have here is coming home.

Well I guess I'll close for now. This is the happiest I've been in a long time.

Lots of love,
Susie

15 Mar 68

Dear Ruby,

I got some more information so I'll write it to you today. I hope to call you Sunday but since I'm working, I may not get a chance to. Personnel called me in yesterday to get the information about a leave that they need to type up my orders. I'm taking 15 days. My port call right now is 30 April and my leave should start the 13th. I start to clear post the 8th which means I don't have too many more days left to work. My port call might be moved to an earlier date and if so my leave would start earlier. I wish something would change by even one day because I just looked on the calendar and I see Easter is the 14th.

I want to drive my car home. Do you think I could sell it there? Everybody here agrees that I could probably get a better price for it there than here and I want to bring my things home myself instead of shipping them. There is no reason why I can't make it easily via El Paso, since I wanted to be there again before I go. It takes 2 days from here to there and I'd like to spend a day there. Then it takes two more days to get home. The worst part would be crossing the desert in Nevada but it would be on the beginning of the trip. I can fly back to the Oakland airport. I clear post and pack before I go on leave so when I get back I'll be ready to go. Keep in mind that these dates could change. I'll get my orders next week and then everything will be definite.

I'm assigned to WAC Company, Special Troops, APO SF 96375 which is in Long Binh, SVN. That's where I wanted to go because it isn't in a city and the girls there wear fatigues. I can't find it on any map.

There are 12 other WACs on the Department of the Army message that came, all from other posts with the same port call date as mine. I don't know if they'll come through here (Oakland Army Base) or not. Some just go straight to Travis Air Force Base.

At the very most I have 29 days left before I can go on leave. I could have taken a longer one but I didn't want to be completely in the hole.

I guess by now you have my letter saying I'm on orders and I bet you're wondering if I'm coming home. That's all for this time.

All my love,
Susie

Note: The remainder of March and part of April were spent doing all the things I wanted to do before I left California. I drove my car home and was able to sell it. I flew from Danville, Illinois to Chicago then to San Francisco. Friends met me there and took me to Travis Air Force Base for the flight to Vietnam.

CHAPTER II

MAY 1968

Long Binh, SVN
0730

2 May 68

Dear Ruby,

I don't know where to start first and I may never get everything said.
The time here is 9 hours ahead of you so to make it easy, just add 10
hours to whatever it is there. I woke up at 0630 so I got up. I don't think
we have to do much today except get our field gear issued. They gave us
helmets last night in case of an alert. We have a fan in our room and it
was on all night so that was all I could hear except the choppers. They
sound like they're coming right in the barracks. I hear a distant rumble
like thunder this morning so it must be the sound of war.

We flew up the center of Vietnam on approach to Bein Hoa. The pilot
told us he had to make a short approach because he didn't want to get
too low. Men started handling our luggage there so that was no problem.
We processed with the officers till we came to the WAC Detachment.
You could never imagine what this place looks like. Everything is dirty
either with mud, dust or bugs or all three. It was 86 degrees when we
landed and is it ever hot. Everything is sticky and wet. My hair is sure
curly now. Since I'm an E-5 I have a room with a roommate. She's pretty
nice-her last name is Murphy and she goes home in July. She took her
R&R in Australia and has a stuffed koala bear. There are 3 dogs here that
I've seen so far, 2 poodles and a short haired tan and white Pekingese.
He sure is cute.

There are about 3 refrigerators here and an ice machine with cold
cans of Coke. The water sure tastes funny and it looks kind of brown. At
least we can have ice water.

My room is real small with bunk beds. I have the top one. There is a mosquito net over it and I have a beautiful bed spread. It's really part of field equipment (a poncho liner) to use when it's raining but it fits the bed. It's the jungle camouflage colors. We have a dresser and tall cupboard/closet between us, a low table and two chairs. It's very crowded but I guess I'll get used to it. There is a large fenced in area around the WAC barracks and they have a movie screen and some sports facilities. One of the dogs sat beside me for awhile. There is one American radio station, AFVN (Armed Forces Vietnam). They play some songs I heard at Oakland.

A girl just came and talked to me for awhile, I think she's Puerto Rican. She seems to be nice and friendly. She's been in longer than me and she's an E-5 also. She knew a girl that I knew at Oakland. Also, remember me telling you about a girl named Marilyn Roth that was listed on my DA message and that I remembered somebody from William Beaumont named that? Well, I met her last night and it's the same one. She's an E-4. It is a small world.

The Vietnamese women are in here cleaning. The security guard at the gate lets them in.

We came here from Bein Hoa in a bus convoy and went through some villages and saw some bombed buildings. It looks worse than old Mexico. We were kind of scared when we landed but I feel pretty safe now. They have a bunker right beside our barracks and the whole area is always guarded.

I sure wish Pat or Barbara were here. I suppose it won't be long till I find friends here. These girls really look sharp in their fatigues.

I feel real good this morning after 10,500 miles. When I woke up I could hardly believe I wasn't just dreaming I'm here. I guess it couldn't have been so hot anyplace else. This paper is damp. Everybody here has a beautiful sun tan.

Well I think I'll quit for now. I wanted to get one letter written before I get busy.

Lots of love,
Susie

Long Binh SVN
1300

4 May 68

Dear Ruby,

I'm sitting here with nothing to do right now so I'll start a letter to you. Yesterday we didn't do anything except sit around again but this morning at 0800 we went to the orderly room and started getting our orientation from the lst Sgt and CO. They are both so nice but 1st Sgt Crawford will be leaving soon. CPT Murphy is young and nice. SFC Benson, who knows SGT Wanty, leaves real soon too. One of the girls that came here with me is from Rockford, IL and enlisted in Chicago. SFC Benson is going to be on some kind of a program on WGN broadcasting from RVN for the 20th WAC Anniversary and she said she would mention our names. The anniversary is 14 May but I have no idea when she'll be on.

This afternoon we go to personnel and probably will get our job assignments. I sure hope I get a good one. We eat at the 24th Evac Hospital mess hall except for the evening meal at the USARV mess hall. So far the food is good but of course it's crowded. They have the same food as every other Army mess hall so there's nothing new to tell you there.

These Vietnamese people are really something. They swarm over the barracks in the morning picking up clothes to wash and boots to shine and they talk constantly. Yesterday I wasn't awake when she (Mamason) came in and she started talking to somebody outside and woke me up. That was a strange feeling. The ones I've seen are real nice but I want to be able to say something to them and they understand very little. Their language is just a mess of sounds run together to me. We had to buy our caps and have our patches sewn on by them.

So far I feel real good except for being lazy from the heat. They keep telling us to be careful and to tell them the minute we think we're sick. I've taken one malaria pill and drank all this water and it didn't hurt me. I hope I stay so lucky. One girl has a rash all over and had to go to Japan because of an allergy to this sun. 1stSgt Crawford says it's been over 100 degrees every day that we've been here. No wonder we're hot. She's going to Fort Sheridan so that will be quite a change.

These fatigues are no hotter than any other clothes and even the boots and wool socks aren't bad. I'm going to love being able to wear fatigues to work every day. Once I go to work I'll never know when I'll be off. I can't go off post at all and I have to be back in the company area by 2230 every night.

The alert system we have will probably sound complicated to you, it did to me. These are all different conditions—white is when everything is normal; gray is when there might be some action; yellow means an attack is likely (get in fatigues with field gear) and red means we're under attack, head for the bunkers. 1st Sgt Crawford said that 3 weeks ago an ammo dump close to here was hit at 0100 and the blast threw everybody out of bed and really tore up the rooms. All the girls automatically got in fatigues and crawled under their beds. I don't exactly like the idea of that happening again but it probably will and I'll do the same as everybody else.

Well I'll close for this time. Write to me often and don't worry about me. At least I'm over here now and you know how bad I wanted to come.

Lots of love,
Susie

5 May 68

Dear Ruby,

You're going to get a lot of mail this week when all these letters get there. Yesterday afternoon we didn't get anything done. We went back to personnel and they never did anything except sent us back home. This morning we went back and they finally got us job assignments. It looks like mine will be pretty good but of course I can't tell from the first impression. I'll be working for a LTC in the Comptroller's office. There is a major, SGT, SP4 and 2 or 3 civilians in the office and there is an E-6 slot. Believe it or not it is my MOS: 71L. It will be mostly typing Army correspondence which I know almost nothing about but I'm sure it won't take me long to learn. The LTC and Major are both friendly and the SGT who will train me is nice too. I'm lucky enough to get one of the few new air conditioned buildings too. It's a long way from the WAC Detachment so I'll definitely have to ride a bus both ways. I hate that. These roads are almost all dirt. There are a few American cars around and there is one white Rambler American. The rest are Chevrolets.

We had to fill out all kinds of forms this morning, among them the post we want to return to. I put Fort Sam Houston, Texas. Also, you are my beneficiary for $10,000 lump sum, and in case I'm wounded, you wouldn't be notified unless it was serious. Those are all standard questions for everyone who comes here. I got my Vietnam Service Medal this morning too. All it takes is to put your foot on the ground over here to get that one. It takes 6 months service to get the other one, (Vietnam Campaign Medal). I didn't go through finance yet. Anyway, there is a new ruling on MPCs (Military Payment Certificates) and we can only put $200 per month in the Soldier's Deposit. If so, I think I'll have an allotment sent to you each month. You can keep it till my debt is paid off then start putting it in my account. Until I start to buy some of the main things I want, I won't be spending hardly any money except the monthly $9 for my maid. There is just nothing to buy. If I make $350 or over, I'll probably make the allotment $100. At that rate, you'll be paid back before you know it.

Last night the VC (Viet Cong) hit Saigon and Bien Hoa pretty hard. The road between here and there is closed and that's the one we came in on. A girl was supposed to go on R&R to Hawaii to meet her family this morning and she couldn't get out of here. From where I work, the window looks out over a valley and the guys said quite often they watch planes dropping bombs over it. It's a beautiful area, all green with grass and trees and I thought yesterday it would be a nice place to go. I changed my mind. It's just hard to believe even with all the noise that I'm right in the middle of a war zone. This is the first time in history that a WAC Detachment has been in the middle of a combat zone. In other wars they have been behind the lines but there aren't any lines here.

I sure wish you could see me in fatigues, boots and hat too. They are so comfortable and look so sharp. We can wear rank pins on our hats too so I'll get one as soon as I have a chance.

I got these envelopes at the PX. I hope they don't stick together. They're in a self sealing plastic sack so maybe they won't. The USARV PX is pretty nice and so is the mess hall up there. They are fairly close to where I'll be working so I'll go to them instead of the Long Binh ones.

The only way to tell it's Sunday here is by the church music on the radio early in the morning.

We stand reveille at 0630 every morning and work from 0730-1930. The sergeant said I would probably get off before that most of the time. I don't know how long the lunch break is. I'll find out tomorrow.

I've heard bombing all day and it's pretty loud. Usually they quit during the day but I guess our guys are after the VC from last night.

I'll quit for now. I hope I get a letter from you soon.

Lots of love,
Susie

Long Binh, SVN

8 May 68

Dear Ruby,

I was so glad to get your letter yesterday. I thought it was about time I got one. I get all my mail in the evening because we pick it up in the orderly room and I don't have time to come home at noon. You mailed it Thursday and I got it Tuesday evening here. I don't care what day you mail letters just so you mail them often. I can't even begin to predict when I'll send yours. I can't remember what day I have mailed the last one. Every day is the same.

I get up around 0530-0545, stand reveille at 0630 and this morning I caught the bus right afterward and went to breakfast. I guess I should start going every day because I don't eat at night. As soon as I can get to a PX, I'm going to get some cans of beans, fruit, etc. to have here. If I went to chow in the evening I never would get home. I get here at 1840 now but when I start working the extra hour I'll get home at 1940. Right now the maids haven't shown up for 3 days so we're doing our own uniforms in our short evening hours. Every time "Charlie" hits close around here, the maids don't show up. That looks as if they are "Charlie" wives. I sure wish they would come back anyway.

My job is more boring than the one at Oakland. Even if I knew how to do all of it, there just isn't much to be done right now. I want to get outdoors so bad and I can't. At noon today I had to go to the 24th Evac Hospital to get a cholera shot (I have a sore arm too) and an SFC Garcia gave it to me. He was so nice to talk to. I asked him if he knew Joe Garcia (from William Beaumont) and he does. He said he'd like to have a WAC working in there but they won't let any WACs work over there. That's where I would like to be. When I'm up there to eat, I never want to leave. I saw another WBGH (William Beaumont) guy, SGT Hubbard over at finance and also a guy from Oakland. I didn't have an allotment made out because the guy said it would be a lot easier to get a money order. The next thing will be to find the post office and have time to get to it. The schedule we keep here is enough to kill an ordinary person. I don't know how long it will take to get used to it. Right now I feel like I meet myself coming and going.

From my window at work yesterday and today I saw choppers shooting rockets down in the valley. There have been ambushes just outside the perimeter here and I suppose you've heard about Saigon being a mess again. I hope my mail is going out.

My first week has gone fast. I only hope the other 51 do. This is no place to enjoy life, believe me. It's going to be a long hard year over here but I have R&R and maybe a leave to look forward to besides all the money and ribbons just from being here.

We have movies here in the company area 3 or 4 nights a week. I saw "Bonnie and Clyde" and last night "The Sound of Music" was on. Of course they're free but I can hardly stay awake through one.

It hasn't been so hot the last day or two and it rained twice today. I like rain here because it cools the air off and washes some mud and dust away. So far I've seen one bird, a little scrawny sparrow hopping around outside my office window. I have my own desk with my name on it.

I got my "secret" security clearance today. I had to write my life history and go to the MP station for fingerprints. They will check my record for a month before it's a permanent clearance but at least I have it. Nobody could figure out how I got here without one.

You won't get this letter till after Mother's Day so I'll say I hope you enjoy what I left there for you and I bet you were surprised. I knew I couldn't send anything from here.

I know how you feel when the plane revs up the motors. I feel a little strange now knowing that I'm a day away even by jet and before it's only been a few hours. I feel pretty lonely sometimes because I miss Barbara and Pat so much but I guess that will wear off. Oakland seems a lot nicer now than it did when I was there. I can't help but think about "Junior" (the car I had to sell) in that car lot too.

This is the "buggiest" darn place I've ever seen. They crawl all over the place, some small and some huge. They look a lot like cockroaches but they're not. It's no joke that you have to shake out your shoes and boots before you put them on.

I probably won't tell you nearly all you want to know. You'll have to write a list of questions but I'll warn you that all I can tell you about is what I can see from here and at work and that isn't much. I just want to get out and explore but unless these peace talks do some good I'll never get to. This country could be beautiful if it was clean and there wasn't a war going on.

I'm glad I didn't bring anymore with me than what I did because anything over here may never survive a year. I keep thinking how terrible it would be if our barracks got hit because everything we have in here would be blown up. At least we have a good chance of being safe in the bunkers. We haven't had an alert yet but we keep expecting one. Charlie is a lot closer to this post than I expected. I'll sure be a war veteran when I get out of here. If I get to liking my job better it will make my whole tour better. No matter what happens, I'm glad I'm here. Now I know I'm fulfilling my obligation to the US and that in itself is a nice thought. I wish some of the slobs sitting around there were over here.

I'll close for this time and I'll write as often as I can.

Lots of love,
Susie

P.S.

There was just a barrage of mortar fire that shook the whole barracks. I wish I could put sound effects in my letters.

11 May 68

Dear Ruby,

I don't have to work today but I have training from 0800 till 1200 so I'm tied up all morning. My roommate is still in bed so I'm sitting outside writing to you. I just figured out that it's 2215 last night for you right now so I suppose you're asleep. When I get off work at 1830 it's 0930 for you. It's easy enough to figure out-just add 9 hours to whatever time you have and that's what it is here.

I got the letter you mailed Monday 6 May yesterday, Friday. It must take 2 days for them to get to SF and 3 over here. It was a nice long letter and I like the article about me. It made me feel terrible to see Junior (my car) in the ad but I'm glad he is important enough to make big print anyway. Also I'm glad he's there and not in Oakland.

I was going to tell you that I do want the newspaper sent to me so I'm glad you got it. They publish a small paper for Far East military personnel called "The Stars and Stripes" which I get to read at work every day. It has national news and sports. The White Sox are playing at Oakland today. How I'd love to be there but I'd probably be working.

It is beautiful out this morning and I wish I could go for a walk. I see every nice morning but I'm never free and there is no nice place to walk around here anyway.

From what I've heard, there are certain countries where we can go only on R&R and not a leave and I want to go to them. One is Australia and another Hawaii. Australia is supposed to be hard to get to because everybody wants to go there. Hong Kong is back on the list and

I wouldn't mind going there. All the transportation is by military aircraft and is free. I'll have to quit now for training.

1000

Well, I didn't have to be at training since I just got here this month so I have the whole day free. I don't believe it. The maids have come back to work but I have a bunch of civilian clothes for my roommate and me in the washer.

Last night we had a movie called "Rosie". It was real good and I saw it at Oakland on 5 Nov, my first Sunday there.

When I finished writing that last letter to you, I went and took a shower and washed my hair. I was just coming out of the shower when I heard explosions real close so I knew we were going to go on alert. Within 5 minutes every girl in the company was at least half way in fatigues and out by the bunkers. I never knew we could all move so fast. The explosions were rockets that landed just down the street from us. The first thing we do is turn all the lights out so we have to find our field gear and dress in the dark. We stayed by the bunkers till about 2300 and nothing else happened. Most of us laid down on the ground, used our canteens or helmets for a pillow and went to sleep. Finally the SGT came through and told us we could go to bed but to leave our clothes on. I've had my initiation to VN now. While we were out the choppers flew over without lights and jets kept going over. When you look up at them you can't help but wonder if they're ours or VC and if they're going to drop a bomb. Our guys killed 86 VC down in that valley that I see from work that same night. I didn't realize that they were so close but they're all over the place. It looks to me like our troops should be able to keep them from infiltrating so far but evidently they can't.

Long Binh is never mentioned in the news and I guess it won't be unless there is a major attack that wipes out half the post.

I keep forgetting to tell you that when I moved into my office there was a switch blade knife in the desk and of course I grabbed it. It is oriental designed and it's different from a Mexican one but it sure is neat. This is a darned poor place to find it though because not only are they illegal but I don't know how I'm going to get it home because they check everything that is taken out of here. Maybe it would be safe to mail it in a package with other stuff.

We have to send film to Hawaii or Tokyo to get it developed so it will be a long time before I can get any pictures to you. When you get the ones you have there, send them to me so I can pick out the ones I want Barbara to have. You can take the cost of all this out of what I'll send you. Either I'll send mine to Barbara and you can send me some of the others or I can tell you which ones and you can send them to her. I'll only want 2 or 3 for her and I don't know how many of them I'll want. I don't even remember what all is on it.

I think I'll lay out in the sun this afternoon. We can only wear fatigues in the mess hall so I'll have to get back in them pretty soon. You can't tell a girl from a guy around here except for the hair and 1SGT Crawford said the only way to tell the girls with short hair is by lipstick so she makes sure we all wear it. I've not had a skirt on since the day I got here. I don't know how I'm ever going to get to church because I'll usually be working and I don't even know where a chapel is except the 24th Evac and that may be for patients. I wish I could go tomorrow.

Well, I'll quit for now and mail this on my way to chow.

Lots of love,
Susie

15 May 68

Dear Ruby,

I guess I'd better get another letter written to you. I've been doing real good getting mail-one from you Monday, Barbara yesterday and you today. Your picture is real good I think. I wish I had a frame for it but I'm sure there is no such thing in this whole country. If all of my pictures are as good as the ones you sent it's really strange because I had such a mess on that other roll. If you want to, go ahead and send them to me. These didn't get hurt in the mail. I'll send a couple to Barbara and the ones I don't want I'll send back to you. That's a lot of mailing but I do want to see them. The first thing I want here is a Polaroid camera. A lot of the girls have them and the heat doesn't hurt the film. The PX doesn't always have them so I'll have to catch it at the right time if I ever get there at all. I just don't have time to do anything. You asked about my day off. I have no idea when I'll get off. My NCOIC is on R&R till Sunday or Monday so it won't be before he gets back. We've really been busy. I'm beginning to like it better though. Twelve hours a day, 7 days a week really adds up to a lot of hours. I'm making up for all the time off I had at Oakland. I am adapting pretty well except I still want to get out in the open and probably always will. I told you that when I got over here I'd probably dream I was back there and I have a couple of times. The other night I was out buying a new car. I have to be here a year to get enough money for that so the war had better not end!

I hear or read most of the national news. I didn't get a paper yet. I don't know how many people here have seen my letter from Oakland but I know the company did and I think LTC Preuss, the guy I work for, did so that's the most important ones. He told one of the WAC SGTs the other day that he is pleased with me and we get along real good so I'm lucky there. He is around 50 years old.

We do have thunder storms and sometimes I think it's thunder and it's really "Charlie" blowing up something. They were raising cane this morning when I was getting ready for work. We had another alert about the same as before. Every time I finish a letter to you and seal it, we have an alert so I think I'll leave this one open till morning.

Last night we had a party for the 26th WAC anniversary. It was here on our patio and they had food and drinks. I was out there till 2230.

I was glad to get the clippings. That sure does look like our sandbar. I hope they make a nice park out of that. It would be beautiful. (This refers to Forest Glen Nature Preserve south of Danville).

I like the people I work with pretty good. Yes, they are all men, LTC on up to a 3 star general. I type his letters sometimes and I sure feel funny typing his signature block when I was used to 1st and 2nd lieutenants at Oakland.

I guess I might as well pay off all I owe you so when I get to send some just keep it till you have all yours back. I really want to pay the $425 worst because of what it's for. This is the best chance I'll ever have to get caught up.

I thought you'd be surprised and happy with the globe. It looked like a real nice one and I couldn't find a separate thing for each of you. You know Aggie (friend and neighbor) and me together can get by with anything. That's why you didn't happen to walk in while we wrapped it. I had it in the trunk of the car a day and a night. I love to do things like that.

Yes, I have girls on the bus and in the mess hall with me. They're nice but I haven't found any to replace Barbara and Grace yet. Barbara wants over here so bad. I sure hope she gets to come this summer. Some of these girls will be leaving so she should be able to get here.

SGT Crawford, our 1st SGT, leaves in about 3 weeks and she's starting another drill team before she goes. She picked a group to be on it and I'm one of them. I sure hope we do get it going. We have our first meeting at 0615 tomorrow. It's hardly worthwhile to go to bed sometimes. There sure aren't enough hours in a day here. I do go to breakfast every day and I try to have a can of something here to eat at night. They have what would be pork and beans except it has sliced wieners in it and is called "Beanie Weenie." It's pretty good, at least it's food. The water doesn't taste so bad anymore. Every Monday morning we take our malaria pills. They're great big pink ones.

Right now I won't say that I want you to send anything but I think of little things now and then and eventually I'll have a list. I hate for you to start sending things very soon because I have 11 ½ months to want things.

I'll close for now. I hope I have more time to write the next letter. This one is scribbled.

Lots of love,
Susie

19 May 68

Dear Ruby,

I guess I'll see how much I can get written to you now. Everybody in the office has gone to lunch leaving me all alone so I can do anything. I haven't had a thing to type yet today. It's about time the work slacked off a little but it doesn't take long for me to get bored. This is my 14th day of work with only part of one day off. It sounds horrible and I do wish for a whole day free but it's really not too bad. I like the job a lot better and these guys are nice to work for and with. LTC Preuss acts like he likes me and the civilian man, Bill Rynearson, is real nice.

I got to go to church this morning but I'll have to tell you a story before I lead up to how. Yesterday we were all supposed to get off at 1730 but the colonel that is the Chief of Comptroller kept sending a letter back to be retyped with different wording. I got out of here at 1802, just in time to miss the bus at 1800 so instead of waiting for the next one at 1830, I decided to start walking. It's a pretty good distance but I figured either I'd get there on foot or somebody would offer me a ride. I hadn't got far before a SGT and 2 civilians stopped for me so after we took the civilians home and got to the WAC Det, the SGT (Tom Simpson) asked me to go to the NCO Club with him and I did. He drives a Dodge truck. They have a few vehicles in the men's companies and if an officer doesn't have all of them sometimes the enlisted guys get one. He took me on a tour of the post. It looks real pretty at night, almost like a city. We stayed at the club till 2215. All of us have to be home at 2230. He wanted to take me to church this morning so I got off work to go. I was the only girl there but it was nice. They had an organ and a small choir of men that really sounded good. It's kind of strange to be in church in fatigues and boots and see everybody else the same way with no women or kids around. The chapel does look like a chapel but it's sure not like anything you've ever seen. I can't describe these "tropical" buildings to you. I hope I can get some pictures so you can have some idea of what they look like. They are not built with solid walls and they don't have windows, just mosquito net over open spaces. Anyway, back to the subject. This guy has 4 ½ years service and is from Louisiana but he worked in Wilmette, IL before he came in. He seems to be nice and I don't see any harm in going places with him. I need a way to see things around even on the post and maybe he's the way. He will probably want to go out every night though and I can't do that. I never would get letters written or anything else done. They had a band at the club last night and they played a song about "San Francisco". I don't know the name of it but I sure like it. I heard it when I was there. Also, there's a song I heard all the time there called "Dock of the Bay" by Otis Redding. If you would, I'd like for you to see if you could get it on a 45 single. You probably wouldn't like it because you wouldn't be able to see what the words say but I love to hear it. Any song that I like now, I know will probably be long gone before I get back and the only way I'll have it is if you can get it for me.

I got your letter and 2 newspapers yesterday. We get mail every day of the week and any time of day. They keep it in the orderly room for anyone who isn't there during mail call so we just go in and pick it up. There are some things more convenient here such as that and no uniforms to wash or iron and no shoes to shine. The way it looks right now, I think I'll enjoy my tour here. I keep reminding myself that I know I'll leave here in a year unless I want to stay and a year really isn't too long. I have had to give up so much to come and to be here but there's just something in knowing that I'm here that at least helps cover everything else up. I miss the car but I wouldn't be back at Oakland now if I could. Well, I'll have to quit for now and go eat.

1300

I'm back from chow and all the officers are still gone so I'll start again. I hope by now you know what USARV means. Up here on the hill in front of the Headquarters building where I work, General Palmer's 3 star flag flies at the door and 2 flag poles are farther out. One is for ours and one for the Vietnamese flag. I hope you remembered to fly your flag yesterday, Armed Forces Day. I didn't think far enough ahead to remind you.

I sure wish I had gotten a bathing suit before I came because whenever I do get some time off I'd love to be able to get sun all over. There is no place here to buy one and I don't have any idea what size I would wear so you can't get me one. It's rather hard to get any sun when I work almost every minute of the daylight hours.

It's going to be pretty hard for me to get a camera I'm afraid because as soon as a shipment comes in everybody wants them. I'll just have to be lucky enough to get there. I sure do want one. Now I have the money and can't get what I want. If I had it, then you could have some pictures. I haven't seen any binoculars at all but maybe they have them someplace. I want some to observe the "war" when I can. For us the war is only when they're hitting close. The rest of the time we're just here. The US is referred to as "the real world."

I don't even remember if I told you that 1SG Crawford started another drill team or not. Anyway, we have practiced a few times and starting this week we meet Monday, Wednesday and Friday at 0615 and drill till the bus comes at 0630. I'm in the front rank at the head of a squad which means I lead my squad in any individual parts. We're doing pretty good and I love it. If we can keep it going with the new 1SG we will get to perform with the band and we might get to tour Vietnam with the WAC band if they come over. That would really be great. The way I love to march I should want to go to Ft. McClellan but I don't want to be stuck out in the middle of the woods. I wish it was in Houston or someplace over there.

Soon two of the NCOs in the company that have dogs will leave and of course the dogs, "Cocoa" Crawford and "Tammy" Efferson will go too. Tammy is a "Vietnamese Pekingese". She's so cute. I still want a koala bear but it sounds pretty hopeless. They only eat eucalyptus leaves and as far as I've found out, they grow only in Australia and California. If I wanted to live in California that would be fine but I don't know how he would get leaves while I'm still over here. I could wait till about 2 or 3 months before I come home and to go Australia then if I thought they'd let me keep him here and take him home with me. There must be some way to get and keep one because I sure want my own live teddy bear. Well, I think I'll quit now until I go home and can read your letter again.

1610

You'll never believe it but I got off at 1400. I went to the motor pool to get a ride home and I got a jeep with some foreign driver. He must have been a Korean national because some of them work here and he sure wasn't Vietnamese. He couldn't speak much English but we managed to talk some. I almost like talking to or at these people and trying to understand them. There are several Australians around here and I love their accent. I sat out in the sun for about an hour so I'm pretty red now. I read my papers while I was out there. They were the 8th and 10th. It's really nice to read them even if they're old.

I don't know who Freda Jennings is and I don't remember you mentioning the Air Force boy but I probably just forgot. I often figure out what time it is there too and what you're doing. No, I didn't know I was so near to being half way around the world from home. It does seem almost unbelievable. I would love to be down at the farm with you but I'll just have to wait. I'll be there again sometime—11 ½ months from now. At least it's under 12 and some new girls have come so I no longer rate in the newest group. I wish you would go horseback riding. I sure wish I had known that was there because we could have gone a long time ago. You always discover something good when I can't be there. I'd love to have a picture of me on a horse.

I've been told to write to you often but not to scare you to death. Have I yet? I want to tell you everything that goes on but maybe I shouldn't. A lot of the girls don't write home anything about how close "Charlie" is but I don't think it will scare you, I hope. Just don't get scared if you don't get a letter as soon as you should because anytime the mail could be held up. They move it by chopper now because they can't travel on the road to Saigon.

My writing is getting worse. I can't even spell and put the wrong word half the time. I'll have to close now. I almost need to mail this in 2 envelopes. I don't know what would happen if it was overweight.

Lots of love,
Susie

23 May 68

Dear Ruby,

This letter isn't going to be long because I still have to take a shower before I go to bed. I have so much to tell you and I never will get all of it said. I sure wish we both had tape recorders so I could just sit down and say it all and send it to you.

I went to the club with Tom last night. We go about every other night. One night they had a band playing Spanish music and the girl that was singing said she was from El Paso, Texas. That almost made me feel like I was back there. Tom is a nice guy. He never tries to keep me out too late and if I tell him I have to stay home and write letters he doesn't argue.

I want all these pictures you have sent, even the ones of me because I was at home. I'll send the one of me standing in the western outfit to Barbara. I have gotten 4 papers but didn't get one today. Maybe they'll get on schedule pretty soon.

I do feel real special being here and it will be even better when I get back and can say "I was in Vietnam". I just hope we can keep the drill team going.

They really had a war the other morning right after I got to work and could watch out the window. Our jets bombed a place about 4 miles from post and we could watch them fly in, drop the bombs and then go straight up out of there. They are really accurate. We could see the fire flash and then the mushroom clouds. I wish I could get a picture of it sometime. That same morning it rained and we had the most beautiful rainbow. We all said instead of a pot of gold at the end, it was probably a company of VC. It's quite a life over here.

I'm getting acquainted with a lot of people. I had a nice talk with SFC Garcia today. I don't remember if I told you I saw LT (now CPT) Eason from WBGH. I see him in the mess hall quite often and he came over to see me last night before I got home from work. SFC Garcia said he would take me on a tour of the hospital if I ever got time off. I'm quite sure I'm not going to get bored.

I found a picture of a '68 Chevelle Super Sport that has everything I want except that I want a Chevy not Chevelle. Anyway, over here we can order a car the way we want it and have it delivered to our hometown on a certain date and it's a lot cheaper. A guy figured one like I want would cost about $3,000 from here and $3500 in the states. I'll sure keep this picture anyway.

It's really hot this evening and I'm about to roast right now. I'm still trying to get a camera. They should get some in next week for pay day. It will probably take me a roll of film to learn to use it.

Well I'm going to quit now because 0545 gets here awful fast. I'm doing fine and I'm really beginning to feel at home here. Keep writing often. Letters mean a lot here. I even like the Commercial News that is a week old. Good night.

Lots of love,
Susie

PS I'm sorry I scribble so much but I'm constantly in a rush.

24 May 68

Dear Ruby,

Everybody is still out to lunch so I'll see how much I can write. I've been watching the war out across the country. The jets were really zooming in. I watched them going in and out of the clouds. Every day the sky is full of those beautiful big white clouds. I was watching what shapes they made and I saw Abraham Lincoln in one. Tom came and got me at noon and after we ate we went to a book store over on the other side of the post. We were going parallel with the fence beside the Bein Hoa highway and on the outside I saw about 4 flag poles flying the yellow Vietnamese flag. That looked strange. At the book store I got myself a world map—50"x33". I didn't have any map with me and I hope someday to have a wall to put this one on. Tom is going to Bein Hoa this afternoon and he's going to see if they have any cameras. I sure hope they do because I'm so anxious to get one and learn to use it so I can send you some pictures.

I don't think I have told you that we have to wear our dog tags every minute of our tour over here. I put my medals on the same chain so I only have one. I carry my comb, lipstick, and 2 pens in this pocket on the sleeve of my fatigues and my ID card and other cards in the left shirt pocket. It's so nice to have all these pockets. The boots and socks are really comfortable now too. These clothes were really made for me. I never did get a rank pin to wear on my hat.

Two days ago I found out that the E-6 slot here is for a different MOS from mine—accounting specialist. It's so far away that I could never be promoted into it even if I wanted to. I'm not in any slot right now because the SGT here is in it. Anyway, I called 1SG Herney and told her so last night she said she's going to try to find me an E-6 slot in an MOS at least near mine. I sure don't intend to sit here and type for a year knowing I can't be promoted. Boy, you can sure run into a bunch of liars because when I came here they told me it was an E-6 slot. Of course they didn't tell me the whole story. It must be pretty hard to find places for a WAC E-5 to be promoted. I just hope she gets me out of here. I like the people in this office but I hate typing all day. I want to be NCOIC of something and I'm not going to be happy as long as I'm under one instead of being one. I know I have the 1SG and CO behind me.

You should hear what we go through to make a phone call. If it's on Long Binh all we do is dial 4 numbers but for anyplace else we have to go through switchboards. I dial a 7 for the Long Binh operator. When he answers I ask for a city and when they answer I ask for the smaller town, eventually I get to where I wanted. The connection is usually pretty good.

Every Tuesday and Friday evening till the end of June, four of us have to go to a class in correspondence at the Education Center from 1900 to 2030 hours. I guess I need it but how I hate having 2 evenings tied up that way. Our section SGT Major decided we would all go.

It pours down rain about once every day now and by the looks of the black clouds across the valley, it's coming now.

This is a lot like basic training except we don't get the physical exercise. I play basketball once in awhile but that's about all we can do.

Well, I'm going to close for now. Maybe this letter makes a little more sense than the one last night. I wrote part of it by flashlight because the lights went out but they came back on. We thought we were going to have an alert but we didn't.

Lots of love,
Susie

2230

I'm finally home from school and the NCO Club. Tom picked me up after school and we went to the club. He couldn't get a camera—they still didn't have any. I got your letter and one from Barbara today. She is as determined to get here as I was. You wonder how I feel about being here. It's really hard to put into words. I guess I don't feel like I'm so far away unless I think about it a lot. It's not nearly as bad as I always pictured being overseas. I don't know what I'll think after 6 months over here. These three weeks have gone so fast. I like your letters even if they are short. I'll quit with this page.

    Love,
    Susie

26 May 68

Dear Ruby,

This probably won't be much of a letter but I have to tell you about my day before it gets old. First I finally got a whole day off and what a day! A group of Special Forces guys were in from the field and had a party yesterday and today for any WACs who could get off to go. They sent Huey choppers for us and believe me my first chopper ride was wonderful. I had an outside seat right beside the machine gun and gunner. I could look right down at the ground and especially when they turned the chopper. It was a 40 minute chopper ride to the beach on the ocean. We wore fatigues and I took shorts and that white blouse with a big neck and no sleeves. We walked along the beach a lot and I got more shells. One of them is really a big beauty. The guys took us around the village in jeeps and I rode on the "jump seat". The jeeps had guns mounted on them too. We ate in their mess hall and of course they had everything to drink out on the beach. Two pilots took us up in little one motor planes called "bird dogs" here. They have room for only one passenger behind the pilot. He tipped the plane completely on its side and he would dip down almost on the water then go straight up and he shot a rocket into the water—that was ear shattering. They took us to their camp and showed us around. I was with the battalion commander most of the time. Later, just before we left to come home, they gave us a set of camouflage fatigues. I got 2 shirts, boy they are neat. One guy gave me his Special Forces scarf too. It's 3 stripes, red, white and blue and looks like a flag. We wore them home and did they ever look sharp. Just before we landed on Long Binh we got in a thunderstorm and rain so we came in dripping wet and covered with sand and salt water. One girl tried to teach me to float. About all I got was a drink of salt water but at least now I have been out in water. How I wish I knew how to swim and I really need a bathing suit here. You wouldn't believe the sunburn I have. I look like a lobster—even my face is red and I mean red. It's burning now and I have a feeling I'm going to have a hot time before it's over. We walked along the edge of the beach with the water splashing on us just like I always wanted to in Frisco when it was too cold. I finally got to look out over the ocean toward San Francisco. It was just a perfect wonderful day, well worth working 19 days for. I'm sitting here in my camouflage shirt and tan shorts. I wish you could see me. I feel so good tonight after I finally got the sand and salt water washed off.

The guys we were with were so nice; friendly, nice to talk to and gentlemen, better than any bunch of guys at a party in the states. I don't know how far we were from here. We were in the choppers about 40 minutes one way so it was pretty far. I found a "tiger tooth" in the sand. They are real and are made into necklaces. The guys wear them for good luck. I have mine on my dog tag chain.

I took pictures from the chopper and on the ground. I hope they turn out. I got to see beautiful scenery from the chopper and plane; hills, palm trees, jungle and some bombed houses and buildings. The guys said the VC were all over down there but they didn't shoot at us. I just couldn't believe it was actually me doing all that. With a day like this, the hard work is worth it and time spent here will be great. I'm not going to answer your letter now. I just had to tell you about my day. The letter you mailed the 22nd got here today which is the 26th, in the AM. Well I'll close for now. I'm a sunburned but happy person tonight.

Lots of love,
Susie

(The following letter is copied exactly as I sent it to my mother)

AVHGF-B 29 May 1968
SUBJECT: The Latest news from your USARV WAC
Ruby I. Earls
2606 Cannon St
Danville, IL 61832

1. I got this idea from school last night. The teacher said if we wrote a letter to our mothers in military form, they would never understand it so I'll see how you do. I can't think of anything to say to make it really hard. He was telling us the reason for writing non-military letters to civilians.

2. After school last night, Tom and me went to the club and they had a band from Nashville. They played real good songs. I was at a table with 5 men—Tom, two of his friends and two of theirs. They were all so nice. I just can't get over how much different men act over here. They really treat a girl like a lady. Usually there are only two or three other girls in the whole club, and sometimes not even that. Most of them go to the USARV club and we go to the 18th MP Bde club more often.

3. Tonight 1SG Crawford is cooking Italian spaghetti for us for a DEROS party for one of the girls. This morning at reveille, 1SG Herney called the dogs, "Ko-Ko" Crawford and "Tammy" Efferson to the front and center of the formation. Their mothers held them there and 1SG Herney read off their unit order numbers, names and service numbers and promoted "Ko-Ko" to Cpl E-4 and "Tammy" to PFC E-3. CPT Murphy fastened rank pins on their collars and kissed each of them. Tammy growled at her. She acts a lot like Rusty did. That was sure a cute ceremony. They did it so formal; just as if it was a real person.

4. Barbara told me a while back that she had something to send to me if I could put it on my wall. I wrote back and said I could so yesterday I got the package. She mailed it 21 May and I received it 28 May by SAM. One thing is a beautiful autographed picture of RFK which she got at Kennedy headquarters in Oakland. Do you remember me telling you about the mat with JFK and the White House on it that Barbara and me saw in San Jose? I wanted it and it wasn't for sale. Well, she found one someplace and that's what she sent. It is just beautiful. It is about 2 ½ feet long and 1 foot wide and it's soft thick material. I hate to have it over here in all this dirt.

Maybe I can keep it brushed off. It must have cost a lot. Now all I have to do is find thumb tacks to put it on the wall.

5. I'm going to close this letter. I bet you don't understand all the abbreviations. Tell me what you don't know. Boy doesn't that sentence make a lot of sense? I'll write the rest of what I want to say tonight.

LINDA S. EARLS
SP5 E-5 WAC
Budget Division, Comptroller

29 May 68

Dear Ruby,

I'll start an ordinary letter to you now. I got my check in the mail today $340. They take off $11.40 FICA tax and $2 life insurance, the rest is mine. I got a check because I haven't been here through a month. I guess I'll get Tom to take me to the bank tomorrow so I can cash it then I'll go to the PO and get you a money order. This check has written all over "Do not mail outside RVN" and "payable in MPC's only".

Boy how I'd love to have beans and onions when you're always talking about them. I get onions on these weird tasting hamburgers. The French fries and hot dogs are pretty good but the hamburgers taste strange. Tom got me a case of orange juice and one of tomato today. When he picks up supplies for his office he gets anything he wants from the warehouse. I'm sure glad to get it. We looked for cameras again but there weren't any. Tom got me a rank pin for my hat. He's always bringing me something, he must like being with me.

I haven't heard anymore about my job yet but evidently they have been discussing it with the SGT MAJ in my office. I guess I'll just have to be patient. I'm making a lot of money now.

Yesterday at 1145 we had a farewell ceremony for General Westmoreland in front of USARV Headquarters. He made a speech and the band was out there and played the "Star Spangled Banner." It gave me such a wonderful feeling to stand there and salute the flag. I've heard so much about him and now I've seen him.

Well, I think 1SG Crawford has the spaghetti ready so I'll close for this time.

Lots of love,
Susie

PS I'm sending you the patch I'll wear the rest of my Army career on my right sleeve after I leave here.

CHAPTER III

JUNE 1968

JUNE 1968

1 June 1968

Dear Ruby,

I had training this morning and I'm off this afternoon. Another girl and me went to the USARV PX and I got a lighter with a USARV emblem and my name, 68-69 and Long Binh engraved on it. It looks real neat. Yesterday the orderly room got in a bunch of sweat shirts they had ordered from Japan about 5 months ago and luckily for me there were extras and I got one. They have USARV WAC Det on them and a big USARV emblem. Mine is dark blue and real pretty. Boy am I ever going to have a collection of stuff by the time I leave here. I see loads of possibilities for Christmas gifts. There are so many things here that I know can't be found in the states.

I didn't get my check cashed till yesterday so I won't get a money order for you till Monday. I don't know what I'm going to do with my money after I have bought the big things that I want. We can only put $200 in Soldier's Deposit or the bank each month. The bank is clear across post and there are no buses running over there so a cab is the only way. I want that 10% interest from Soldier's Deposit but I can't get any money out of it until I return to the states. That would be all right except right now I plan to order a car from here and I'll need the down payment. I'd like to be able to drive a bunch of different ones first and if I get to Hawaii I can but they are so much cheaper from here I almost have to take advantage of it.

My sunburn has been peeling except my face, lower arms and legs. Maybe I can hang onto that much. If nothing happens, 3 of us plan to go to Vung Tau this Wednesday. One girl, Jan, and me have DNCO and

CQ Tuesday night so we're off Wednesday and the third one is too so we hope to go. This would be to the town of Vung Tau. I hope we get to go but here it's never safe to plan ahead.

I don't remember whether or not I told you about the guy who has the tape recorder for sale. He's had it 2 months and it sounds like what I want. He works down the hall from me and I've known him since I got here. He was stationed at Presidio in San Francisco before he came here so we talked about that a lot. I just found out a couple of days ago that he wants to sell his tape recorder so he can get a tape deck outfit. It's a Sony and that's a good brand—4 track stereo. I'm supposed to go see it tomorrow and if it's what I want I'll get it. He's asking $145 and in the states it would cost around $250 so it must be a good one. I hadn't intended to get one so soon but I guess I might as well have it now as later.

I gave our room a good cleaning this afternoon and gave myself a haircut. My roommate took the picture I'm sending. The puppy is "Callie" and I have on my jungle shirt. The money is 20 piasters. We get some money converted each month to pay the maid and I had some left. Look through the white area and you'll see a face. I don't know yet how much that is worth but it's not much. The smallest denomination we have in MPC's is 5 cents. There is no tax on anything and all prices are even numbers.

We're having another company party tonight, this time for our outgoing cadre. I think I probably made Tom mad because he wanted me to go out tonight and I cut him off pretty short when I told him I was staying home. He has guard duty tomorrow night. I just get tired of going out.

I wish you had told me a long time ago that Aggie's birthday was so soon. I'm sending her a card, the best I can do for now but it will be late. I didn't think about finding out when I was home. The sample of material is real cool and pretty looking. I am happy wearing fatigues. I love blueberry pop-tarts. Whenever I decide to have you send me something I want some of them. We have a lot of yeast rolls here and they are real good but the bread is hard and horrible. It must be made by the Vietnamese. There is no nice soft American bread over here.

I think our drill team has fallen apart because too many of the girls wouldn't get up and out at 0600 for it and that's about the only time we have. I sure wish we could keep it but if everybody won't come we can't.

An Australian accent is more English than anything else. I'm pretty good at getting across a message to the Vietnamese and understanding them. We use a lot of hand signals and they understand some English words but not sentences.

I want the record of "San Francisco" too but I don't know who sings it. How I wish you had a way to tape my favorite records and send them to me. If you ever hear of anybody with a tape recorder grab them. You and Aggie together should be able to figure out how to run one. I'd give anything to have some of my favorite albums on tape.

Well I'll quit for this time.

Lots of love,
Susie

Sunday
0830

2 June

I brought this letter to work with me and there is nothing to do so I'll start writing. I didn't expect a letter from you yesterday. I got 2 newspapers. I still don't get them every day and they run about a week behind but I like to read them. I saw where somebody in Georgetown had a Pekingese for sale for $25. I wish I could have him. I just discovered that I brought your old letter instead of your new one to work so I can't do much toward answering it. I am so glad you went to Eugene. I didn't suppose you would. Next year I hope I can be there for that. Whether I extend here or come back to stay, I'll still have a 30 day leave. I just hope the rest of my time goes as fast as this first month. I have seen 3 "freedom birds" this morning. They are the jets that bring us over and take us back. They are usually TWA or Trans-International airlines but one day I saw an American Airlines jet and it was a strange feeling to look up and see "American" on it.

We had our company party last night and what a party. The CO presented gifts and plaques to the outgoing sergeants and gave each of them a bottle of champagne. They opened the bottles and brought them around and gave each of us a drink. I got SGT Benson's. I hate to see her go most of all because besides the fact that she knows SGT Wanty, she's such a nice person. She is going to Fort Monroe, VA, 1SG Crawford is going to Fort Sheridan and SGT Efferson is going some place in the east. They all got to feeling pretty good with their beer and champagne and they told stories about their 18 months over here. They were really funny. You sure never find this closeness between girls and their cadre at any post in the states. CPT Murphy calls us by our first names and a stateside CO would never do that. I don't care if Tom is mad, I had a nice evening and I want to have some time with the company. I guess I should call him today if he doesn't call me.

I wanted to go to mass this morning so much and thought I could but LTC Preuss and me are the only people at work so I sure can't leave. He's writing letters too. There is an auditorium in the building next to this one and they use it for a chapel so I could have gone so easily but SGT Hall decided to sleep this morning. I'm sure they don't have mass in the afternoon or evening but I'll go check at noon. It's really a challenge to try to get to church around here.

I see a guy from Albuquerque won the race. I was for the one from San Jose but at least the west won. I still want to go to that race sometime.

Well I'll quit now and answer your letter when I get home tonight. MAJ E. just came in but I still can't leave.

1635

I'm home now. I got off at 1550 but it took about 45 minutes to get a ride home. While I was waiting I had a nice talk with an SFC who was stationed in El Paso at the Defense Language Institute at Biggs Air Base. He left there 29 Mar 68 so we really had a nice conversation. He wished he was sitting up on Scenic Drive and so did I. I'm always running into somebody that has been where I have.

Jerry, the guy that has the tape recorder came at noon today and took me down to see it. It's really a beauty. It has tone controls like Aggie's stereo, speaker and jack input places and 2 microphones for recording in stereo. Also it can be used as an amplifier for a speech or to amplify music. It sounds so good. He's going to bring it and all its parts to work tomorrow and I'll give him the money and we'll get a truck to bring it down here. Now you know what I'm going to want—my 2 tapes. At least some of the songs I like are on them. I suppose they are in the chest. I don't want the empty reel, just the 5 and 7 inch reels with the tape on them. Just reinforce the outside with cardboard, wrap them up and mail them. Don't send anything else this time. I haven't seen any of those pre-recorded tapes over here. I wish they had some. I wouldn't want to get any the same as my records but I could find some good ones.

Tom called me this morning and he wasn't mad. He has guard duty tonight so I'll finally have a whole evening free. My roommate is going to a party so I'll have an evening alone.

I'm mailing you a cute card. You'll probably get it with this. Also, I'm sending a sample of Vietnam red dirt. I don't know what it will be like by the time you get it. I guess I'll leave all this space and quit. I don't have anything else to say.

Lots of love,
Susie

1900

I've just been messing around all evening so I'll answer your letter now. It is practically a questionnaire. Some of the bands at the clubs are good, some are terrible. Yes, they are usually full of smoke and Tom smokes too. I'm getting fairly used to always feeling wet and being hot. It's disgusting to come out of the shower and can't tell you were ever dry. We have a fan on all night in our room. Otherwise we couldn't sleep at all. I can't believe that you're going to a show. I saw "The Sons of Katie Elder" in El Paso and I saw it again at Oakland. I liked it and the scenery is beautiful. I love Westerns because of where they're filmed. Don't forget to fly the flag on Flag Day. I am closing for sure this time.

Love,
Susie

4 June 1968

Dear Ruby,

This is just a short note to go with the money orders I hope to get today. I'll probably have to sign my life away to get them and send a registered letter. This money is in MPC's now, then it will be a money order, then you will convert it to American money and finally it can be spent. It is really a pain in the neck to do anything with money over here. It would be so simple just to put some in an envelope and send it but you couldn't very well use MPC's.

If you would happen to find a pre-recorded tape of the Dr. Zhivago sound track I wish you would get it for me. My record skips so I'd like to have the tape and I know it would be beautiful. It has to be stereo and would probably cost around $6 because they're about $5 in a PX. You should start a "Vietnam Fund" or something and each time I send you money, keep some out to use for me. Also I'd like to have my account forwarded so I know how much I owe you.

If you're ever around tape recorders, see if you can find a Sony 260 stereo and see how much it costs.

One more thing—I'd like to know the price of a Polaroid 220 camera. There are none in this whole country unless they're really hiding because 2 guys have checked Saigon and Cholon and they didn't have any. I hope I can look at Vung Tau if I get there tomorrow but I doubt if they have any.

Last night I watched a movie in the company and Tom came over at 2100 after school and we sat outside and talked.

Well, that's all for now. At least when I mail this I'll have started paying you back.

Lots of love,
Susie

0900

6 June 1968

Dear Ruby,

I'm at work with nothing to do so I'll start writing. The air conditioning is off and we're about to roast. By the time you get this letter it's going to be awful far from the last one but it's not my fault. Tuesday I got the money orders for you, a $100 one and a $50 one. I registered the letter and mailed it. This morning the postal officer called me and said the letter had been lost. He said he had everybody in the USARV post office including the officers looking for it till 0200 this morning and they can't find it. He asked me what was in it and I told him. He said he will come up tomorrow morning with the paper work to fill out so I can get the money back. Then I'll have to start all over. Maybe sometime you'll get the money. I don't remember what all I told you in the letter so you will probably never know.

Tuesday night DNCO wasn't too bad. Guys on switchboards call from all over the country just to hear a female voice. They want to talk and talk and at first it's all right but I get tired of it after awhile. We never did get to Vung Tau yesterday. We got a chopper from the USARV helipad that was going to stop at a MACV compound in the edge of Saigon, pick up a general and go on. When we got to MACV, 2 generals and a colonel got on so we had to get off. We walked to an Air Force bus stop, got a bus to Tan Son Nuht Air Base and spent the rest of the morning trying to get out of there. We gave up at noon, went to the PX, and then got a flight back. The company was supposed to call and get a flight for us but they didn't and that's how we got messed up. Anyway, it was fun. That's the first time I have hitch-hiked by chopper and we got to see Tan Son Nuht and Saigon. Saigon from a distance looks like any other city but the closer we got the more shelled and mortared buildings we saw and one place we flew over an area full of mounted guns. They have cemeteries all over the place and I saw several churches that looked real pretty. I think this country would all be beautiful if everything wasn't ruined. I'd hate to be on the ground in Saigon but it's fairly safe from the air. So now when you hear Saigon and Tan Son Nuht mentioned you can know that I have at least seen them and I've flown in and out of TSN.

Yesterday morning our 3 sergeants left. I never saw so many people hate to part so bad. The girls that had known them longest all cried and CPT Murphy hung on to 1SG Crawford. I hated to see them go and I only knew them a month. They were really attached to the company and the girls.

I didn't hear that Bobby (Kennedy) had been shot till yesterday evening and I still don't know what time or day it was over there. When we get the paper today I'll find out.

1230

I'm back from chow so I'll continue. We've been listening to the news all morning and it doesn't look too good for Bobby. Somebody must have a conspiracy going against the whole Kennedy family. I'm glad it didn't happen in Oakland or San Francisco. At least they have caught the guy unless they fool around and let him go. Here we expect to be shot at and we're prepared but at home nobody suspects anything till it's too late. Between Bobby getting shot and all our cadre leaving last night our company was quite a "depressed area." We had a movie and it wasn't even good but everyone sat outside anyway.

My roommate has a dog that she raised in the area where she works. So since 1SG Crawford and SSG Efferson left with Ko-Ko and Tammy yesterday, she got to bring her dog, "Reddy" to live in the company. She sleeps in our room at night. Once she started to "wuf" but Tanya quieted her. She's just a plain dog, medium long hair and a reddish brown color. It's nice to have her around. The little puppy is getting more friendly and playful now. She licks my face when I pick her up.

Yesterday I met a girl from Champaign. I'm not too sure she still lives there but she went through school there and of course she had been in Danville many times. I've never met anybody that lived that close to Danville before.

What address would I use to write to Rev. Meyers or his church? I might write them a note sometime when I get ambitious. They are a pretty nice bunch. I like for everybody possible to remember that I'm over here.

Well, I'll quit for now and answer your letter when I get home tonight.

2000

I'm home now and soaking wet. When it rains it pours and that's just what it did when we were going to and from the bus. I heard the news at 1800 that Bobby didn't make it. I got a nice long letter from Barbara. She says Grace and Pat both told her they're going to write to me. Surely Barbara will get here too as soon as she has a year in and can request it. She says she keeps looking west and wanting to come.

This little article I'm sending came from a "Western Horseman" magazine that I was looking at. I saw Danville, California and kept looking and there was Danville, Illinois.

I was wondering if I'd ever get a refund from my insurance. SIC will probably send something eventually. I'm sending you so much little junk that you'll run out of places to put it. I'm sending you a piece of grass from TSN.

Yes, USARV Headquarters is on a hill. It sure makes a good view. Yes, I knew there was a Memorial Day even though there was no ceremony here. I'm glad you sent the 2 programs. I'll keep them.

I occasionally see a sparrow and there are some weeds out in the yard with little tiny purple blooms but very few of them. Somebody had a rose in the orderly room. I don't know where they got it. My roommate brought home a bunch of fried chicken from the mess hall so I'll have something good tonight.

Well, I guess that's all for tonight.

Lots of love,
Susie

9 June 1968

Dear Ruby,

I guess it's letter writing time again. I'm sitting outside and it looks as if I might get rained on soon. It's getting so it rains everyday now and it almost never fails to pick a time when we have to go outside. It's just like having buckets of water falling out of the sky. I don't care except the cards in my pocket and my watch get wet. It steams up inside every time it gets wet but so far it has been all right.

I've been off today so I went with my roommate to an orphanage near Bein Hoa. A lot of the girls used to go there till it was put off limits. As long as the alert and road conditions are white now we can go. There are hundreds of kids there of all ages. I don't like the tiny babies but the older ones aren't too bad. I kept trying to find a cute little boy and every time I thought I had, "he" would turn out to be a girl. That's as bad as you and Aggie with the cat. Anyway, I did give one a bath and dress it. That would be a great place to practice medicine. Most of them have a rash or sores where they've been bitten. They lie in metal cribs on straw mats and flies just swarm over them. Two captains took us out. One of them wants to adopt a little girl but the nuns say he can't because he's not a Catholic. It's run by nuns and all the kids are Catholics. They sure wanted our watches and rings. We drove through the city of Bein Hoa but it's completely off limits and is it ever a crowded mess.

Some way or other I managed to get a cold, probably from my roommate because she has one. Don't think it's not a miserable feeling to have a cold in this hot weather. I bought some Contact capsules and have been taking them so maybe I'll get over it soon. Everybody is supposed to get a cold when they first get over here but I've been here too long for that.

Some of my sun burn peeled but I'm still pretty brown. If I just had a bathing suit top it would help with the tan but I feel funny getting in water with shorts on. I guess I shouldn't because others do it too. We do a lot of things here that we couldn't in the states.

Tom and me went to the club last night and they had an extra good band called the "Rat Finks." They played several western songs and "San Francisco" and "Unchained Melody." Somebody besides me likes that song a lot because they kept requesting it. I think Tom had to go to Cholon today. He hasn't called me yet. One night at the club we met a nice kid from Fort Wayne, Indiana. He wanted to know if I was doing anything the next night. Of course I was.

I have kept each issue of the Stars and Stripes with anything about Bobby in them. I don't know what magazines you take that would have pictures but save any you get. We don't have much variety in magazines over here.

I guess there is a chance that the letter of mine with the money orders might have gotten through. If it did, I don't know if you can cash them or not since they've been reported lost. If it didn't get through, it will be 60 days before we can get the money. I sure wish I had some other way to send money to you.

I never told you to write "Tape—Do Not X-ray" on my tapes when you send them. By the time you get this letter you'll probably already have them mailed. Also, you don't have to send anything air mail because it comes fairly fast by SAM (Space Available Mail).

I never have remembered to tell you that we have frogs out here around the company and they evidently speak Vietnamese like that blackbird spoke Spanish because they sure sound different from any other frogs I ever heard.

My newspaper still comes about a week late but I'm glad to get it anyway. I got a nice long letter from Grace yesterday. I got a letter from Edie the other day too. She gets out about the 29th of this month.

The other morning CPT Eason came to my table and talked to me in the mess hall. After he left one of the girls sitting with me asked me where I knew him. I told her and she said "did you know a girl named Smyth?" I said I sure did so we had a long discussion. This girl ran around with Lilia when she was stationed at McClellan last year. I was sure surprised and so was she.

I just went and got my mail and another letter from you. From the article I'm sending you, you can get a pretty good idea of our reaction to Kennedy's assassination. We're over here fighting and dying to keep our country and the world free of communists and then some idiot shoots our own leaders. That guy deserves the worst kind of death but that won't bring Bobby back.

I'm glad you got to see Dean. Yes, we do wear patches on our fatigues but usually they are black and green instead of colored so we don't really feel like we're wearing a patch.

Yes, $340 is my regular pay. Starting 1 July we get another raise. It should be about $355 then. I got all my back pay when I processed in.

Well, I'll close now. I didn't get rained on yet.

Lots of love,
Susie

PS AVHGF-B is our office symbol. The letters have no meaning. You had SAM right. DEROS is date eligible for return from overseas. MP Bde is Military Police Brigade.

12 June 1968

Dear Ruby,

I have an hour left to stay at work and there isn't a thing to do so I'll start a letter. LTC Preuss is the only other person here and he's writing too. SGT Hall was off today because he had guard duty last night and I rather enjoyed being the only enlisted person here. I got to run around a lot more. Every morning somebody goes to the snack bar at 0800 to get a turn-over for LTC Preuss to eat with his coffee. This morning I went and I thought I'd be glad to wash the general's car or even sweep sidewalks just to be outside. I'm out so little because it's nearly dark when I get home, especially when I get off at 1930.

Last night the club had a real good band from Vancouver, Canada. They played country western music and one young guy played a fiddle. They are going to be at our favorite club tonight so we're going. Today I was talking to the guy I bought my recorder from and he asked me if I went to the club last night. I told him I did and he wished he had known so he could go. He doesn't know I was with Tom. I was in his office and he had 2 .45 cal. Pistols so I got to look them over. I sure want a pistol or something to bring home but I don't know where I'll get it. Tom may be able to get me a bayonet or jungle knife. You know what a scavenger I am. The only trouble is that a lot of the stuff I want is not authorized to be shipped out of the country. Most people do manage to get just about anything out one way or another but it takes some planning.

My cold is much better. I almost lost my voice one day but it's back now. Everybody seems to be getting a cold. It must be the monsoon season.

I forgot to tell you that in Edie's letter she said SGT Hayes had left for Germany and he told her he would write to me from there. I had sent him a letter but I doubt if he got it before he left. I'm glad he got to go because he wanted to.

I'm having a terrible time trying to get my roll of film developed. The PX's don't have the right size pre-paid mailing envelope and it is so hard for me to try to get to the main PX where they develop film. I'm trying to get together a few things to send to you and if I don't have it developed by then I'll probably send it. I guess if you don't get that letter with the money orders I should get a small one and send it so you have money to use for me at least. I should go to Finance and have an allotment made out to you.

I know I'm sending you an awful lot of newspaper clippings but every time I read a paper and see something that I wish I could show you I cut it out and send it.

I just heard a jet and looked out and it's a TWA "freedom bird" coming in. Today I typed a letter to the San Francisco Procurement Agency, Oakland, Calif. I never heard of the place but it was nice to type it and address the envelope.

Well I'll have to quit now and put things away so I can leave.

2000

I thought I might get a letter from you to answer but since I didn't I'll close. We got a letter from our three sergeants today and they were wishing they were back here. They all caught colds and the dogs were freezing.

Lots of love,
Susie

16 June 1968

Dear Ruby,

I have 2 letters from you so I guess I'd better get them answered. First of all, about the money orders; the same day I got your letter telling me you had received them, the CPT from the post office came over and said they had been notified from Champaign that the letter was received so, since this post office has that information you can cash them and all the tracers on the letter have been withdrawn. The guy here put that brown paper on the envelope before I mailed it. I really don't think it's any better to mail a registered letter than a plain one—they always get through. I'm so glad you got them because I sure wanted you to have that $150.

The more I think about it, the more I think I should go back to Ft. McClellan and get in troop work but I don't know what I could do because I don't think I could ever make a platoon sergeant. That's what I need because I could be outdoors and marching. I'm never going to be happy in a darned office job because I just despise sitting behind a typewriter all day. I wish I had re-enlisted for medical school but then I couldn't have gotten over here. I sure envy these nurses stationed out in these field hospitals. What I want to do, a girl just can't, such as be a chopper pilot or on a med-evac chopper. There are so many exciting things going on that I can't do.

I was off yesterday afternoon but had to work all day today so I missed church and a farewell ceremony for General Palmer. I did get some more sunburn yesterday. It sounds like you've been having Saigon weather. Wait till next winter when you have—10 and we have 90 degrees.

I still haven't found out who the girl is that sings "San Francisco". That is the full name and a guy that sings it is Scott McKenzie. If you could get it by him it would be okay. I'll be glad when I get your loan paid off, it will be the first time since 1966 that I haven't owed you money.

I got a ride home in a jeep tonight. I love riding in them but I sure want to drive one. Sometimes when I see the Army cars sitting out in the parking lot I want to get in one and take off so bad. I feel like it's already been years since I drove a car. I supposed you never found out where Junior went. It's nice not to have that payment to make but I can't help but wish I still owned Junior. I want a TV and camera from over here. When I get back, I'll have 2 ½ years to go and in that time I hope to accumulate all the main things I want and have a car paid for so I'll own everything I want.

Well so much for my thoughts of the day. I sure hope Tom doesn't call tonight because I most definitely don't want to go out and I don't want to argue with him on the phone when I tell him I won't go.

I'll quit for this time.

Lots of love,
Susie

18 June 1968

Dear Ruby,

I'm going to get a money order for you this afternoon so I'll write something to go with it. I'm going to send it in a plain letter. We got paid this morning, 2 days early for some reason. I got $358, $19 leave rations. I found out that we can put money in the Bank of America in Saigon through our orderly room so I opened an account and put $350 in. We give the money to the company clerk and she takes it to Saigon. This way I can write a check to you and I won't have to fool with money orders anymore. This seems to be the easiest way. The bank pays 5% interest so that's not bad.

We had a unit picture taken before pay call. I don't know what that was for.

Yesterday a Jewish Women's Association in Los Angeles sent us a whole bunch of things-make up, lipstick, lotion, powder and ball point pens. Some organization sends things often. It's really nice because usually they send what we can't get here. I had wondered how I'd ever get anymore lipstick. All of the stuff is Max-Factor and it smells so good. I guess several people in the "real world" know we're over here.

Would you believe it's possible to go to a drive-in movie in Vietnam? Well it is. The other night we went out in the truck (another couple) with Tom and me and parked it off the road in an open area. Paul had a little portable TV that runs from a battery and he set it up in the front. We all sat in the back seats and watched TV. We even had hamburgers to eat. It was nice but I bet anybody that saw us thought we were crazy. We expected the MP's to come after us but there is no regulation that says you can't watch TV in a truck. Nobody thought of it before. There wasn't a no parking or off limits sign so I think we were pretty safe. It was sure a different thing to do anyway.

CPT Murphy is still trying to find someplace for me to go. I can be released from here as soon as a replacement comes in which should be within the next 2 weeks but as far as I know she still hasn't found anyplace for me to go. Somebody really slipped when they sent me over here because there is supposed to be a slot waiting. I'm glad they did anyway. If they hadn't sent me without a slot I never would have gotten over here.

I hope I get a letter from you today. I'll close for this time and read the Stars and Stripes before I go to chow.

Lots of love,
Susie

19 June 1968

Dear Ruby,

I'll start a letter to you while everybody is still at lunch. I stopped by the barracks at noon and got your letter so I have it here with me. When I mail a letter on Friday what day do you get it? I just wonder if there is a difference from that and when I mail it on Thursday.

I'm glad you remembered to fly the flag on Flag Day. I wish I had some tiny little red, white, and blue thing to wear on my shirt pocket on holidays but I don't know what it could be. I could get by with it if it was small enough.

I can't figure out the price of that camera. Are you sure it's the real Polaroid and not a Swinger? They cost about $100 here and I don't see how they could be that much cheaper in the states. Anyway, if that is it, I'm going to want you to get it for me. I don't need the flash attachment because they take pictures inside without it and I have seen some here if I would decide I wanted it. There is plenty of film here too. The biggest problem is that I can't send you more than $50 this month without going through the orderly room and CO and getting a certificate authorizing me to send over $200 out of the country in one month. We can't do anything with money over $200 without a certificate unless we spend it on small items. That is sure a stupid thing because everybody over here with any rank at all makes over $200. They do this because too many American people were making money off the black market. I think a $300 limit wouldn't be bad. Anyway if you would get the camera before next month I'll send you $50 this month and $150 or maybe more next month. It will probably be July before we get this all figured out and done. While you're at it, see what a Polaroid 250 costs. That's the best camera and I think it's in a leather carrying case. When you find out everything and decide when you would get it, tell me all the details so I'll know everything at once. Just be sure it's a standard Polaroid and not a Swinger. I don't think it would hurt it to be mailed if it was packed good. Before I get out of this place you're probably going to get very tired of finding and mailing things for me. It sounds like a good idea to keep $25 to use for me. I have everything I want to send to you now if I ever get them in a box and wrapped. It's just some little things so you can have something from here and Aggie's delayed birthday present.

I sure hope that bathing suit fits. If it does I might learn to swim yet because there are several pools around and Tom knows how to swim. If we ever get an afternoon off together we could go to the pool. Trying to swim in it wouldn't be quite as bad as the ocean. At least it wouldn't be salt water.

I'm really enjoying reading my newspapers. It's the first time since I've been in the Army that I could read a paper regularly. I'm even following the comic strips that I like. Mary worth is in the Stars and Stripes. I see articles about or pictures of kids I went to school with in almost every paper. There has been a complete turnover at WTHS now since I was there.

We get cards from our three sergeants all the time. The last ones were from Tucson and from there they were going to Ft. Sill then Chicago. I finally got a letter from Lilia. She is going home on leave on 8 July. I sure envy her being in that beautiful desert. She sounds like she's really bored. I don't have a chance to get bored but at times I sure wish I was back in civilization.

I heard "San Francisco" by Scott McKenzie again yesterday so he must be one of the main ones that sings it so if you can, get it by him.

Monday evening when we all got home, we gave our latrine a good scrubbing. The maid does it each day but she never gives it a real good cleaning. Our room is right beside it and all the bugs that got run out of their homes came to our room. Our floor was just crawling so about 4 of us stepped on them, swept them out and sprayed bug spray. I saw one of the biggest black hard shelled bugs. I swear it was 2 inches long. Boy, high school kids should have a chance at these for their Biology classes. After we finished we had a cook out then sat in the rain and watched a movie. We have a very casual informal life here if nothing else. Yesterday morning we watched the war again. Three jets were making air strikes over across the river and we could see the fire flash. It goes high in the air and they are at least 4 to 5 miles away. I'd sure hate to be under them. They don't scare me but I have noticed that every time there is a sudden "boom" or even if somebody drops something with a loud noise I jump and I'm ready to spring out of the chair or bed in half a second. If I'm writing, a line goes across the page.

I wash my hair about every other day. It takes a lot of shampoo but they sell Prell in the PX unless they run out. My hair looks real nice. I keep it trimmed off and this sun is giving it more blonde highlights. I had thought the humidity would make it curly and terrible but it didn't.

Well I'll quit for this time. I never got interrupted except once by the phone while I was writing this.

Lots of love,
Susie

PS I keep forgetting to tell you that we have praying mantises all over the place. I just saw one out by my window and it reminded me. They are all green and very healthy ones.

22 June 1968

Dear Ruby,

I'm sitting here in the office with nothing to do as usual so I'll start a letter. I am determined that somebody is going to get me out of this office. Since 1SG Herney can't seem to do anything I'm going to get an appointment to talk to the CO Monday and she should do something. I have 2 real good reasons for wanting out of here—no chance for promotion and since I'm not working in my MOS I have no chance for proficiency pay. I could never make it in the states because my test score wasn't high enough but here they don't go by a test. That would be around $30 a month. I saw in the paper that the Illinois Vietnam veteran bonus is still going. As soon as a person gets the Vietnam Service Medal, which I have, they are eligible for the $100 bonus. I don't know where we get it from or how. I guess Dean should know. Only 3 other states have it. I'm sure surprised that Illinois is one of them.

Last night was my last class in that correspondence course and I'm sure glad it's over. Now I won't have 2 evenings every week tied up with that. I get most of my letter writing done at work now but if I'd happen to get a job that kept me busy I'd have to write in the evening. Yesterday evening after I got out of school, Tom and me went to the service club and watched TV—Combat, Bewitched and Lucy. It's nice to do that once in awhile instead of going to the club. The last night we went that Canadian band was there again and they were the best yet. We had a table close to them. How I would have loved to tape that. Last night on the radio I heard "San Francisco" and "Love is Blue". They play a lot of good songs on AFVN. One thing about it over here, nobody can argue over radio stations and TV channels.

I don't know when I'm going to be off again. SGT Hall is on company duty, Reactionary Force, every night this week so that means I have to work till 1930 every night. It wouldn't be so bad if I had something to do. I think I would even transfer to MACV in Saigon if I knew I was going to an E-6 slot. Some women that come in here do go to MACV because there are no jobs for them at USARV. They are usually E-6 and above. I'd hate to take the chance of getting into something a lot worse than this and I know so many people here. Also if Barbara gets over here this is where she'll be. Oh well, it's very unlikely anyway. They must have a slot some place in USARV. I wish a WAC could be an officer's driver but of course we can't.

I'm sending you an article from the paper about a Kennedy book. Maybe you already saw it but you can be sure I want it. It sounds real good and I still want anything and everything I can get about them.

I just found out that I have the whole day off tomorrow. I don't believe it. This will be my first day to sleep late in 12 days. On Saturday and Sunday when I do work, I don't go to breakfast so I can sleep till 0640. Tomorrow there are a number of things I could do. I intend to go to mass at 1030 then in the afternoon I could go to the orphanage or possibly get a chopper ride. There is another girl that loves to ride in them too and we could come up to the pad and see if we could get a ride. Since we might wait all afternoon and never get one, I should go to the orphanage. At least we drive through the town of Bein Hoa on the way. It's off limits but we can go through as long as we don't stop. It still has VC in it someplace but it's full of MP's too. There is a rumor that Charlie is planning another offensive around the 1st. Maybe we will get to celebrate the 4th with live fireworks. There was quite a bit of banging going on last night just before I went to bed. The girl in the room next to me asked somebody "Is that ours or theirs?" The other one said "It's ours" so she went to bed. I'm getting a little better at distinguishing ours from theirs but I'm still not sure. Our guys shoot flares into the air along the perimeter and they sound like mortar rounds.

Well, I'll quit for now and continue this later.

23 June Sunday 1800

Well believe it or not I got to do everything I wanted to today. I got up at 0930 and went to mass then watched the welcoming ceremony for the new USARV commanding general. They always play the Vietnamese National Anthem before ours and we salute through both of them. Theirs is real pretty but you can sure see arms and backs straighten when ours starts. I got a ride back to the company in a jeep with a nice MSG. The buses weren't running so I went out on the road and had only walked about 2 steps when he came along. It's usually pretty easy to get a ride in some kind of vehicle around here.

This afternoon a bunch of us went to the orphanage. There is a little tiny baby only a few days old and he's cute now but he won't be long. I found another cute little boy but I just can't get interested in kids like the other girls do. They make over all of them. They're too dirty and make too much noise.

I just went and got my mail and had 3 letters from Illinois, Texas and California. I got yours day before yesterday. Sometimes I don't get any mail for several days and think I never will then I get it all at once.

I don't know where to tell you to look for my tapes. I just hope you find them. One is a 7 inch reel that I recorded on Edie's recorder. I'll be waiting for the package you mailed. I can't remember when I mail letters to you or what I said half the time.

You were sure writing early in the morning. How I'd love to be there and out at the farm on a nice summer morning and smell the corn fields. I will sometime.

I'd better quit now. That Canadian band is at the club again tonight so we're going.

I don't care if you didn't have much to put in the package. I'll be glad to get anything from home. Keep writing real often.

Lots of love,
Susie

26 June 1968

Dear Ruby,

I'm at work and there is nothing to do so I'll start a letter. I just read 2 good articles in SGT Hall's Sports Illustrated. One was about Lee Trevino, the golfer from El Paso and the other was a guy telling about his trip from Yuma Arizona to Mexico City and back up through Monterey. I'd love to do that sometime.

After work last night I finally got to talk to the CO. She didn't have any idea that I'm not in a slot here. They never tell the company anything about where they assign us. She said she was glad I told her and she would start today to see if she can find anything for me. She said she couldn't promise anything, which I know, but at least she's going to try. She is so nice to talk to. Unless she extends, she'll be leaving in October. How I wish I had got here last October like I wanted to. I am glad now though that I was stationed at Oakland because the west coast is our link with home and practically everybody has been in San Francisco.

I guess we will get paid Sunday. It seems like this pay day came real fast. In the states when I was running on my last gallon of gas they were slow but now it makes no difference. I think when I get over 4 years in my base pay, without any of this extra, will be a little over $300. I just need to be able to make E-6 because I would really be making money then. I won't want to come back to the states because I'll lose $100 a month. I think now that whether or not I'll extend over here will depend mainly on where I get orders for. If it's someplace I really don't want, I'll extend 4 or 6 months and try again. My roommate was supposed to leave for Ft. Lewis, Washington next month but she extended till

November so she can ETS at Oakland. A lot of the ones on their first enlistment do that.

We've really been having a lot of noise around here the past few days. There have been a lot of air strikes but not where we could see them. This building shakes like it's in an earthquake and I expect the clock to come off the wall right into my lap. So far everything is holding together.

I mailed the box to you yesterday by SAM. I had to put a customs tag on it telling what is in it and the value. There are more complications trying to get anything out of this country. You'll probably get this letter before you get the package. It really isn't much but at least you'll have something from here. You'll have to open each little box to see who they belong to. While you're sending things to me, I wish you would put some bubble gum in one of the packages if you haven't mailed everything when you get this. If you have don't make a special package for it. I can wait. We can't get bubble gum or candy bars over here. Plain gum is usually plentiful. Hard candy is easy to get but there is no variety in anything. We can get potato chips and pretzels but only in cans.

By the time I leave here and get back to civilization I won't know how to go in a store and buy anything. All the people working in any PX here are Vietnamese and most of them understand very little English. Yesterday I went to buy a new cap. After a conversation of few words the girl got the cap for me, told me the price and I had to sign a paper for it. Sometime I'll try to tape some of the language. If I could ever be in my room when the maids are outside talking I could get them on it.

I found out that we can't go to Bangkok on leave, only on R&R so I think I'd like to go to Hong Kong on leave. I don't even know where it is from here. Malaysia is supposed to be a good place too. I wish we could go to Formosa or the Wake Islands. I did see them on the way over. I'd give anything to have about 2 months just to travel over here. I'm so close to so much and can't do anything about it. Well, I guess I'll quit for now. These lines are so close together you'll probably have a hard time reading this.

1840

I'm back at work now for the last hour. I go home at 1700 supposedly for chow and come back at 1815 so it isn't too bad. I have that hour at home to read my mail and papers and do anything else I want to.

Tom gave me this felt pointed pen at noon today. He got it at a PX someplace. He gets to run around all the time because he's the outside plant inspector for the telephone management agency. He sometimes goes to other posts too. I guess we're going to the club tonight. Tom didn't call yet so I don't know what we're doing. He has school tomorrow night so I can stay home for once. I get tired of going out but I would get tired of spending every evening sitting around the barracks too.

July will be here before I know about the camera so I won't have to wonder how I could send you the money. I think at the end of this week I'll get another money order for you so it will go on this month's credit and I'll have $200 of next month's free.

It's 1900 now and the sun is about to set. The sky has black clouds and the sun shining down over the river and the green valley is so pretty. I always wish I could go out there but it's rice paddies and Charlie is out there. It's really a shame that a country as beautiful as this could be has to be all torn up.

Well, I'll close for this time. I hope I get a letter from you tomorrow. I forgot to tell you in the other letter that we do wear clean fatigues every day.

Lots of love,
Susie

30 June 1968

Dear Ruby,

Well, it's the last day of another month and tomorrow I can turn a calendar page. When I got here I thought it would never be time to turn this one with the cats on it because it has 2 months but they are gone already.

I got my bank book and check book yesterday. This is the Bein Hoa not Saigon branch as you will see on the check. Whoever cashes it is sure going to look at it I bet. Until I find out about you getting me the camera I don't know whether to put that $50 on our account or not. I don't think I will because I want you to get me a camera. I'm tired of waiting for one and it looks as if they might never come in here. If you do get it, send it airmail. The package you sent never got here yet.

Tom had guard duty last night so I got to stay home. I wrote letters and listened to tapes. Boy this recorder of mine is really a beauty. My roommate has one tape I love, the "Sons of the Pioneers" singing the best western songs. I wish I had a way to record it. Maybe I can before she leaves.

I'm off today, that's 2 Sundays in a row. I don't believe it. I'm going to quit now and iron some clothes. I wish I'd get a letter from you today.

2145

Well I certainly had an interesting afternoon. I went to chow at 1200 intending to come back and go to the orphanage. CPT Eason came and sat down beside me and wanted me to go to his ward so I did. I met CPT Love who was at Beaumont. She recognized me and 3 other guys recognized me. I stayed at the ward and he took me on a tour of the hospital till he got off work at 1500. Then we went for a nice long walk all around the area up there. He showed me his quarters and a bunch of pictures he has taken. We really should have a Beaumont reunion over here. We had a real nice afternoon talking about Beaumont and everything else. There aren't very many patients on each ward and the wards are air conditioned and real nice. Some of the guys are really battered up but it doesn't bother me to see them. This evening a doctor from Mexico City cooked a bunch of Mexican food so CPT Eason had me stay for some of it. Boy was it ever good, almost better than what I had in El Paso. I don't know where he got all the seasoning but he even had hot green peppers in it. I got home around 2030 and Tanya said Tom had been here looking for me. I hope I hadn't told him for sure that I would go out tonight. Half the time I forget if I made a definite date with him or not.

I see my name is checked on the mail roster for a package but this is the one night that they left it locked in the mail room so I won't get it till tomorrow night when I get home from work. At least we know it finally got here. It's only a week behind the letter you mailed the same day.

Well I think I'd better close for now and get ready to go to bed.

Lots of love,
Susie

PS While we were touring the hospital I saw where the VC prisoner patients are kept so I have seen "Charlie" now. They are really fenced in and guarded but he said 2 of them escaped once. I didn't know they were right here on post.

I hope I wrote this check right. It's the first one I've ever written so feel privileged.

CHAPTER IV

JULY 1968

1 July 1968

Dear Ruby,

This won't be much of a letter because I just mailed one but I got yours today. I got 3 newspapers and your letter and package. The bathing suit is a little tight but I think I can wear it. I sure won't look any worse than anybody else. I'm determined to get a tan over as much of an area as possible. I had heard about that surfing dog but I haven't seen it. Almost every company has a dog.

As for the camera—go ahead and get me the $74 one without a carrying case. I sent you a $50 check because I didn't want to mail a bigger one. Later in the month I'll send another $50 one. Please get the camera as soon as you can and send it air mail. I'm so anxious to get it and send you some pictures.

I guess I did get a good price on my tape recorder. It plays ordinary tape on a reel, not cartridge. I think pre-recorded ones are a 7 inch reel but anything less than that would be OK too. I think I have everything clear about the camera and tape. It takes so darn long to get answers back and forth. You would think we're on opposite sides of the world or something!

I hadn't seen anything about Mr. J. in the paper. They run too far behind. It may be in one I got today and didn't read yet.

Did you listen to my record? I'm glad you've at least got it. I have never heard it on the radio here and very few of the bands play it. I hear San Francisco fairly often.

At 1700 every day now we have a thunderstorm. It gets as black as night, the wind blows dirt all over everything and then the rain pours down in sheets. It's still raining lightly now at 2030. Usually it stops after an hour or two. I really enjoy the rain here because it's so refreshing.

Today I saw a red Falcon in the parking lot and with very little imagination it looked like Junior. The CID personnel drive the few civilian cars around here.

Your letter smells good, I wonder if you scented it. I'm sure glad I got that bottle of Tweed. I wear a lot of it and the "Original" and switch to some of the others now and then. All the pleasant smells possible are needed here. This place is really hard on soap too, it just melts.

Aggie will probably read this but tell her thanks for the magazine and the use of her bathing suit. I bet she never thought it would be worn in Vietnam. It smells like moth balls. Maybe it will knock off a few of our bugs. If I had a bottle to put one in, I'd capture one of these fine specimens of bug land and send it to you.

Well, I didn't think I had much to say but I've gone on for quite a few pages so I'd better quit.

Lot of love,
Susie

2 July 1968

Dear Ruby,

I sure didn't expect another letter from you today but I was glad to get it. I would rather have them often instead of waiting for a long one. I don't know what to tell you about the tapes. The ones you found were recorded on my little recorder and they aren't worth much. I know the 2 I want are there somewhere but it's hard to tell where. I didn't think you would like my record. The song isn't pretty but the words are so good, about "the Frisco Bay watching the tide roll in". I've done that so many times.

I guess I'm running up quite a charge account with you. I'm glad my credit has always been good. Barbara asked me if there was anything she could send me and I said yes, a '68 Chevy SS. She said she tried her best to get it in an envelope but it just wouldn't fit. I think everybody over here wants something they can't have. What we can get in canned goods is very limited, in fact everything is. They just have certain things and not always them.

This Saturday I'll have training so I'll have the afternoon off and work Sunday. 1SG Herney told me at noon today that she has the people in personnel working on finding me a job and she won't let them forget about it. She said my SGM told her I'm doing a good job here. I don't know who couldn't with so little to do. I want to get to another job and get settled so I can get the leave I want this fall. Wherever I go, I hope to be able to find some binoculars for you.

All of us over here have a very sentimental feeling for anything connected with the states. I just wonder how it will be when it comes the time that I would usually be going home. December will be the longest I've been away. Maybe it won't be too bad. As long as I keep getting mail I don't feel deserted and that's the most important thing. This is no ideal duty station but I wouldn't leave if I could. In fact, the thing I think about a lot is what if something would happen either to the post or me that would get me shipped back. I would lose everything I came over here to gain. I went through everything to get here so I sure want to stay. A few of the girls wish they could go home but not many.

Well, I'll close for now.

Lots of love,
Susie

7 July 1968

Dear Ruby,

I'm sitting here at work with nothing to do so I'll start answering the letters I got yesterday, yours and one from Edie. She is a civilian now and she's happy. She says being married gets better all the time. 1SG Crawford was asking her about me so I guess I'd better get busy and write to her. I might be stationed with her again someday.

Yesterday morning I had training and the first hour of it was an inspection in our summer uniforms. Some stupid man, the Headquarters Commandant, is trying to make us start wearing them so CPT Murphy is compiling a 4 page report on why we shouldn't and she wanted to see how many of us could get into them if we had to. Not very many could. She says she has a good argument and she thinks she'll win. I sure hope so. Besides the fact that I enjoy wearing fatigues, Class A uniforms just weren't made to wear in this place. Every time we sit down we get red dirt on the back of us and those uniforms would wilt in the rain. Besides we can't get nylons over here and after the maids hung our cords on the barbed wire fence to dry a few times, there wouldn't be anything left. After we got in fatigues and went out under the parachute for the rest of training CPT Murphy asked which we liked best and everybody yelled "fatigues!" We about roasted out there because yesterday was an extra hot day. In the afternoon I thought I'd get to take a sun bath but I got recruited to help set up the area for last night's party. I did get some sunburn and something, I suppose heat, broke out on my back. I guess it's gone today. After that, I took a shower and changed clothes and got my mail. The party started at 1900. I had a real good time at a table with

4 other girls. Tom was in Saigon and didn't get back till 2130. He came over then. One of his friends, Chico, is in a Roadrunner Platoon here. He had a little white pin with the roadrunner on it and I asked where I could get one. He brought me one the other night. It is so cute.

Friday night we had a delayed Fourth of July. About 2230 I had just got in bed and I heard a whistle and a loud boom. It was a lot closer than ever before. You should have seen how fast I got off that top bunk and out the door to see what was going on. There were several more booms then nothing more. We thought sure we would go on alert but we didn't. That was the closest I've heard yet. We found out yesterday it was ARVN artillery right outside the gate so no wonder it was loud. I'm just glad it was going out and not coming in. Anyway for a little while we were ready to hit those bunkers. I saw the other day that the tin lining in them is from Granite City, Illinois.

Yes, the moon looks the same as it does there. Sometimes there are clouds around it and it's real pretty. When you see a jet going west it really has a long way to go to get over here. Every morning when I go out to stand reveille the sun is just coming up and I look east.

1320

I had to quit there so I'm back from chow and going to the PX and snack bar three times for LTC Preuss so I'll start again. Tom took me to eat. We went over to the PX at the 24th Evac and I almost got your binoculars. They had 3 different kinds and one was what I want to get you but they didn't have the book or all the straps that went with them and I want all of it so I didn't get them. We even asked the manager and he didn't know where the rest was at. They had a "zoom lens" and you can focus then bring it up as close as you want. I'll keep looking. They still don't have any Polaroid cameras. I expected them to come in by truckloads since I have told you to send me one but I guess they won't.

The USARV PX got some tapes in the other day and I got 2 at $4.98 each. I'll send you the list of songs on them if I don't forget. They are real pretty. I dreamed last night I was home and had a new car and we were over in Indiana someplace driving on gravel roads. I never dream anything about this place.

By the time you get this letter I hope you have my package. I wish you would wear that ring if it fits. I have one like it. I finally quit wearing my class ring. I don't know what these brown ones are made out of but I think they're real pretty and quite different.

Well I guess I'll close for now and I won't write anymore tonight because I have covered everything I can think of.

Lots of love,
Susie

1330

9 July 1968

I'll have to start a letter to you. I went home at noon and my name on the mail roster was checked for a package. I thought it was too soon to be getting anything then when I saw the box I thought it was my camera. I sure got a surprise when I opened it. Another girl was with me and when she saw the percolator box she thought that was what was inside. I told her I don't even drink coffee so it couldn't be that. I sure like everything you sent. The only things in it that we can get here are the jelly beans and M&Ms. Sometimes we can get nuts but not any of the rest of it. I'm especially happy with the bubble gum. I'm chewing some and it's so good. I'm glad everything you sent is bug proof at least till it's opened. I'll have to find a cookie or cracker can with an air tight lid to put anything I open in. We have little tiny ants in our room now along with the rest of the bugs. Boy do I ever get tired of seeing everything crawling. It's not too bad till one crawls on your tray in the mess hall and that is horrible. The more it rains the worse they come inside.

I'm so happy with the package you sent. I already put your picture in the frame and I cut your return address off the paper and kept it. I hated to throw away any part of it but I don't have room to keep wrapping paper. You can send anything over here but to send a package out I have to give a complete inventory of it. Let me know if they had taken the tag off the package I sent you. I sure wish I could have gotten those binoculars for you. Getting that package really put a bright spot in my day. I was so bored all morning just sitting here but I feel a lot more alive now after getting the "care" package. Thanks so much for it.

I don't know if I told you I have DNCO Friday night. I'll automatically get Saturday off and Sunday will be my regular day off so unless a lot of work suddenly comes up, I should get both days. If I do, I sure won't stay around the barracks Sunday. I may have to spend the day at the orphanage but I'll go anyplace to keep from being called to work. It would be too good to be true to get 2 days off. Tom is supposed to go up to Pleiku today or tomorrow. Everybody in this office except Mr. Rynearson and me has a cold. He says we're the only healthy ones. Everybody has a cold or something half the time. I guess this is just an unhealthy place. The girl that got the sun poisoning when I first got here has come back from Camp Zama, Japan now. Another one went there for something. If they have anything that takes prolonged treatment they go there.

Well I just found out that I have to come to work Sunday. SGT Hall says the colonel thinks we're getting too many Sundays off. There is never one thing to do on Sunday but sit here and now he wants 2 of us working instead of one. He said I could go home if there was nothing to do but I bet I can't. I knew I'd never get 2 days off. The guys have so many details in the company that they get off for but all I have is DNCO about every 5 weeks. I never thought I'd see the day that I'd rather pull DNCO than work but I would now.

The other morning I was on my way to the snack bar to get breakfast for LTC Preuss and the band was playing out in front of the building. I stood there and watched them. Two songs they played were "Yellow Rose of Texas" and "Somewhere My Love". They must have known I was out there. One night at the club the band played a medley of songs that was very pretty.

I hope I have a letter from somebody tonight even after the package at noon. I always enjoyed anything you sent me in the states but it means so much more over here. I'm anxious to get home and look it over better. Where did you get that pen? I really like the verse on it.

1850

I didn't get a letter but I finally got my pictures back and they are good considering the vibration in that chopper. I'll send all I can and you can keep them.

Lots of love,
Susie

14 July 1968

Dear Ruby,

Well I'm happy now. I got both packages from you, the case yesterday and the camera today. The letter you sent with 6 cents got here yesterday in the AM. The airmail one you mailed the 10th got here yesterday afternoon. It took that plain one 8 days so it was practically ancient history. It's a pretty stamp anyway and I like the airlift ones. I couldn't imagine what I was getting yesterday. I didn't think I needed a case but I'm glad you got it because it will keep a lot of dust and dirt off the camera. I opened it and then I read your letter about the strap. Since I don't know what it looked like before, it looks perfect to me. The foam is really stuck. Thanks a lot for the case. I feel almost like a professional photographer now. I'm waiting for Tanya to come home and show me how to load it. The instructions don't make too much sense. I'm trying to keep all those boxes you send because they will be handy to use to mail stuff to you. Between Tanya and me we almost have the space under the bed full. Reddy tries to sleep under there among boxes, boots and shoes. Tanya got me a new pair of jungle boots so I'll have them to bring home. We're authorized to take back one set of fatigues. I want more than that, especially the shirts because they make nice jackets.

I listened to my Dr. Zhivago tape. It's beautiful. I can just see that snow. I'm sending you another check and that's all till next month. I hope I don't want anything for awhile.

Sometimes I think I'll never get an answer to any questions I ask you. This is slow communication but I guess we'd better be satisfied, it could be a lot worse. I bet you did see Junior. How I wish I was out driving someplace right now. You put that good smell in your letter again and I still don't know what it is unless it's that Hawaiian perfume. Tanya smelled it across the room when I opened the letter.

Tell Wilma that I didn't forget about her wanting the earrings. I tried to get her some to send with your stuff but they didn't have any for pierced ears. If I could get to the II Field Forces PX I could probably get her some with real stones. Ask her if she would want them or just plain ones. None of them cost too much here. You said at one time you would like a diamond ring. I need to know what size and an idea of a style so if I have a chance I could get you one or another kind of ring.

We don't have anything we can keep locked. About the only thing we have that could be stolen is money and I keep mine locked in my bag that I brought over. The maids can't steal anything of any size because they're searched by the guard on their way in and out of the company area. There isn't much danger of anybody taking anything here because there's no place to go with it. Tom is on R&R so I can't take a picture of him.

DNCO was quiet and uneventful Friday night. I was off yesterday but had to go in today, quite a day. All I did was read the papers and go to the snack bar for LTC Preuss. They finally let me go at 1430. LTC Preuss even got a driver to bring me home.

1845

I went to the mess hall with a couple of girls and just got back. We started out walking and got a ride. Just after we got in the mess hall the rain poured down. It has quit now and it's cool and pretty out. I can see why people count months, days, hours and minutes till they get out of here. At least my 9 ½ months sounds pretty good and I know I'll get out of here twice before then. I'll survive but I know I'll sure be glad to get back and I doubt very much if I'll extend. Maybe I will for a week to get another month's pay and to be home over Memorial Day. I have my mind on going to the Indianapolis 500 and I'd love to go to Eugene. About all that keeps any of us going over here is the thought of what we have to go back to. It gets kind of old having bugs and dirt in and on everything. Aggie should be invaded by some of our fine specimens. She would do more than call you.

Well, I'll close for now and make that song list for you. I'll probably forget some I'd like to have.

Lots of love,
Susie

15 July 1968

Dear Ruby,

I won't have much to say after mailing a letter this morning but I want to tell you about the camera. Tanya showed me how to load it, real simple compared to the directions. I took a picture of her and her dog in our room last night and it turned out real good. At noon today I took one of a girl outside and it was perfect. It's sure nice to just snap a picture inside without a flash bulb. I don't think I have it fitted in the case right but I can't figure how else to do it. It does fit OK but it looks wrong. I filled out the guarantee but I had to use my address. There was only room for one and I couldn't mail it here using your address. I guess it won't matter. I can't wait to get color film in it. I hope it's as easy to use as black and white. I want to get a picture of USARV HQ and the flags flying in front in color. If I ever get up in a chopper again, the case will be real good to drop pictures and everything else in. I feel a lot safer having the camera protected in it.

This month is going by fast, half over today. I hope they keep going like this. Well, I guess that's all I have to say.

Lots of love,
Susie

16 July 1968

Dear Ruby,

I'm working till 1930 tonight and when I was home at 1700, I got your letter and 2 newspapers. I drank a Fizzie and read them. It makes me feel like I live at least an hour of a normal life to come home and read the paper leisurely. I sure never read that paper before like I do now, even the K-Mart ads.

It takes 4 or 5 days for a package to get here by PAL and forever by SAM. Anything I send after this will be by PAL. I am eating what you've sent and enjoying every bite. Those little chocolate cups are like Ronnie used to always eat. The little bags of candy are really nice because they stay fresh and it's a nice variety. When I opened my camera in the percolator box, Wanda, the same girl that saw the other one said "Well I know it's not a percolator this time." Tanya said you must have bought a lot of them. I was at the little PX today and they have stacks of color film for my camera so I won't have any trouble getting it.

We have a movie almost every night for anybody who wants to watch it and I listen to my tapes and read anything I can find. Tom is gone on R&R so I'm home every evening and enjoying just being around the barracks.

When we have parties there is usually a band and we have food and drinks. We sit at the tables in groups and eat and drink. It may not sound like much but it gives a feeling of togetherness and it's nice. Two new girls have come, SP5 Ruth McKenney and Sp5 Pat Powell. Them, Wanda, and I stay together a lot. It seems as though I can't get away from people named Pat and Powell.

I have worn my ring all the time and the top is scratched and 2 pieces of the white came out. It probably is tortoise shell. I see where you smashed the bug. Boy if I smashed one on the paper you wouldn't have to look for the spot. Besides all the bugs we have rats running around all over the place. There is poison out but they must not eat it. I think we have a mouse in our room. We have never seen or heard it but Tanya had some pine nuts and something hollowed out a bunch and stacked them in a corner of the closet. I think we need a cat.

When you tell me about going to the farm or sitting in the yard, I can just see it and do I ever wish I was there. I thought coming over here would make me appreciate home more and it has already. This is almost like a sentence of a year. I'm glad I got here but will I ever be glad to go. It would really take something awful big to get me to extend over here. I like to live and have fun too much.

CPT Murphy leaves tomorrow for R&R in Australia and we have a Warrant Officer (female) for our acting CO. WAC officers except nurses aren't too plentiful over here.

Well I'll quit now. It's almost time to go home, 1930, and it's almost dark outside.

2000

I'm going out to watch the movie so I'll end this.

All my love,
Susie

22 July 1968

Dear Ruby,

I just got back from chow so I'll start a letter to you. I was sure happy and surprised yesterday when I got the tapes. I also got a letter that you wrote on 5 July; evidently the day or day after you got my package. I don't know where in the world it could have been all that time. I was glad to get it even if it was 2 weeks old. If you wonder why I don't answer your questions sometimes don't give up. I got a lot of mail this weekend, 2 letters from you, and one each from Grace, Edie and Susie Collum. I was real surprised to get it and until I opened it, I couldn't imagine who she was.

I didn't realize I had so many good songs on that big tape. I wish I had filled it up at the time but I didn't anticipate playing it in Vietnam.

I think I have found somebody I'm going to be real good friends with. She got here about 3 weeks ago, Ruth McKenney. She's 28, in her 2nd enlistment and came here from Ft. Bragg, N.C. She's a real nice girl and we seemed to hit it off from the start. We walk to the mess hall from the barracks a lot and she likes to be outdoors and walk just like I do. She seems to like to be around me so I hope we will stay together and get to be like Pat and Barbara and me were. I've enjoyed this past week a lot and I haven't felt nearly as tired as before. I don't know if it's because I've been here longer or what. I don't go to bed a whole lot earlier but I sure feel better. As long as I was going out so much I was never around the other girls to get in a group and get to know them. Friday night one of them came to my room and invited me out to a small beer party they were having, about 5 people. We stayed out there and drank and talked till bed check at 2400. I'm better acquainted with the whole company now and there are about 6 girls I like real well. We all do a lot of things together. None of them want to go out. Some have boyfriends at home and others just want to stay away from these guys.

I'm sending you an article that was in the Stars and Stripes yesterday. It's well written and most of it expresses my thoughts perfectly. I wish I had been around for one of the pictures. If I only had a job I liked everything would be fine.

I don't really pay much attention to the days I write to you. I just write when I have something to say and the time. We've been having a lot of noise around here recently. It's getting like it was my first weeks here. We go to sleep listening to the artillery again. I wish I had your letters here to answer but since I don't, I'll quit for now.

1900

I'm home now and I just barely got in before the worst rain storm we've had. It is just pouring down and the wind is real strong. There is a river outside my door. The rain usually brings cool fresh air. Some places around here stink pretty bad but not every place. There is always dirt in the air.

I'm reading your ancient letter now. You probably forgot what you asked me in it. Yes, I can get plenty of soap and they even have Prell shampoo. I'll have no trouble getting any of that kind of stuff. It's just clothes that we can't get at all. If they ever get the women's section of the PX re-stocked they might have something but probably not much.

I fitted your ring on my left hand and just hoped that would be the right size. Yes, the fastener comes on the tiger tooth but the one I found came apart and I don't have any glue to put it back together. I bought that one for you. If you wear it I'm sure it would be noticed.

I'm listening to one of the tapes now. I wanted to finish this letter before my roommate got home or Tom called. I'll close for now.

Lots of love,
Susie

27 July 1968

Dear Ruby,

I guess I'll start writing to you now. It's Saturday morning and I'm off till noon and that's all for the whole weekend. I just ate a Pop-up, I have 2 left. I'm listening to my tapes sitting here with the door open and a nice breeze blowing in. It would be real nice if I had the whole day off.

Last night we had a DEROS party for our company clerk who leaves in a few days. They had 35 Vietnamese entertainers, a band, singers and dancers. It was really nice. Of course they played American music too among the songs "San Francisco". Ruth and 2 other girls and I sat together.

I half way have a cold again. I started catching it and took Contact for 2 days. It stopped my nose running but I was floating around and so sleepy. Now I'm kind of hoarse so I don't know if I'm going to win or not. Everybody over here gets so many colds. I guess it's mostly caused from the dirt in the air. It's sure going to be disgusting to go on for a year like this.

Boy how I would love to be taking all those long walks with you. There is a song called "The Green Green Grass of Home" that is played often over here. I told Ruth if I ever touch the green grass of home again I'm just going to lie in it. There isn't much grass around on post and it's not fresh and clean anyway. Rain can be pouring down one minute and the next dust is blowing in our face. When I was 9 months from my ETS it didn't seem long but 9 months here sometimes seems forever. At least I'm one quarter through now.

Yes, ordinary room lights are OK for taking black and white Polaroid pictures but you have to have flash for color ones. My camera case is covered with red dust all the time so that would all be on the camera without it. I don't know when I'm ever going to get to take a bunch of color pictures since I'm not off tomorrow. I want some of me in fatigues and I have to have somebody around to take them.

I sent Miss Thomas a card when I first got over here and I got a letter from her this week. I also got a nice long letter from SGT Hayes in Germany. It took it 6 days to get here through both APO's. He's the one that got my license plates for me. He went to Germany in May and I thought I'd never hear from him again.

It's cloudy out practically every day now so I couldn't get any sun even if I was off. I'll have plenty of time to get a good tan after the monsoon season ends in January but I want more now too.

Well I guess I'll quit for now and do something else. "El Paso" is playing now. While I'm thinking about it, there was a picture in the Stars and Stripes of the USS Enterprise going in under the San Francisco/ Oakland Bay Bridge. When it left there in April I was there and I knew it was coming back in July. Now I'm here and it's there. It was a good picture of the bridge so I kept it.

1850

I'm back now. I got your letter at noon and one from Aggie tonight. When I got off Ruth and me walked down and looked over the new barracks. They are pretty nice. They are in an area of small trees and just plain jungle. I hope they leave it there. We just barely made it back without getting rained on. The wind was blowing dust but it was cool.

It sounds like your song fest would have been fun. I should have been there with a drum.

I don't have any idea what time of day they take the Saigon temperature reading but it has to be at night or early morning.

Ruth is sitting here in my room reading a book right now. We're both still in fatigues. Tom called and we are going to the service club tonight. Well the rain just got here, it's really pouring. Ready even came inside.

These pictures I took are just around in the room and company area. I wanted to get color film in the camera. In Aggie's letter she said sometime she would send me some pictures. You can keep any and all pictures that I send you.

Well, I think that's all I have to say so I'll close and mail this tomorrow morning.

All my love,
Susie

30 July 1968

Dear Ruby,

I was surprised to get your package yesterday. I didn't think you had even mailed it yet and there it was. Ruth was with me when I got it so we opened it together. She was as excited over it as me and she said she wished somebody would send her a package. Anyway she had fun seeing what was in mine. I'm so happy with all of it. The monkeys are so cute. I have the big one tied on the end of my bunk on the mosquito net bar and the little one sitting on the dresser by Barney. They won't show dirt like the rabbit so that's good. I'm glad you sent the pickles. Sometimes we can get them but not always. I didn't eat any cheese yet. The plastic containers are perfect. The money clip is just what I wanted. I'll put in my time trying to keep it shiny. The key case is nice too. I just love to get a box of stuff like that. Of course over here everybody does. I guess I won't need anything else for a long time now. It sure takes a lot of postage to send all this stuff.

Ruth got a different job so she has to eat earlier than me now and we don't see each other except for a minute at noon. Sunday night her and me and a few other crazy ones sat out in the rain and watched the movie. We had our ponchos on so we didn't get wet. It's getting so it rains right at movie time too.

Tomorrow is payday again, not that I really care. I'll send you a check as soon as the bank gets my deposit and this one can start going on my account again. I'll sure be glad if I ever get it paid.

I worked all day Sunday and finally got that 20 page report done. Boy, sometimes I feel like I work a 7 ½ day week if it was possible. I've had one ordinary day off this month with 2 half days. It's getting less and less. SGT Hall leaves around the middle of September and then I probably won't ever get a day off. A few of the girls get a day and a half every week and the rest of us hate that.

I went to the club with Tom Saturday night and haven't seen him since. Alex is over here now at Camp Black Horse, far from here.

1920

I'm home now and got my mail, a letter from you. I usually do look at marriage licenses but I don't have that paper yet. If you do want to get a GED I would advise you to go to school because you can learn a lot more in a class with other people than from a book.

I'm glad you don't think the postage on my packages is bad. It seems an awful lot to me. I hope you've listened to "San Francisco" by now. There's a song they play here that has this in it "We've gotta get out of this place if it's the last thing we ever do.

We all sing that part because it's so true.

You're not the only one who would give anything for the outdoor life we had. I'm just so thankful I have the memories so I at least know what it was like. I have seen Dr. Zhivago 3 times and I'd see it again if I had a chance.

I'm going to the club tonight with Tom and Ruth is going too. She's so tired but she wants to get away for a change.

Well, I'm going to close for now. Thanks for everything in the package.

Lots of love,
Susie

PS Ruthie says "Hi". I forgot to mention the mouse trap. I sure didn't expect to find that. We'll put it in the closet and see if we get anything.

CHAPTER V

AUGUST 1968

4 Aug 68

Dear Ruby,

I'll try writing to you on this paper. The Orderly Room handed it out and it's OK except I can't see lines through it and I'll probably be writing all over the page. I think it's cute anyway. It's 1345 and I do have the whole day off. Tanya has been at the orphanage all day so I've had the room to myself and it's nice. I scrubbed the floor and gave the whole room a good cleaning this morning. Ruthie is working but I went to chow with her. We walked up there and back. Then I washed my hair and read my newspapers. I saw the picture of the Zayre store. I bet that shopping center is going to be real nice. By the time I get back Danville might be a big city. I'm listening to Dr. Zhivago. I love to listen to my music while I write letters. It isn't too noisy around here right now. Usually somebody always has a radio blaring.

Last night 5 of us went to the Service Club and played Bingo. One girl, Eileen, won several things but Ruthie and me can't win even once. We both said we're not going back. They have a piano there and we were messing around with it. Ruthie is a real good singer and she loves to have a chance to sing. Sometime I may want you to send me some music. We were about ready to come home when a call came that we were on a practice yellow alert so we found a guy with a truck to bring us home. We stood in the back of it in the rain. By the time we got back the alert was almost over. On a practice one all we do is come home. Things have been pretty hot around here lately. One day this week the jets were bombing out in that valley again only much closer than ever before, about a mile away. After they would drop a bomb and come back up, they circled right over headquarters. When they start doing that everybody stops working and watches. Last night there were a lot of flares being shot up over at the 90th "Replacement Company and the ammo dump. We have been expecting another major offensive since 4 July and nothing has happened yet. It keeps us kind of on edge waiting and wondering. It seems impossible that Charlie could ever get on Long Binh but I guess we can't be sure of anything. I don't really worry about it, there's no use to. It bothers Ruthie quite a bit but she's only been here a month. I don't know how her and me got together but I'm sure glad we did. I haven't known many girls as nice as she is. She sure doesn't seem 6 years older than me. She gets tired of being around so many people all the time too and we have the same views on a lot of other things. She's from Oregon. If we ever get a chance we're going to take some pictures and I can send you some. Every time we're off it's either dark or raining. We can't ever get a day off together. Judy Roberts from Oakland got here the other day. I haven't seen her much but she said Barbara and all of them told her to say hi to me.

I can hardly believe it's already August. Soon it will be fall for you then you have winter to go through and when spring comes, I'll come too.

I guess I never told you that I'm in the E-6 slot in my office now. HQ, USARV is cutting down on the excess personnel so since SGT Hall leaves in about 50 days they took him out of the slot and put me in it. I don't know that I'm any better off. I know nothing about accounting and have no desire to. You know how I always hated math. They're supposed to hire a civilian typist and if they do that will leave me as Chief Accountant and NCOIC of Budget Division. There's so much to do that I don't know anything about. If I would get promoted there, it would change my MOS and I'd really be in trouble when I get back to the states if I couldn't get it changed back. If I stay there I'm almost sure I'll get the Army Commendation Medal which I really want so I guess all I can do is just stay there and take what comes. It is very disgusting more often than not but the way the other girls talk their jobs are no better. I was real busy this past week and time went a whole lot faster. I'm getting to be an expert typist.

I've only been out with Tom once all week. He has asked me but I just tell him I already have plans to do something else. He tried to take Ruthie out and she wouldn't go either.

I have a bottle of hot sauce. They have it in the mess hall and I said I wanted some so one morning a girl that was with me just picked up a bottle and carried it out.

Your letter smells good. I wish I was there to help you get everything done. I never get to do a thing around here. I'm sure not going to get any sun today because it's cloudy and it's going to rain. It has rained every single day for 2 or 3 weeks and I guess it won't stop till December. Yesterday I walked by some freshly cut grass up at HQ and it smelled so good. There is quite a bit of grass up there but almost none around the barracks. This is really a desolate area. There are a lot of trees around our new barracks and if we ever get to move down there I hope they leave the trees there. We were supposed to move 1 Aug, now it's 1 November. I wonder if we'll ever get down there.

Well I'd better close for now or I'll have to send this in 2 envelopes.

Lots of love,
Susie

5 Aug 1968

Dear Ruby,

I'm at work for my last hour so I'll write you a short letter. You wrote the end of your letter and mailed it Friday and I got it today, Monday, so I feel like it's not so old this time. While I was home this evening Ruthie and I decided to give up waiting for the sun to shine and try some color pictures anyway. It was real cloudy and it rained just after we took the last picture. I think they turned out real good. We took one of CPT Murphy too but I don't know if I can get 3 in one letter or not. Ruthie wears glasses and she didn't have them on so she doesn't look natural to me.

We're going to have another practice yellow alert tonight and we had one 2 nights already. I guess they are getting us prepared in case there is another offensive like Tet. I sure have good excuses not to go out with all these alerts going on. Last night Ruthie had DNCO so I went on the club rounds with her. We were just leaving the USARV club when they called the alert.

Boy the rain is pouring down. It's only 1905 but it's dark outside because of a big black cloud.

The blue and white trailer in the pictures is where the CO lives. The pink and white one has a tailor shop and gift shop run by Vietnamese.

This is all I have to say for now. I mainly wanted to send the pictures and if I don't forget I'll send a check.

Lots of love,
Susie

7 August, 1968

Dear Ruby,

I guess I'll see how much I can think of for another letter. You should get this one Monday if I mail it tomorrow.

We have heard part of the Republican convention. I'm sure Nixon is going to get it. The whole thing seems to us to be happening in another world that we aren't even part of.

Our barracks SGT is leaving in a few days so we got a new one. Ruthie is her assistant but since she has to be at work at 0630 most mornings, she can't be there to take reveille. She asked for me to take it for her whenever she has to so both of us are going to have the job. I'm anxious to get to do it and a little scared too. I've never been in front of a platoon of girls. We stand up there, take reports from the squad leaders and give the report to the First Sergeant with all the salutes, etc. that go with it. On inspection mornings it would mean giving the platoons the commands for the position for inspection and then going with the CO to inspect. I hope I don't get stuck with that for awhile at least. It's been so long since I've done anything military that I sure need a chance to use it again. I think I will enjoy being in charge of a platoon. That's one way to find out if I can do it. I probably won't have to do it very often because the barracks SGT should be there.

I don't know how much you have heard about making MARS calls from here. It is possible and some of the girls have. There is no way to tell when one can get through because they are always booked hours ahead. Usually a night on DNCO is the best time to try. It usually gets through after midnight so it would be sometime in the afternoon on your end. I'd like to try it sometime. It goes through a radio so you have to say "over" after each thing you say. You get a briefing on what to do before the conversation starts. They are limited to 5 minutes and you are charged an ordinary collect call from wherever they put it through. Sometimes the connection is good but if it's real poor the radio operator acts as a go-between. If I don't try it before, if I ever make SSG I'll get a call through somehow. Don't hold your breath waiting. It would be my luck you wouldn't be home the day I did try.

They have started something new in Comptroller now. Each week an officer, and NCO and a typist are on call all night in case of an alert or anything that has to be typed right then. Even for practice alerts, we have to come back up the hill. They are supposed to send a car for us. I start it Saturday night through next Friday. I don't care for having to stay home but I don't love the idea of having to leave the company and come up here for an alert. Of course I'd have to wear my field gear and probably be the only WAC in this building. I hope if Charlie hits he does it when I'm not on call. I used to wonder how it would be to have alerts like they do in Germany but there they are just a game. Here we never know when it will be real.

We have been invaded by a bunch of local nationals (Vietnamese) who are painting the office. They are making it white of all colors. It was a dirty green. I wish I was doing the job instead of sitting here watching them. Maybe you'll have a paint job for me next spring.

Ruthie and I were discussing MACV in Saigon. She wished she had gone there and so did I. Now we wish we could both go but we can't unless we would extend for there and I have no intention of extending. Besides, I think I'd better stay here in this E-6 slot and hope it does some good. You hope real hard too and maybe someday I'll make it. They have an E-6 board now so if I get put in for it I'll have to go before the board and answer questions.

Almost every night Ruthie and I open a can of something and heat it and have supper either in her room or out under the "chute". 1SG Herney is always joking about our campfires. I think we're going to pop corn tonight. Somebody sent the company an electric popper and we can get corn and oil. Morton's salt is a failure over here, it gets all stuck together and impossible to pour. Oh, we didn't catch anything in the mouse trap yet. I'm not too sure the mouse or whatever it was is still around. Ready might have chased it out.

I have training this Saturday and if nothing happens Ruthie and I will have an afternoon off together for the first time. I don't know what we'll do but we've been wanting a day or half day off.

The smell of this paint and being the time of year it is reminds me of my school days so long ago. Well I'll close for now. The painters are about to reach me.

1930

I'm home now and I'll close this and put it in an envelope.

Lots of love,
Susie

11 August 1968

Dear Ruby,

It's Sunday morning and I'm at work so I'm catching up on my letter writing. Yesterday morning I had training and in the afternoon Ruthie and I were both off so we went around to some of the PX's. She got a hot plate and a cooking pan so maybe we can fix some food without heating it in cans now. Whenever we move to the new barracks Ruthie, Eileen and I want to move into the same room so it will be a lot nicer. There will be 4 or 5 people to each room but they are big so it shouldn't be too bad. We're supposed to get rid of our bunk beds too. We might move by the end of the month. Some officers are going to get our old barracks and they are in a hurry for us to get out. It's really going to be a mess when we move.

1345

I quit writing there to type something and after that I went to church, then to eat. LTC Preuss and Major Warren have been the only ones here and I don't think LTC Preuss is coming back this afternoon. This is a real good Sunday for me to work. I was just reading in the paper that if a person extends over here for 6 months, they can get a non-chargeable leave to anywhere in the free world, transportation paid. That would be wonderful if I wanted to stay over here that long and didn't want to go home.

Friday morning I was a platoon SGT for the first time in my life. I was scared but everything went just perfectly. I'm a permanent squad leader and assistant platoon SGT so I don't know how often I'll be doing it but enough to get used to it I hope. I mailed you a couple of pictures this morning. Ruthie and I were messing around yesterday and decided to put on our field gear and take pictures. I think they turned out perfect. Ruthie buys film for me so I give her the pictures she wants. I'm perfectly willing to take pictures for anybody as long as they furnish the film. It gives me more practice.

You must have had a monsoon rain. I can't imagine that much water all over town. I sure would have been out exploring if I were there. I didn't get the paper yet of course, but I will read about it.

Would you believe that after only 3 paydays over here, I have $470 still in the bank even with all I've sent you? I wouldn't have had that in a year without being over here. If I could only make E-6 I would get $420 a month. I hate the thought of losing all this extra pay but I can't stay here forever.

I'm getting so many letters collected and I sure hate to get rid of any of them but I'll just have to because we have so little space. We have to burn all our letters because the Vietnamese go through the garbage and some of them are probably working for the VC. If they would get our home addresses they might start sending propaganda so if you ever get anything you'll know they found my address someplace.

An SFC that Ruthie works with is going on R&R, I can't remember if it's Singapore or where. Anyway, he's going to try to get binoculars and a set of walkie-talkies for us. He says the binoculars are $9 a set there. We've wanted walkie-talkies but can't find any. We could have a lot of fun with them.

I'm going to watch a movie "Wait Until Dark" tonight. It's supposed to be real good.

Well I'll quit for this time. Everything will be dry by the time you get this letter.

All my love,
Susie

15 August 1968

Dear Ruby,

I'm sitting at work and there is nothing to do so I'll try writing to you. Well, I survived my first inspection as a platoon SGT. CPT Murphy was real nice. She knew it was my first time. Two girls had buttons undone and one had a pants leg not bloused, otherwise they were fine. CPT Murphy turned the platoon back over to me when she was through and as we saluted each other she said "Your girls looked real nice this morning." That made me feel good. I actually enjoy having charge of the platoon. If I'm going to have to be out there every morning, I might as well be doing that. It's really good training.

Yesterday at noon there was a skinny little kitten in the bunker by the barracks. I called it and it came to me. When I petted it you should have heard it purr. It's a calico color and could be pretty if it was fat. It sure looks like a Vietnamese. This morning after inspection CPT Murphy was holding it. She said "I'm not saying we can keep this cat but if we feed it, maybe it will stay around." 1SG Herney got some milk for it. CPT Murphy loves cats too. I sure hope it stays around. It's the first one I've seen around Long Binh.

Tanya got 2 watermelons from the mess hall and put them in the refrigerator so we ate some before we went to bed last night and was it ever good. I never thought I'd get any over here. We sure don't get any sweet corn.

Saturday night Ruthie and I and some others are going to a senior NCO party down at the AG Company. I don't usually go to parties around here but this one sounds pretty good.

One evening this week the bus left a minute or two early at 1830 and we were right by the flag poles for retreat and they have a bugler stand by the HQ USARV sign. That's the first time I've been out there and I'd like to be every night but I can't. I've got to get some pictures of the flag poles and buildings up here so you can see some of the pretty parts.

Well this month is half gone already. This time last year I had 2 weeks left. I've sure been around since then. A year from now I hope I'm back in Texas. Awhile ago I typed a preference sheet for LTC Preuss on where he wants to go and his first choice is the same as mine—Ft. Sam Houston and after that anyplace in the 4th Army area. He leaves on 16 February. He wants to retire in Texas or Arizona.

I'd like to get a portable tape recorder to keep over here and send my big one to you. I don't like the idea of having it over here in this dirt for a year. Besides that, I want a portable one so I can carry it to different places and record things such as the bands, maids, work, etc. I saw one in a PX catalog that looks pretty good. I'm very tempted to try it. I'm going to quit now till I can read your letter again.

Later

I'm supposed to be off Sunday and I have DNCO Tuesday night so I'll have some free time for once. If I mail this letter tomorrow you should get it Tuesday I think and if you do, it will be Tuesday night here and I'll be keeping watch over the WAC DET.

I'll close for now and go watch the movie with Ruthie.

1020 Friday AM

I couldn't send this letter without telling you the interesting thing that happened to me yesterday. First, I don't think I had told you that they opened a commissary here on post. Yesterday I was sitting here in the office and a LTC walked in. I thought he was looking for LTC Preuss but he introduced himself to me and said he wanted to see what the other side looked like. I couldn't imagine what he was talking about till he mentioned building K. Officers live on the other side of the downstairs floor of our barracks. Anyway we were talking about food and cooking and he said he'd come back later and take me to the commissary. There wasn't anything to do and SGT Hall said I could go. We bought some stuff and took it to the barracks. When we came out he was carrying a small tape. He said he was asleep one Sunday afternoon and he woke up and heard voices in my room so he turned his tape recorder on. He got about an hour of conversation between an E-4, Tanya and I. We didn't say anything worthwhile and I'm glad. Who would think about a LTC on the other side of the wall recording it? Tanya, Ruthie and the other girl couldn't believe it. We're almost afraid to talk in there now. The whole thing was funny but it might have been embarrassing. The commissary is nice but not well stocked yet. I got some Pop Tarts among other things. I even got 2 US pennies in change.

I'll have to quit for now.

Lots of love,
Susie

1400

18 Aug 68

Dear Ruby,

I'm sitting here listening to my tapes with the door open and a fresh breeze blowing in from the rain. I really enjoy these Sunday afternoons when almost everybody is at work or sleeping and it's so nice and quiet. I've been off all day and got off at 1630 yesterday. Ruthie had to work today.

When you mentioned the rug you got I couldn't help think how many different things you'll have by the time I get back. Even my own stuff will be like going through some I never saw before because I'll forget I ever had half of it. It's going to be a mess to mail Christmas presents from here. It shouldn't be too hard to buy them. All I need is the time because it won't be hard to find them. Each box will have to have a customs tag on it.

Tom finally got a rain jacket for me. He got it up at Pleiku and it's US made so I won't have any trouble getting it home. It's olive green with an off-white lining, snaps and has a hood. It's real nice. He's gone to Can Tho for 3 days now.

Last night we all went to the NCO party in the pouring rain. We had on civilian clothes but changed to fatigues because it was raining so hard. We had a real good time even with the water and mud. The band couldn't play but they had tape recorded music and would you believe I danced with a bunch of different guys? We got home about 2230. I knew I didn't have to get up this morning so I really made the most of the party. An SFC brought Ruthie, me and another girl home.

CPT Murphy took the cat to live in her trailer so I never see it. I'm glad it has a good home now. If she doesn't take it when she leaves in October, I wish I could inherit it from her.

I'm going to close for now.

Lots of love
Susie

22 Aug 68

Dear Ruby,

I'm at work but I'll start a letter. Boy, Charlie is really going to work around here. For 3 days and nights we've heard bombing and artillery all the time but last night it was really loud. I was sound asleep as was everybody else at 0110 when there was a horrible blast that woke us up. The buildings all shook and so did our beds. When I looked around I expected to see everything including me on the floor but nothing was. Dust was so thick we could hardly see. This morning at 0545 it started again real close. We didn't even have reveille and this was inspection morning. None of us slept too good after that first blast. We didn't go on alert but everybody got up and went outside. The big blast was Charlie hitting the Bein Hoa ammo dump and this morning it was ARVN artillery going out from outside one of the Long Binh gates. Things are really getting hot and it looks as if another offensive is under way. Saigon really got mortared last night. I guess all of us here should be thankful we are here instead of Saigon. Casualties are just pouring in to the 24th Evac. Anyway, let me warn you again that it could get to the place where planes can't get in or out so the mail could get slowed down or stopped. I hate to keep telling you that but I want to make sure you remember. I hope it never happens because I sure don't want to be without mail.

My night on DNCO was a quiet one. We heard artillery all night but nothing happened. When I got off yesterday morning I went to bed and slept till 1330. There's nothing like DNCO to wear a person out. It makes a 25 hour day and that's a long day, especially here. Tom hung around till 2215. The LTC from the other side of the barracks comes by and talks to me now and then. We hear his music a lot.

I had to quit writing then. It's 1300 now and I'm back from chow. I got to go at 1100 with Ruthie today. We had roast beef, potatoes, rolls, jello salad and cake and ice cream. I don't like mess hall roast beef but the rest was good. They have a lot of good salads.

A lot of windows in the complex of buildings up here at Headquarters were knocked out. They're all unbreakable so the LN's (Local Nationals) are putting them back in today. They'll probably get knocked out again tonight. A lot of the ceilings fall in but the one in my office has been fixed so it can't.

This pen I'm writing with is a new felt tip I just got. Ballpoint pens don't last too long here, the wet weather does something to the ink because they leak and don't write good very long.

I don't know when I'll be off this weekend, probably Saturday afternoon. I hope so because Ruthie is off all day Saturday.

Well I'll close for this time. Don't worry about the situation here, we won't let Charlie get us.

Lots of love,
Susie

25 Aug 68

Dear Ruby,

I'm sitting out in the sun trying to burn some new spots today. Yesterday afternoon I got off at 1430 and was out here in my bathing suit for an hour. Only the front of me got the sun because I couldn't find anything to lie on. The same is true today only I'm sitting with my back to the sun. I got off at 1230 today. We've had 3 straight days without rain and I don't believe it. It's partly cloudy but not all the time. This sun is hot but it feels good for awhile after being in that air conditioned building all morning.

The letter that you mailed last Sunday evening wasn't postmarked till Monday the 19th so maybe you don't even have a Sunday evening pick up anymore. All of us think our mail is being slowed down someplace.

I bet the floor sure looks a whole lot better with a rug down. You are really getting classy around there. I hope you continue to like your job. How nice it must be to have a choice of whether or not you go to work on Saturday. Well, I just spoke too soon about the rain. You will see the drops on this paper. It came so fast I couldn't' get out of it. It's been exactly 15 minutes since I wrote that other sentence. I'm so happy that you have finally decided to get an extension phone. I have no idea when I'll try to put a call through but I sure will after you get the phone. The price isn't high at all. Ruthie has called her mother twice. She thinks it's fun and we probably will too once we get used to it. One of Ruthie's calls went through Hawaii which is rather expensive but they usually go through somewhere in the states. They are limited to 5 minutes so it wouldn't cost too much.

Yes, we get fresh fruits. We get some Vietnamese fruit from the people that work in various places. Their bananas are delicious and I wish I had a way to take a grapefruit tree home. The grapefruits are covered with about 1 ½ inches of skin, green on the outside. The fruit itself is about the same size as American ones but it is so sweet and juicy. Tanya got about 5 of them and I'm going to cut one after awhile. We had Vietnamese corn on the cob in the mess hall yesterday. I won't call it sweet corn because it wasn't. It really didn't taste like anything. They eat it raw. The horrible things these people live on would kill an American in one day. We get a lot of USA oranges and apples in the mess hall and we even had grapes yesterday. The lunch you carry sounds real good. I ate my cheese spread on Ritz crackers.

I doubt very much if anything could make me stay over here an extra 6 months. I have too much to get back for. I fully intend to be at home at least 25 days when I leave here depending on where I have to drive. I have 247 days to go now. It's about 15 minutes later and the sun is shining and you can't see any evidence of rain.

I wish Ruthie was there to sing and me with my tape recorder for your song fests. They sound like fun. You hadn't already told me. I guess we both repeat ourselves but it doesn't matter.

You'll think I'm nuts but it's raining again. This is getting ridiculous.

Well, I'll quit now. Tanya just said it looks like I'm writing a book.

Lots of love,
Susie

1300

28 Aug 68

Dear Ruby,

I think I start writing a lot of letters to you at this time. Usually LTC Preuss comes in and I have to go to the snack bar and get him something to eat but he has a meeting today so he won't be back. I wonder if my letters to you are getting slowed down. Yours are running about a day behind. The reason is all the increased activity. My papers are slower yet. I have never figured out whether I get all of them or not. I think I do but they don't come in order and I don't pay much attention to the dates on them. I don't read them for the national news because it's history to me by the time I get them and the local news doesn't need a date. I got the one advertising the Georgetown Fair the day after it was over. I never told you that Sears in El Paso sent me a coupon for ½ off anything in the store on a certain day. Of course I got that a week later. Ruthie got a Phillips 66 gas credit card yesterday that she had sent for months ago. She really needs it here. I found the letter from the Veedersburg GI and it's really a good one. That's the way all of us feel. I've been reading about the "Yippies" in Chicago demonstrating about the convention. I never heard of them before.

I have 244 days now and it's 4 months tomorrow since I left. I guess I don't need to remind you though. I have 1/3 of my tour through and I have no doubt that the rest will go as fast as this. I guess I won't be calling you on Labor Day this year and it's the first one except when I was home.

Our weather has been pretty nice the last few days. It isn't raining so much and even though it's hot it's a little more pleasant. I'm so used to being wet with sweat when I'm not at work that it doesn't bother me too much anymore. Sometimes the air conditioning in our office gets so cold we open a window. When we go out at noon the heat hits us like fire. No wonder we all have colds so often. I'm going to quit mentioning when I have one because I'll lose count before the year is over. What will be fun is this winter when you're under a foot of snow at 10 degrees and I'm still roasting every day. I pity anybody that leaves here in the winter.

I was glad to hear you say you don't worry about me. I suppose you do to a certain extent and I do too at times but it's really useless. I know this post is probably not as safe and secure as we like to think it is but I feel that I am safe and nothing will happen to me. If the VC ever got inside the post the evacuation plan is for generals first then WACs to be evacuated by chopper, probably to Cam Rahn Bay. They wouldn't just leave us sitting here. Pretty soon we're going to have a war going on all over the world against communism and in the US it's the stupid hippies and yippies and black power that are causing our own war.

Dogs and cats over here look different only if they are living with the Vietnamese and are skinny. When we take them over they get fat and they look like any others. CPT Murphy sure keeps the cat in her trailer. I see her emptying the kitty litter now and then.

Ruthie, Eileen and me all want a bicycle so bad. There are a few in the company but they won't let us ride them to work and keep them all day and that's about the only time we can ride them. They are available on the black market in Saigon but we have no way to get one there. We're getting very tempted to each order one from Sears. I hate to when I have 2 there but I could sure get a lot of use out of it. Sears sends us special catalogs for APOs. Eileen and I walked to work a couple of days. It takes 35 minutes of a good pace to get up here and we hardly have time. I don't know what we'll decide. I'm going to close now at the end of this page.

Lots of love,
Susie

29 August, 1968

Dear Ruby,

I'm sitting here not doing anything so I think I'll type you a letter on this pretty pink paper. I just got through typing a 14 page draft twice. I should buy myself a typewriter over here if they are any cheaper.

Last night at about 1900 the ARVN artillery started firing real close and they kept it up all night. It's such a pleasant experience to go to sleep to the soothing sound of artillery fire. I don't even put the fatigues I take off in the laundry bag at night anymore because I'm likely to need them in the middle of the night and I don't want to put on clean ones to go sit in the bunker. So far we've been real lucky and haven't had an alert through all of this. At this rate, we will never be able to get off post. I had hoped last month it would quiet down and we could but this offensive will no sooner be over than it is time for TET again. I sure want to get to see some of this country as does everybody else.

Ruthie and I have gotten so disgusted with our mess hall that we have decided to open a can of something at the barracks at noon and eat there. The mess NCO always gives us a fight about getting in before 1200 because that's when the doctors and nurses eat. At 1200 it is so full of patients and men in from the field that we can hardly find a seat. Her lunch time is 1100-1230 and mine is 1130-1300. This way she goes home and eats and heats a can of something for me so when I come in I go to her room and eat and we sit there awhile. She goes back to work and I have another half hour to read my papers or whatever I want to do. It's a lot more pleasant than the rush of the mess hall. Neither of us needs all that food anyway. We will probably get tired of this then we can do something else. Sometime after the first of the month we're getting ourselves a small refrigerator from SGT Hall. A lot of people have their own so that way you can keep what you want without it walking away. We'll put it in Ruthie and Eileen's room because they have more space than Tanya and me. I'll sure be glad if we ever move so I'll be in the same room with them.

One year ago today I had one day left and 4 years ago it was my last day at home. Boy that seems like history yet these 4 years have all gone so fast. Eight months from today is my DEROS so this is an important day in my life. I don't think I told you about my "short timer's" calendar I made. Everybody over here has one to count days on but the men mostly have a picture of a girl. I couldn't hardly have that so I traced a map of the US and numbered it 365 down to 1. Each day I color in a number. That's how I always know how many days I have left. Illinois has the numbers 4, 3, 2, and 1. One is the area around Danville. I'll continue the countdown to 29 April even though I intend to extend about 15 days. Ruthie hopes to extend 6 months and take her 30 day leave when I leave so we can fly home together. She has put in for an R&R at the same time I want to and she hopes to have her mother meet her in Hawaii. If LTC Preuss concurs with the idea I'm requesting R&R from 3 to 9 December.

We had our weekly inspection this morning and it went very well. I'm not even scared of my job as platoon SGT anymore. The more I think about it, the more I wonder if I could someday make a drill instructor at McClellan. That wouldn't be as bad as Platoon Sergeant. I know I would love it if I could do it. They are anxious to get anybody now because of the increase in trainees and the decrease in career women.

I got a card from Barbara the other day and Grace wrote to me just before she went on leave for 2 weeks. They should both be back by now so I should get a letter soon. I sure wish I had been with Barbara going through Disneyland and across the country.

Well I think I've carried on my one sided conversation long enough. It is so much faster and easier to type a letter. I don't know why I don't do it more often. Everybody in the office knows what I'm doing anyway.

Lots of love,
Susie

CHAPTER VI

SEPTEMBER 1968

1 Sep 68

Dear Ruby,

I'm off today and I'm sitting in my lawn chair outside my room. It's been raining off and on so it isn't worth the bother to try to sun myself. I just ate half of a Vietnamese grapefruit. I'm going to send you some of the seeds and you can try to grow them. That would be quite different to grow a Vietnamese grapefruit tree. We had a Vietnamese girl visiting us this morning and I took some pictures of her so I'll send you one but not in the same letter with the seeds. I don't think I told you I finally got one of the jackets I have always wanted from here. It's black with hand embroidery work on it. It has dragons on the sleeves, a tiger and US and RVN flags on the front. On the back it has a map of RVN and above that is the wording: "When I die I'll go to Heaven because I've served my time in Hell." Under that are "Long Binh" and "Bein Hoa". It's all in red, yellow and green-quite colorful. Everybody that has ever been over here gets one. I think it's real neat. I don't know what you would think of it. I hope I hadn't already told you.

By the looks of the weather reports you did get some cool weather. This is sure a hot sticky day here.

I can dance fairly good with some men and not with others; it depends on how they lead. I am not picking up any new boyfriends. I like to go to a party and meet a guy and stay with him through the party and then never see him again. So far I've had pretty good luck that way. Every girl needs a man for an escort around here but that's all I want and Ruthie is just like me. The guys can't understand that but I couldn't care less.

Yesterday afternoon LTC Preuss and I were the only ones in the office and I enjoyed it. I like to do everything besides type and I can't when the other two are there. SGT Hall has about 20 days left.

I ordered a pair of shoes from Sears, the slip on kind that I always wear. They came the other day and they are so pretty I hate to wear them around here. The ones I brought over fell apart. I'll order any clothes I need and you won't have to get them for me.

I don't know what you can get to send me for Christmas. Maybe I'll think of something. Everything in that package you sent was fine so remember what that was. We will have to mail them during the first days of November I think before the Christmas rush is on. I doubt if I'll be able to wrap my things to you but I can send them anyway. I hope we're in our new barracks by then. I have one very special thing in mind for you but it's in Bangkok. I hope I can get it someway.

Well, I think I'll close for this time.

Lots of love,
Susie

3 Sep 68

Dear Ruby,

I don't really have much to write but instead of just sitting here I'll see how much I can write. SGT Hall gave me the plastic covered mat that he had on his desk so I have a place to put pictures now. I have the one of the entrance to Texas, 2 California post cards and the card with the rose picture that Liberty Church sent me. I'd like to have one of home and one of you if you can find some. These pictures are on public display because a favorite pass time of everybody is to stop by a desk and look at pictures. My desk looks so much more like it belongs to me now.

Today I filled out an order for the portable tape recorder and one pair of binoculars from the Pacific Exchange System in Japan. It will take at least a month and maybe longer to get them if they aren't out of stock. If the binoculars are what I hope, I'll order another pair for you. They are only $12.50.

I sure had a surprise this morning. Ruthie called me and asked if I knew a SFC Nolan. I said I sure did. He had been in her office and asked about me so she told him where I work. A few minutes later he walked in the door. If you don't remember me talking about him, he was my NCOIC at OAB. He just got in-country a week ago. Almost that whole transfer station is over here now and most of us are on Long Binh. He is at the 90th Replacement Company which is where everybody processes in and out of VN. It isn't far from my barracks. He said he has a real good friend in the reassignment office here and if I couldn't get the assignment I want from here, he could help me. He also said he should be able to help me get the R&R flight I want. I just hope they don't move him. He's a real nice guy, friendly. He acted happy to see me and he brought me up to date on the Transfer Station. It's so nice to meet somebody like that over here.

I think Ruthie has given up her idea for R&R because it's going to cost her too much to get her mother to Hawaii and pay for a room and food.

I have so many plans for when I get back and I know they will probably all change but I have to plan things anyway. In about 2 more months I'm going to have you paid back and a lot saved. I hope to save enough this year to pay at least $1500 on a car and still have money left.

It's 1800 now and it just thundered so we'll have our usual rain when it's time to go home. It hasn't been raining quite so much and a lot of people say this is a dry monsoon season. I'd hate to see a wet one.

Last night we saw the movie "Wait Until Dark." I have always wanted to see it and it's good but it scared everybody half to death. If the ARVN artillery had started shooting in the middle of it we would all have been under our chairs. I saw in the Stars and Stripes that Dr. Zhivago is back on the circuit again. I sure hope it comes to us. It makes us all homesick to see snow in movies and especially when they show Christmas scenes. I love the westerns that are filmed in Arizona or New Mexico.

Tanya got me a little RVN flag yesterday. It's about 8x11 and it's just what I wanted.

I think I'll quit for now. I might add more later.

1900

I'm home now and I got your letter so I'll answer it. Thanks for the flower. It smells good and it's not dried up but it's brown. You have sent me one of them every year and I had wondered if you would this year.

I'm always dreaming about being home and in fatigues but last night I dreamed you, Mom and Aggie were over here. How about that? You didn't know you traveled so far did you?

The activity has calmed down some but there is still a lot of noise. Maybe it won't get any worse this time. I have been writing this half in the dark outdoors so it's not too neat. Ruthie says to say "Hi" to you.

Lots of love,
Susie

(Sunday)
1330

8 Sep 68

Dear Ruby,

The letter I got from you yesterday is sure a long one. Thanks for the gum. I like that kind and we don't have it here. It wasn't even sticky.

Yes, I remember the little twig I picked. I don't remember you keeping it. If I don't forget I'll put some grapefruit seeds in this letter. How glad I'll be when I can have my own home again and grow things and have a cat. I had better go back to somewhere in the south where I can afford to live off post. I have put exactly $1,000 in the bank over here and with all the checks I've written to you and ordering things I still have almost $600 in there. Next month I get my "over 4" raise.

I bet those two rooms look real nice with rugs down. They would look better without plastic drapes too. You are really fixing everything up.

Do you ever think about Vicksburg? I sure do and how quiet and green it was there. I'd love to take that whole trip over with no time limit so we could stop everywhere we wanted to. I'd also like to go to Virginia and the Shenandoah Valley. In school I always hated history and geography but since I've been traveling I've learned so much and gained such an interest in both just by seeing for myself.

All the sports broadcasts here are a week or two old but yesterday SGT Hall had a football game from Chicago on and the announcer said "This is WGN, Chicago." That sounded so funny here.

The PX is getting Reader's Digests in a month behind now so I got the August one. It has a 396 Chevy in it advertising the PX ordering system. All our magazines are special overseas editions. I'm quite sure that is still the car I'll want when I get back. I thought I wanted a gold car with a black top but I like that beautiful bright blue that is popular in that type of car.

I got a long letter from Barbara yesterday telling me all about her leave. It sure made me homesick to hear all the places in California where they went that I had gone. She sent me a roadrunner keychain like the one I gave you from Albuquerque so long ago, a roadrunner decal and some postcards.

Last night Ruthie and me and some others went to a party at a civilian's trailer. The guys were partly from my office and the rest 101st Airborne guys. One of the girls goes with a SSG from the 101st at Bein Hoa so he brought along his little brother and his friends. The little brother was so cute, blond and blue eyed but looked too young to be in the Army.

The LTC who recorded us left for Hawaii yesterday. He bought me a tape of real nice music and said he wanted me to have it so I would know he appreciated having a quiet considerate neighbor. He called me to say good bye just before he left. SFC Nolan came by to see me again yesterday afternoon. I sure enjoy talking to him.

I'm trying to talk somebody into taking me to Saigon on "official business." The only way we can go is through our office. Comptroller has a lot of things to coordinate with MACV in Saigon so maybe I can get there. LTC Preuss is in Okinawa for a week. It would be quite an adventure to get to Saigon. I may not get there this week but I bet I will sometime if I keep after them. Mr. Rynearson will help.

I'm off today. This morning I cleaned the room and washed some clothes. Tanya is at the orphanage so I have the room to myself.

Well I think I'll quit for this time.

Lots of love,
Susie

Monday
1245

10 Sep 68

Dear Ruby,

I'm sitting here in the office all by myself. LTC Preuss is still in Okinawa, MAJ Warren is in Saigon and everybody else is at chow. I got your letter at noon today and I like the pictures. The small rose fit perfectly under my paper weight and it's so pretty. I put the other 2 on my desk top.

Yesterday I got to go to Saigon. A major down the hall was going in to pick up a plaque and Mr. Rynearson asked him if he would take me. He said he sure would so we took off in the office carryall with the driver at 1000 and got back at 1430. It takes about an hour transit time each way and it took him about 5 minutes to pick up the plaque. We drove in through Cholon and I saw so many things I've heard about and seen pictures of-all the hotels and the American Embassy. We went to the Cholon PX which is really nice compared to ours here. MAJ McGee took me to lunch in the International House, a big fancy restaurant and club. It was so beautiful with thick carpets, tables with soft chairs, chandeliers and a combo playing soft music. I couldn't believe I was still in Vietnam. Almost all of the people in it were civilians working in the embassy and we looked kind of strange in our fatigues. We went through John F. Kennedy square and by a statue that I have a picture of and you have on a post card. We went over the Newport Bridge which is famous for getting blown up. I saw all the buildings that have been mortared and burned. It really isn't as bad as everybody makes it sound. I don't know where the MACV WACs live but they have more freedom than we do. This post gets to be so much like a prison that I'd be happy to go anyplace to get out in the open. I saw rice paddies and water buffalo all the way there. The worst part was that I didn't have my camera with me and I had no way to get it because I didn't have any idea I was going until I got to work. I'm sure I'll get to go again sometime so I can take pictures then. It was sure a nice day. SGT Hall called the orderly room and made it sound like I was going on official business because that's the only way they let us go and then they have to call and check road conditions first. Anyway, I made it there and back safe and sound.

Sunday night we had the movie "The Green Berets." If you ever get a chance to see it, do. Besides having John Wayne it's a real good movie. If the ARVN artillery had started firing while we were watching that movie all of us would have hit the dirt.

Our mail seems to be back to normal now. You mailed your letter Friday and I got it today, Tuesday.

Well I'm going to close for this time.

Lots of love,
Susie

1400

14 Sep 68

Dear Ruby,

I'm sitting here at work with not one thing to do. It's a beautiful day outside. The sun is bright and there are big fluffy clouds. I'd love to be out lying in the sun. I had training this morning and came to work at noon. I have tomorrow morning off and have to come in at noon so I sure can't get any sun. It has stopped raining as much as it was and the days are sure getting shorter. It's dark now at 0630 when we have reveille and the sun is setting at 1830 when we get off. I don't know how much shorter they get but if they keep up the only time we'll be outdoors in daylight will be at noon. It's about that way anyhow. Other than that, there is no change of season at all except it will soon be dry. I bet this is going to be the longest summer I ever saw. It started in March and won't end till next fall depending on where I'm at then. Being in the Army has sure kept me out of cold weather but I have a feeling I'll make up for it someday in Alaska or Germany.

I just got some work so I'll have to stop writing.

Sunday 0945

As you can see, I never got back to writing yesterday. They kept me busy the rest of the afternoon. Yesterday evening Ruthie and I walked to the club and sat there about an hour and ate a pizza. When we walked home the sun had just set and it was so pretty out. The rest of the evening we sat outside and watched the fireworks. One plane made

2 trips dropping 12 rockets on each trip one right after the other. For awhile we thought he was being shot at from the ground.

You wrote your letter on Sunday and I'm answering it on Sunday. I hope the pictures Aggie and you took do turn out. Usually they take when it's hazy, just not as sharp.

The moon is in the southwest at night here if that tells you anything but last week when you wrote that letter it was in the northeast at about 2000. There are usually clouds around it that make it real pretty. We don't see too many stars because of the clouds.

I have been talking to CPT Murphy about her cat. She would give it to me when she leaves next month if I had a place to keep it but I don't. In the daytime the maid would let it out when she opens the door in our room and at night Reddy sleeps in here. That isn't as much of a problem as the maid. I'd do anything to have that cat for mine but it looks pretty hopeless. She hopes the new CO will want it. At least they would be willing to let me keep it in my room if I could.

I keep having that dream that I'm home from here and the car I am going to order isn't there and I don't know where it is.

I wish I was off this afternoon so I could lie out in the sun. This coming week is the last for SGT Hall so I'll be working 0730-1930 a lot more often. I'm going to need an R&R out of this place long before I get it. At least when December finally gets here I'll be far on the downhill side.

I envy you and Aggie taking your evening walks. This time last year I was with you.

I guess I'd better close for this time. I don't mind your letters being short, just so I get them.

Lots of love,
Susie

1200

18 Sep 68

Dear Ruby

Everybody else has gone to chow and I don't go till 1230 so I'll start a letter. I'd rather eat at 1230 because the mess hall is much less crowded and it also makes the afternoon a lot shorter to come back at 1400. Today is the last day for SGT Hall to work so I should get 1230-1400 most of the time from now on. The mornings always go faster than the afternoons. You talk about Wednesday being the hump in the week. It doesn't mean a thing to me. The only thing I can look forward to on a weekend for sure is not standing reveille so I can sleep about 40 minutes longer. We're supposed to get off at 1730 on weekends but I can never be sure of it just as I can't be sure of getting any time off.

I enjoyed the little comic and the Farmer's Wife. She describes everything perfectly. Yesterday I got your letter and a card and letter and one of those little Treasure Books from Liberty. It's a real nice one with the prettiest pictures and poems. I really am glad they write to me. It seems you should have had a letter from me before you mailed your last one but maybe not. I hope they didn't stop the one with the grapefruit seeds in it.

I know what you mean about working so hard and not getting but about half as much done as someone who has been there a long time. That's the way I was at typing 214's when I got to Oakland but by the time I left there I was best and nobody could keep up with me. You're supposed to be wearing that tan jacket of mine if you want it.

From the way it looks our monsoon season is about over. This is supposed to be a dry year and if they are over it sure will be. It's been boiling hot the past couple of days and with no rain to cool it off it just stays that way. 1SG Herney said we had better be ready for a long dry summer. This is really going to be strange for me to be going into the dry part of the summer while you're going into fall and winter. I have 223 days to go. They are going down pretty fast.

1400

I quit at the end of that page and went to chow. Whatever the meat was, it was pretty good for once. The only way to know what it is supposed to be is by reading the menu and I never do. We're using paper plates and plastic utensils now because there is no water in the mess hall for some reason.

We had a brand new air conditioned bus today. It's so clean and it has a beautiful sound especially in third gear. I'd love to have a chance to attempt to drive one of them. It would be all right except on sharp corners.

SGT Hall just came in from the PX with a bag full of cookies and fig bars in little snack packs and he's handing them out. One of Bunnie's (she's the civilian) friends is supposed to be bringing her some Hershey bars this afternoon. Everybody here is always crazy for them because they can't be bought over here.

1730

As you can see there is quite a time lapse. I got busy and just now got finished with everything. I have a feeling I'll be a lot busier after SGT Hall is gone. I'll get to run around a lot more because he has always done all of it just to get out of the office. I would be glad to do that. I would be much happier if they would make me a SSG to fill this job as NCOIC.

Well I can't think of anymore for now so I'll close.

Lots of love,
Susie

1500

21 Sep 68

Dear Ruby,

It's Saturday afternoon and I'm all alone in the office. I'm off tomorrow and just have 2 ½ hours to go now. I just got through telling you in a letter that I can always sleep later on weekends. Well this morning I had to be up and out at the Orderly Room at 0600 to get a plague shot. That was disgusting. I don't mind the shot but I sure hated getting up so early. SFC Garcia comes to the Orderly Room and gives shots because there are usually a bunch of people to get them. I knew I would be due for one soon because April was my last one. Cholera will be coming up soon and I guess we'll get flu shots next month. Between the weekly malaria pills and all the shots, we should be immune to everything for life. I'm glad I don't mind getting them.

After that it was still early and the sun hadn't even come up yet so I decided to walk up to the mess hall. It was so pretty out. It reminded me of being at Oakland the few mornings when I was outside early, mostly coming in instead of going out. I got a nice letter from Grace today. I sure hope she and Barbara are still there when I get back. I don't think either one will try to come here and I don't really want them to now. I think they're happier where they are than they ever would be here. It's almost a sure thing that Ruthie and I will part after we leave here. We agree that leaving friends behind is one of the biggest disadvantages of service life.

Thanks for the pictures and gum. I have the cards and decal on my desk and I'm chewing a piece of the gum. It was sure a fat letter. I'm glad you got the grapefruit seeds all right. It's probably illegal to send them to the states because they could possibly carry a plant disease but I don't know who else in Danville grows grapefruits so I don't think it would matter.

I have taken care of your countdown for you as you can see when you open the other envelope. There are only 9 days of September left and fall begins tomorrow. Next month is the one I'm looking forward to because when it's over I'll be going on the downhill side.

Whenever the 1969 cars come out, I still want some books on Chevies. Since I'm not going to get to Hawaii I won't get to look at a car.

We have never had fog but some mornings it's real hazy over along the river. If it is fog it looks different from what I'm used to. In the mornings the grass is so wet with dew and I'd just love to go walking through it barefooted. One morning I ran my hand over some and it was so cool and fresh. That's up here at Headquarters. Down at the barracks all we have is dirt and a few patches of grass. I guess we are spoiled with the freedom of open country and I'm sure I always will be no matter how long I'm away from it. I know I was sure never made to have an indoor job but I don't know of many outdoor jobs a girl could have. Even a meter maid is in the city.

I'm surprised you went to the Coal Branch homecoming. I know I should be able to think of who Fred and Josephine Bolton are. I remember their names but I can't think of their faces for anything. I know too many people in too many places and I can't keep them straight. I can't say for sure that choppers are jet powered but they sound like one when they warm up to take off and they have an exhaust like a 727. I think they are but they may just look and sound like it.

I hope you do go down to Liberty sometime. Yes, I remember Harold Miller. I saw his picture in the paper since I've been here. Is Morey Chapel the one by Jenkins Community Center? I suppose you saw about the car crash that burned Mt. Carmel church. Keith Collins, who was driving it, was a sophomore the year I graduated. I'm always seeing something about somebody I went to school with but never the ones I wonder about such as Darla.

This has been a hot but beautiful day. I hope it's like this tomorrow and I can get another sunburn. They say that once the monsoon season ends there won't be a cloud in the sky. I can't imagine that because there are always big white ones now.

I guess I never tell you a lot about my days either but they're almost all the same as far as work goes. I'll close for now and I think I'll mail this tonight so it will go tomorrow.

Lots of love,
Susie

23 Sep 68

Ruby,

I decided that you need a short timer calendar too so I have made you one. Since I have mine as a map of the US I thought it would be nice to make yours on a map of RVN. Besides, that was the easiest to find. I made all 365 days so you can see the progress so far. It's up to you what color you want to make it. You may need a magnifying glass to find some of the small blocks. Mark off every single day as they go by. I figure you will be sure to have this by Sunday, 29 Sep so I will give you the days left for that day. 213 will be the number you color in on Sunday. Just keep going from there.

Love,
Susie

24 September 1968

Dear Ruby,

I'm sitting here with nothing to do again so I'll start typing a letter to you. I have done a little work this morning; typed a DF, totaled reimbursement vouchers for one Assistance-In-Kind Fund cashier, and signed for and took inventory on all the property in the office. CPT Hobbs, our Admin Officer is leaving soon and he had to sign the property in each office over to somebody so I got it here. I hope nobody carries off a desk or chair or something because I'm responsible for it now. I didn't realize we have so much stuff in here till I started counting it. LTC Preuss just went on sick call with a sore throat. He is always having a cold.

Boy we really had some bombing last night at 1825 just as I went out to the bus to go home. The jets were real close and going right over us. Of course we could see the fire flash of every bomb and the smoke came over and covered the whole post. It made everything look so strange then this morning we had a ground fog and was it ever thick. I could barely see my platoon standing in front of me at 0630. Nobody had ever seen fog like that here before.

There was an article in the Stars and Stripes yesterday about Lauhoff exploding. I'm sending it so you can see Danville makes international news when something blows up. I wonder if you heard or felt the blast. If I had been there I would have thought an Ammo Dump had been hit.

SGT Hall goes over to the 90th Replacement this afternoon and flies out for Oakland to get discharged tomorrow. He is so happy to leave and to get out of the Army.

Tomorrow morning we have to be in formation in alphabetical order at 0545 to get our flu shots. I thought they would wait till October but they sure didn't. That is the most ungodly hour to have to get up and get a shot. Everybody dreads getting it. I don't for the shot itself but the way we all have a cold or half way have one all the time, the shots won't help any.

I just looked out across the river to what I guess must be a rice paddy and there was a water buffalo running across it. It's real far away but that's what it had to be. The rice paddies start at the very edge of the post perimeter on this side and the river is farther. It was sure pretty when the fog started to lift around the river this morning.

1420

I had to quit there and do various things then go to chow. I got your letter in the morning mail. I could smell the Cinamint gum through the envelope. I read the article about the girl.

For Christmas for me about the main things I can suggest are a lot of homemade cookies and assorted candy and some packages of dried fruits, especially apricots. A few dates would be OK and some figs. I love the ones that come on the wire made into a circle. Don't send too many nuts because they are inclined to attract even more bugs. On second thought, I could keep them in the refrigerator. The same goes for the cookies. They keep real good in there because Eileen's mother sent her some. I want something I can keep though besides things to eat and there I can't think of anything. I guess you did very well without my suggestions last year. It doesn't make any difference about me having to bring anything back because it will be shipped anyway and I won't have to carry it. I am going to have a heck of a time trying to do my Christmas shopping because I have so little time off. I need to go to several different PX's and it's hard to do. I know all I need to do is get there and I can surely find things easy enough. What I really want for you I can't get in RVN and if I go to Bangkok in December it will be too late to mail it for Christmas. They have all kinds of jewelry real cheap there and it's supposed to be about the best anywhere. I'll get something done.

I'm sending you several little articles from the paper. That's about all I can think of now.

Lots of love,
Susie

29 Sep 68

Dear Ruby,

I'm at work and nobody has come to life yet this early on a Sunday morning so I'll start a letter to you. I'm working the whole weekend because of a briefing for a general tomorrow. Yesterday I had to type a 20 page report on mats to be reproduced. I started at 1430 and finished it at 1630. Today I don't think I'll have much typing to do but I have to be here because the others will be up in the conference room practicing. Klunder had guard duty last night so when the conference is over he will go home to bed. I have DNCO tomorrow night so at least I'll have Tuesday off I hope. I do have quite a bit more to do with SGT Hall gone but the worst part is a situation like this weekend with only 2 of us here.

Tanya was admitted to the hospital Wednesday with a 104 temp and diarrhea. She woke up freezing to death and her face was red hot so instead of getting the flu shot she went on sick call. They have never given her a diagnosis yet except fever of unknown origin. I've gone to see her every morning and noon and taken things she wanted to her. She got dehydrated so they had an IV going for 2 days. Yesterday they let her out of bed and she thought she might get to go home today. Her and another girl were supposed to leave today for R&R in Australia. This was sure a terrible time for her to get sick. I've been taking care of Ready too.

I had a cold Wednesday when I got my flu shot and I was afraid it would make it worse but it didn't. My arm didn't even get sore.

Ruthie and I were discussing Christmas presents and came up with the idea of having somebody send us wrapping paper. I don't know if it goes on sale early enough or not. I guess I should mail my things during the first couple of weeks of November. If it won't be in stores maybe you have some from last year. It would be a lot better than not wrapping them at all.

I was going to ask you if you had found out anything about my ballot and I see you did. I'll probably have to have an officer witness it or something.

Well I guess that's all I have to say for now so I'll close.

Lots of love,
Susie

PS I'm sending you this article about the geese because my office provided the money to buy them and I typed a lot of paper work about them. We had a lot of fun over it. I saw Tanya at noon. Her doctor didn't come in this morning so she didn't get out.

Love,
Susie

CHAPTER VII

OCTOBER 1968

0130

1 Oct 68

Dear Ruby,

You can see by the time that I'm on DNCO. This has been quite a night so far. To start with, I'm acting barracks SGT this week since SSG Howard went on leave. We are trying to collect money and get together a farewell party for the CO and since Tanya is still in the hospital, I had to find somebody else to take my platoon in the morning. About 2230 I guess, to put it in plain language, all hell broke loose. That is the time that all men have to clear the area. A new PFC had just come in and we were getting calls of incoming mortar rounds at one of the bunkers and alert messages to write down. One girl came in so drunk she couldn't walk so she made a nice scene and most of the girls were outside trying to see where all the activity was. Two girls were outside the gate talking to their boyfriends after 2230. I went out and told them to get in "right now". They didn't so I wrote them and the drunk on my report. All this time we had a background of mortars and artillery. I think the new girl was scared to death but I didn't have time to say much to her. For awhile everything calmed down. At 2400 I had to take bed check and it was pouring down rain. Ready had to follow me through all the barracks and she was fine till we got in the dayroom of the E4 barracks. There of all things was a cat. Of course she took off chasing it under the beds and I grabbed her collar and it came off. The cat disappeared somewhere and I finally caught up with Ready and got her collar back on and got her outside. We both got soaking wet. On top of that a girl loaned me her radio for the night and I took a flying leap off the bottom step and the radio and me landed on the wet ground. It didn't hurt me but the radio won't play. This just wasn't my night. Right now mortar and artillery fire is still booming but it's farther away. This is only the 2nd time we've had incoming fire since I've been here and I'm very surprised we didn't go on yellow alert. I just hope nothing happens the rest of the night.

Now for the better parts of the day. One of the girls who came over with me has a "Sharpe" portable TV set which is almost brand new. She's selling it for $90 because she needs the money to send home and I'm going to buy it. It's the kind I've been looking for because it isn't real tiny and it runs on a rechargeable battery as well as electricity. It will be nice to have it.

This morning was pay call and I got my usual $358 and put $300 in the bank. You'll have a check coming soon. Oh how I wish I could make E-6 so I could save that much more money. I get a raise for half of next month anyway.

Tanya still has a fever and diarrhea so she doesn't know when she'll get out. She is sure tired of being there. I wish she could come home too. I think I'll sleep all day after I go see her when I get off duty.

Ruthie didn't feel good tonight so she went to bed right after she got home. Somebody is always sick around here. I get it too, only twice so far that was worth mentioning. I was on quarters one day with "viral gastroenteritis". I sure hated to go on sick call but didn't feel like working 11 hours. I always wait till anything is history to tell you so you won't worry about it. I don't think a person over here ever feels really good for a whole week at a time. I think it's as much tension and nerves as anything else. We seldom show it but each of us has a fear inside. I know I can't imagine how it will feel to get out of this place and be able to go to bed at night without wondering if I'll be called out before morning. It will take a long time to learn to relax and get back to normal living after a year here.

Well I'll quit for now. It's 0210. This should be a pretty interesting letter.

Lots of love,
Susie

0600

The rest of the night was quiet.

3 Oct 68

Dear Ruby,

I don't know how much I'll think of to write but at the moment there is nothing else to do so I'll see. I almost never write a letter at the barracks anymore. I like to know that I don't have to do anything during the few hours that I'm at home and I have a lot more time here usually. Some days I'm busy all day long and others there is nothing going on. If the officers aren't doing anything I don't have anything either. Two other offices of Comptroller will soon have a WAC Sp5 in charge of them. All of us are pretty good friends so that will be nice.

I took my ballot over to the JAG (Judge Advocate General) office yesterday and marked it and got the CPT to sign the envelope so my vote is on its way. Right now I'm sitting on my desk top because the maids are scrubbing the floor with soap and water. When they come in everybody moves out because if we don't we'll get mopped out or get tangled up in the buffer cord. LTC Preuss is back in his office but he's the only one.

Tanya thought she might get out of the hospital today but at noon her doctor hadn't been around so she was still there. Any day now I'm supposed to be moving to another room by myself. The girl who is in it leaves tomorrow unless something delays her. 1SG Herney asked me if I'd like to move Tuesday morning and I said yes. The room is upstairs right by Ruthie and Eileen. We sit out on the balcony up there in the evening and since they have our refrigerator 1SG Herney knew I'd like to be up there. The only bad part is telling Tanya I'm leaving her. I hate to in a way but I can't let the opportunity go by. She and I have our

167

things so combined it won't be easy for me to move. I hope she gets home before then. My TV works beautifully. We only have one channel so there is no choice but they have some good shows on. If I remember I'll send you the piece from the paper about Long Binh being hit. It would happen during my night on DNCO. I still don't understand what kept us from going on yellow or even red alert. I was just lucky. They hit right down over the hill from USARV HQ. That night I wasn't scared at all. I guess I was too busy.

I have decided what to do about my Christmas shopping. I have found what I think will be perfect presents for all of you in the PACEX order catalog where I ordered my tape recorder from. I am going to fix up the order and send it next week so you will have a good chance to get it before Christmas. I'll have Aggie's separate and sent to her house. I still want to get something from here so you will have it personally from me. I would still like to have the wrapping paper. Also, I would like to have a tape of Christmas music before Christmas, as early as possible.

My time is going by so fast that I'll probably still be trying to get things done when it's time to leave. I know my winter will go a lot faster than yours. If I can just make E-6 I will be really happy. I want it so bad before I go on R&R.

Well I think this letter is long enough so I'd better close for today.

Lots of love,
Susie

6 Oct 68

Dear Ruby,

It's still early on Sunday morning and while everything is quiet I'll start a letter to you. I had the afternoon off yesterday so I got all moved up to my new room. I really love it. It was a filthy mess so I cleaned it good from top to bottom before I started moving in. It is so nice now the way I have it fixed up. There were 2 wall lockers in it besides the closet and I didn't want them so I asked 1SG Herney if I could get them out. She told me to put one in another room and she would get the other one out Monday. The bed has a top bunk but there is nothing on it. Mine has a big thick mattress with a board under it. I have a desk lamp on the dresser with my pictures and animals sitting on one side and the TV on the other. I have so much room I hardly know what to do with it. Last night Ruthie and I sat in there and watched TV. It was so nice and relaxing and her room is right beside mine. The girl who was here before left behind a few things I am glad to inherit, an ironing board (with no pad or cover), a real pretty Vietnamese painting and a little stuffed Koala bear. It is smaller than I wanted but it sure is cute and at least I have one now. I'm so happy in my new home. I'd like to stay in that same room till I leave but this will probably get us moved to the new barracks. Down there E-5 and below will have 4 or 5 in a room and E-6 will have 3. They are real big rooms so it wouldn't be too bad but I sure wish I could just stay where I am. 1SG Herney and Ruthie and I get along so well.

You won't believe that I finally got my state bonus paper signed so all I have to do now is put it in an envelope and mail it. One girl works in personnel and she offered to take it down and get it signed so I let her. I think the check should go to you because my address here isn't on the paper unless they use it from the envelope.

I'm so pleased with the way the office has been running since SGT Hall left. If anything it is smoother because I don't argue with LTC Preuss the way he did and Klunder and me get along fine. I haven't run into anything I can't do yet. If I didn't think I would ever make SSG I could be converted to a SGT E-5 now because I'm NCOIC but I hope very much that it won't be too long till I make SSG.

I'm glad to hear you're planning to send me another package. I won't ask you to unless I really want something because I know it's more bother since you're working but I would be happy to get another one. I'll always share it with Ruthie and Eileen. I have one piece of bubblegum left from the other one. I don't know what I'm keeping it for. If you haven't already sent it before you get this letter, I wonder if you would get me a small box of crayons. I need them to color my map. Also, if you can find a cheap ironing board cover I need it. If you have already mailed the package this can wait till you send my Christmas stuff. The Hershey bars will be all right till I can get them in the refrigerator. We all love them.

Your idea about us staying at Dolkart's for a few days is really a great one. I can't think of anyplace I'd rather go. I don't know why I never thought of that. Don't let anything happen to the idea or we will have to rent a camper and camp out somewhere. I never get to spend as much time out there as I want to and we're never out there early in the morning or late in the evening. That will be a perfect time of year too.

I have so much to look forward to when I leave here but most of all just coming home and stepping off that plane with my ribbons and stripes and the wonderful feeling of knowing I've done my part.

Thursday night at 2300 I was asleep and I woke up and thought I had dreamed we were under attack but the booming didn't stop when I woke up so I went outside with everybody else. It was outgoing artillery but it was so close it sounded like it was going right over our heads. We could sure hear the whistle from it. We all stood on the balcony and watched it awhile then went back to bed. The only time it really scares me is when it wakes me up like that and I'm scared before I get awake enough to find out what's going on.

Tanya finally got out of the hospital Friday. She's pretty weak naturally, but she doesn't feel too bad otherwise. I'm glad she got home before I moved out.

Tonight is the DEROS party for CPT Murphy. She leaves around the 15th. If I had gotten here when I wanted to, I would be leaving with her. In a way I'm glad I didn't get here then. At the end of this month I'll have my Vietnam Campaign Medal and one overseas stripe. I hope you are coloring your map.

The girl here who is from Champaign is being medically evacuated for some kind of a disease in her blood. She will go to Saigon then Japan then home. I have heard that a person has to be here 10 months to get credit for the tour and she has only been here 7 months. I think anyone who serves any time here deserves some credit, especially when it isn't their fault that they have to leave.

I've been feeling real good lately. I'm pretty tired at night because I'm working till 1930 a lot more than I was but I'm a lot happier than I used to be so that helps.

I saw the weather report on TV last night and Chicago was 59 with frost warnings. It must be getting pretty cool. It's still raining here some but not as much as it was. Sometimes at night it gets real cool but not always. It's real hot out today and the sky is such a bright blue. I'm hoping to get some time off this afternoon too if Klunder isn't tied up with the general's briefing. He has to run the slide projector.

Well I think I had better quit before this letter gets so long you never get it answered or even read.

Lots of love,
Susie

8 Oct 68

Dear Ruby,

This seems to be letter writing time so I'll write one to you. I was busy all day yesterday and this morning but I finally got everything done.

Sunday night was CPT Murphy's party. It was a pretty nice one. We had all gone together and bought her several going away presents and some of the girls presented them to her. I used Tanya's flash attachment and bulbs and took a whole bunch of Polaroid pictures of CPT Murphy. They turned out just perfect. I'm so proud of them and my ability as a photographer. I can't send you any because Tanya wants to send all of them in to have copies made. That camera is the greatest for anything close up or in bad lighting. I'm going to order myself a flash attachment from Sears because Tanya will leave soon and I have to have one.

The more I read and hear about Bangkok the better it sounds. It seems to be the best place for stones so I'm going to hope to get your diamond ring there. Before time comes for me to go I want either a cheap ring to use as a size or a string or something so I can get it perfect. One ring that a lot of people get there has 5 separate stones in it all a pretty good size and it costs $20. I don't especially care for the design of it but if the prices are all that low I will have a ball. I want a ring with a ruby in it myself and I'd also like to have a blue star sapphire. They are beautiful. I want to get you a pin and earrings of different stones and also something for Mom. If she has any preference for a special thing, tell me. Also if Aggie wants anything specific tell her to put her order in. I will get Wilma some earrings then if not before. I looked for some in the Cholon PX but they just don't have any for pierced ears. I'm glad I'm going to Bangkok instead of Hawaii. There will be a lot to see along with everything else. It is only about 500 miles away so half the time won't be spent in the air.

LTC Preuss has a new name for me-"Lynda Bird." I like for him to call me that. He is nice to me. We have 2 little tables in this office, one in his room and the other one out here. The one out here is broken on the bottom but I thought I could fix it so I asked if I could take it home. He came out and told me to take the good one out of his office because he didn't need it. I have a nice little table by my bed to put my clock on now.

I was afraid my maid would forget that I had moved and not bring my clothes back or even get them but she did a beautiful job. She's real good. Some don't do any more than they have to but she does.

I got a letter from Barbara the other day with a picture of her at Sequoia Park, California when she was on leave. She had on one of the fatigue shirts that we wore for jackets when we were running around San Francisco. I sure wish she and I could be together again.

Ruthie has a cold and has been coughing her head off. I hope she gets over it pretty soon because all she wants to do is sleep.

I'm so happy in my new room I wish we would never move.

Well, I'll close for this time. I like to write to you whenever I have the time and something to say.

Lots of love,
Susie

11 October

Dear Ruby,

This is another busy morning so I guess I will start typing a letter. I got your package this morning. It is sure a big heavy one and am I ever anxious to find out what is in it but I don't want to open it here. I'll probably not go to the mess hall at noon and go home and open it. It's a week today since you mailed it. Let me give you a suggestion about the Christmas package. Send anything that needs to be opened or eaten upon arrival separate from the rest so I won't have to open everything before Christmas because I know you have to send it so it gets here long before.

Today I have 200 to go. In twenty more days I'll be halfway through. Technically 182 is the middle but I use 180. I feel like an old-timer compared to the girls that come in now.

Last night our movie was "The Night of the Generals". It stars Omar Shariff and Peter O'Toole. I've seen it before and liked it. Ruthie and I watch TV a lot and it sure is nice. "Bewitched" was on last night at 1900 so we watched it before the movie. She says it makes her feel more like she's home to be able to come home and watch TV. I should wait till tonight to open this package so she could be there too.

Our new CO was supposed to arrive at 0300 this morning and CPT Murphy, 1SG Herney, and SFC Gold got up and dressed to go to Bein Hoa to meet her and found out the plane had been delayed. The new arrival time was 0700. When we went out for reveille this morning, CPT Murphy was sitting out in the yard drinking coffee. She had never gone back to bed because she couldn't go back to sleep. We're all anxious to see the new CO. I hope she is half as nice as CPT Murphy.

I have training tomorrow morning and I'm off tomorrow afternoon then work Sunday. I haven't had a chance to sleep in for 3 weeks and I wish I could. I can sleep till 0730 tomorrow I guess.

I don't have your letter here so I'm going to quit for now and bring it back with me at noon.

1820

I'm back now for the last hour and I have 2 of your letters to comment on. I opened the package while I was home awhile ago. I sure didn't expect to find a Christmas tree in it. I like those little trees, they are real pretty. It's in perfect shape and so is everything else. I wanted to make one of them at Oakland last year but I never did. I put the Hershey bars in our refrigerator. The comb is in the pocket on my shirt sleeve replacing the black one. It's a neat little comb but I don't think the Covington Grain Co. will be likely to get my business. The bag of candy is nice because they are individual little packs. Thanks so much for all of it. You can't imagine how much I appreciate getting anything from home.

It sounds like you had a real nice time going to Liberty and to Smith's for dinner. I'm glad you finally went. You complain about the chintz bugs biting, well you should have something crawling or biting every time you move. They don't bother us at work because they can't get in here except spiders and we're always getting hung up in a web or having a spider come sliding down beside us. The big bugs, some cockroach variety and ants are thick in the barracks. You open a drawer and see at least 6 scramble for cover.

Today I fixed up the orders for your Christmas presents from Japan. They will have customs tags on them whenever you get them. If you could, I wish you would take them off without reading them so you won't have any idea what is in the package. Just before Christmas I'll send you a sealed note telling you who belongs to what. I want you to unwrap them first and see if you can guess which one is yours.

I'm so glad you finally got yourself a good typewriter. It will take some time and practice to get used to.

How was the turtle? You didn't say. Boy I think that is one thing I wouldn't even want to try. It sounds absolutely horrible to me. I guess I never had any around there did I? I hope not!

When the phone was ringing it sure wasn't me trying to call. I won't till you get the extension. I don't know how soon I will then. It just depends on the situation and whether or not I can get on the list to get a call through. I wouldn't get you up in the middle of the night to go downstairs to answer it. I wonder if you would be awake enough to know who you were talking to.

I hope I'll be a typical Army SSG by the time I leave here. I love to be over people and that's the only way I ever will. I want to supervise, not be supervised. Being platoon SGT gives me the most chance right now. I would kind of hate to quit that if I do make E6 because I enjoy it and it's good training but if I didn't have to get up till 0630 I don't think I would be dedicated enough to continue getting up at 0540 to do that. This place sure adds some seasoning to a soldier. The re-enlistment rate in our detachment is sure high. In the states almost nobody re-ups at their ETS but here almost half the girls do. Our WAC DET is really one of the greatest. I just hope it keeps the reputation of the "Best in the World".

Tanya will soon be gone. I'll sure miss Ready. She comes up to my room now and lies on the floor while we watch TV. I think she had almost given up on Tanya ever coming home and had about decided to be my dog. Ruthie had to go on sick call for her cough and cold. She got some Cherol and I guess she's going to survive. I wish we didn't always have something going around. Whenever I get the crazy idea that I might be wise to extend over here I just think of a few of the pleasant things like diseases and bugs and I'm ready to leave. I could sure make a lot of extra money by staying but I hope I never need it that bad. I don't think I would want to know I had to come back once I got home.

You must be getting real fall weather now. I don't think I'm especially going to like having summer all winter especially when you start talking about snow. Always before I have been where I could at least go up in the mountains and see some but I can hardly do that this year. I don't think it snows in Bangkok and that's the only place I'll be going.

Thanks again for the package. Ruthie hasn't seen it yet but she will be happy with it too. I'm going to close now. It will take you an hour to read this.

Lots of love,
Susie

13 October 1968

Dear Ruby,

I just want to write a short letter to go with the stuff I'm sending.

I went to church today, 3 weeks in a row, and went to chow at 1100 with Ruthie.

Yesterday afternoon while I was off I didn't do much of anything, listened to tapes and washed some clothes. I went to the Long Binh PX and they actually had OD (olive drab) towels. I have been trying to buy them since I got here and could never find any. I got some wash cloths earlier in the week so I don't have to ruin all my white ones now.

Tomorrow night at 1900 "My Three Sons" is on TV. I hope I get off at 1830 so I can watch it. I saw most of it last week.

A girl that just moved into the room next to me has some real good records. One has movie themes. I want to record them. One of the girls recorded the band on her portable one this morning and I recorded it from her. "The Yellow Rose of Texas" is on it.

We are enjoying the candy. Ruthie especially likes the Hershey bars. My maid has been doing such a beautiful job on my uniforms and boots lately that I was going to give her a couple of bars but she didn't come to my room when I was there. Maybe she will yet. I like to reward her when she's doing good.

It has been clouding up and now it has started to rain. I'm supposed to go to a Comptroller party tonight but I don't want to so I've decided to go home. I'd rather watch TV or the movie.

While I'm thinking about it, would you do some research for me if you can find anything. In Bangkok there is a bridge on a river called Qui or something that sounds like that. There was a movie called "Bridge on the River Qui" (maybe Kwai) and the theme music was the COL Bogey march. I want to see the bridge when I'm there but none of the literature I can get mentions where it is. I have never seen the movie but I hope to sometime. I sure want to see the bridge.

Lots of love,
Susie

15 October 1968

Dear Ruby,

I'm typing a letter again. This makes it sound like I'm real busy and all the officers that walk in here can't tell that I'm not working. Mine in this office don't care but others might not think it looked so good. I really don't know as it makes any difference. If there is no work all the officers write letters too. I type some of their personal letters.

Your typing had improved on the last letter. It won't take you long to get good on it. I bet you enjoy typing on the new one a lot more than on that poor little old one. It was terrible even for me. I hope when I leave here I never get another typing job. As an E6 NCO I shouldn't have to. To me, anybody can be a typist and I don't want to do what anybody else could be doing just as well. You probably don't think that way. I don't mind typing but I hate to have everybody think that is my main purpose.

You should have my fatigue pants to wear to work. You would have pockets and I think they look pretty neat even without wearing them bloused like we do. All of us will have permanent ridges around our ankles from the boots and the springs or whatever we use to blouse our pants. They are real comfortable as long as they aren't too tight or too loose. I hope to be able to get at least 2 uniforms and 2 boots home. The boots would be great to wear out on the farm.

I just thought of a suggestion for Christmas. I would like one or two of the stockings you can buy that have toys and miscellaneous little junk in them, not the tiny size but not a real huge one either. I enjoy putting together and messing with the little things out of the Cracker Jack and

I got the idea from that. I have some real cute things out of them—a magnifying glass, a telescope, a rabbit in a hat and out of one of these last boxes, a cardboard buffalo. If you could find some kind of a game that 2 or more people could play that would be good. I don't know what it would be. They are just ideas; you don't have to stick to them.

I think I'm going to be able to get a cross bow from a Montegnard tribe. A guy who knows Bunnie goes to a village some place about every two weeks and she said she would ask him to get me one. They cost $3 there and $12 here on post in the souvenir shops. This would be the real thing. They are really sharp looking. I used to see guys come through Oakland carrying them.

I'm glad you finally got the phone. As I said before I'll never know before when I might try to call so don't expect it till you get it. Sometimes the girls say they get a real good connection and other times it's bad. It just takes luck.

I have my tape recorder set up on a foot locker now so it is a kind of table and I fixed a cover for it out of some paper that has a waxy coating. The poor thing is so dirty inside. The first thing it will need in the states is a good cleaning. I hope all the dirt doesn't hurt it. The TV doesn't have so many openings for dirt to get into. The camera is in fine shape in its case.

Tomorrow morning we have to fall out for formation at 0600 to get ready for the change of command ceremony for our COs. From the way it sounds some of the generals from up here are going to come. All the women of all ranks have to stand this one so some of the upper grade NCO's should be the platoon sergeants.

Well I guess I'll close for now. I'm about ready to go to the snack bar on my daily run to get Mr. Ryerson a tuna sandwich on toast and a "fat boy". He wants the same things every day and I go get them. It makes me a nice little walk before I get to go to chow at 1230.

Lots of love,
Susie

17 Oct 68

Dear Ruby,

I don't think I have much to write but I might as well try. We have a lot of this paper in the office and I can't find any other use for it so I'll see how it is to write letters on.

The main thing I want to tell you is that I got the binoculars from PACEX yesterday. They are really great. MAJ Warren said they were the best ones I could have ordered to use for general viewing. I looked out across this area where they bomb and I could see a bunch of people working in rice paddies and the dense jungle beyond that. They are just perfect. I'll order the same thing for you but I think I had better wait till I at least get the tape recorder. They only cost $12.50.

General Lemay is supposed to be out here in our VC village in about 5 minutes. I wanted to get a picture of him but I just got informed that no cameras are allowed for security reasons. I'm not sure I'll even go look at him now. Security guards are all over the place. If anybody has to be that heavily guarded they aren't worth the trouble of trying to see them. I just looked out the window and I see they are getting the last specks of dust off the general's car to go to the chopper pad and pick up General LeMay. There have been a lot of choppers flying around this morning so I guess they were checking out the area. In my opinion the guy is probably safer over here than at home. LTC Preuss and Mr. Rynearson are both looking out the window watching for the car to leave. If anybody else goes to look at him I will too. I can't risk missing anything.

At this time this day last year I was sitting at the RMS waiting for them to get my orders. If I had come here then I would be going home with CPT Murphy today. She leaves this afternoon. She has been by far the best CO I've ever had. As of yesterday my base pay went from $291 to $304.

Well, I just went out to try to see General LeMay and the security guards chased us all away so that's the end of that. He supposedly comes to talk to the troops and they won't even let us get a look at him. All I saw was the motorcade with machine gun mounted jeeps taking him around to the front door.

I'm back again. I finally found a place to see him. An office down the hall has windows right beside the VC village so we watched and General Mildren and him walked right by. They even have security guards on the roof of these buildings and there were at least 4 secret service guys with him. The excitement of the day is over.

Klunder leaves in 15 days and they still don't have a replacement and not much hope of getting one. If they don't that means 6 months with not a day off except my R&R and the day after DNCO. I can't handle this whole office alone. If they would get a typist it wouldn't be so bad but she would be a civilian so I wouldn't get any time off. Next month I have to type the Yearly Budget Execution Review which is about ¾ inch thick when it's put together. I'll need my R&R by the time that's over. Thank goodness I'll be half way through.

I think I'll quit now. I hope I can go to chow soon.

Lots of love,
Susie

19 October 1968

Dear Ruby,

This is a slow Saturday afternoon so I'll start writing. I forgot to bring your letter back with me at noon so I can't answer it here. This is a cloudy misty day and to sit in this air conditioned building and look out, with a little imagination it looks like it's going to snow. All of us feel like we are living in another separate world because we know it's no longer summer in the states but we feel as if it should be. I'll never realize that you have had a winter because even though you talk about the weather and I'll read it in the paper, it's all so far away.

About the Christmas tapes, I would love either the Roger Wagner Chorale or Ray Connif. They are both good.

Last night at about 2145 I had already gone to bed and Tanya came up and told me there was tear gas in the area. The ones that were out in the yard watching the movie discovered it first when their eyes burned and their noses started running. They went and got their gas masks but it didn't last long so I don't think anybody put one on. It never reached upstairs where I was. Boy you never know what is going to happen around here and whatever does is always at night. At least when they're firing at us we can hear it but there is no way to detect gas till it surrounds you. I didn't know they used gas over here and some of us wonder if there was another riot at LBJ (the stockade) and it drifted to us from there. Wherever it came from, it's not a pleasant thought to have gas floating around. This morning when we were waiting for the bus a "bird dog" which is a light observation plane, was flying around broadcasting the "Chieu Hoi" program. It's a method of psychological warfare where they broadcast in Vietnamese trying to get the VC and NVA to come over to the SVN side. One day they dropped leaflets and a lot of them came down around HQ and I got one. I wish I knew what they said. The VC are all the way down in the delta now and I don't see how they can infiltrate that far south. They don't have planes so either they come in from Cambodia or they go on foot all the way down. The only thing a bombing halt would do would be to give the VC a great opportunity to take over the south. Well that's enough war stories for today.

Tonight at 1800 there is a Julie Andrews special on TV that Ruthie and I want to watch. I'll get off at 1730 but Ruthie isn't sure she will. We both love Julie Andrews. Our movies haven't been too good lately except "A Man and a Woman." I really wanted to see it but the rain was just pouring down and our parachute is torn up so there was no shelter at all. I didn't want to see it bad enough to get soaked so I just hope I get another opportunity.

I finally ordered the walkie talkies out of the Sears Christmas catalog along with my flash attachment and a few things I'll need for R&R.

I didn't check my account yet to see how much $100 to you will leave. I can never remember. It will sure feel good to know I don't owe anybody anything. I intend to keep all of my November pay out for R&R. It has to be converted from MPC to American dollars here at the R&R out processing center then to Thailand money in Bangkok and coming back it's all over in reverse. I can pretty well figure the value of piasters but it will be harder with Thai money. I intend to get you a ring you can wear all the time. I can't do much about a design till I get there and see what they have.

I'll quit now until I can read your letter again.

1230 Sunday

I'm sitting in my room listening to Dr. Zhivago so I'll start writing again. Ruthie is on my bed going to sleep. She just got off work a little while ago. Boy did we ever have a rain last night with the wind blowing. My floor is all wet today and everything in here is damp. We heard a lot of booming real close last night and Ruthie says Long Binh was hit again. She didn't find out where or how many rounds came in.

Now I'll get to your letter. It was a nice long one. It sounds like you're really getting ready for cold weather. I guess it was pretty cold last year when I was there. I wonder if I would ever get used to real winter weather again. You don't have to send me any of the stuff I asked for unless you do send it with the tape. I don't have to use my ironing board but since I have it I do want a cover for it. Yes, I do get along well with my superiors and I always have. It's a good way to be. I can get along with about anybody if they give me half a chance.

Yes, I colored the green VN map on that envelope. I wondered if you would notice it. It would be at least 9 days before you get an answer to your letters because if you mail one on Monday I get it Friday and even if I answer it that day it would be 9 days or over. It's sure a good thing they go by air or we would never hear from each other.

All of these few days I keep thinking about where we were last year. I would love to have a chance to get out in the open with my binoculars. I never will here but whenever the planes bomb again I can sure watch them. I keep them (binoculars not the planes) locked in the file cabinet at the office. I can't wait to get some to you.

Well I think I've said everything I can think of. We did get to watch Julie Andrews last night for an hour, she was real good. I have all day off today.

Lots of love,
Susie

22 Oct 68

Dear Ruby,

I'll start a letter although I'll be going home shortly. All afternoon about all I have done is play photographer. I bought 1 color pack and 3 black and white packs of Polaroid film from the same guy I bought my tape recorder from. He had sent his camera home and wanted to get rid of the film. I paid him $5 for the whole thing. It would be worth $13.10 so that was quite a bargain. MAJ Warren asked me if I would bring the camera to work and take a picture of him so I did. They turned out real good. I'm sending you one of me that he took. He wants to buy me a pack of film so he can have a picture of everybody in here. LTC Preuss got out his camera and took some pictures. We had a real nice afternoon.

As of tomorrow we will have a civilian typist in the office. I just barely got to meet her today. Boy am I ever glad to see her coming. I'm pretty sure Klunder won't have a replacement so I'm taking over his job. Once I can remember all the different places to post things and the file folders everything is in I should get along pretty good.

1905

I quit there and came home to find out that as of tomorrow I am barracks sergeant. 1SG Herney told me and I said, even though I'm not an E-6 and she said yes, because I've done such a good job with the platoon every morning and she's sure I'll do the same with the barracks. That makes me feel good. I want to be a leader so badly and I'm finally getting responsibility handed to me all around. Also, Ruthie and I have both been appointed as members of the WAC Det Unit Fund Council. There are about 8 members who make decisions about company parties, how to spend the unit fund money, etc. so that is an honor too. I hope I can do as good a job as I want to in the company and at work too.

Ruthie is sitting here and she said to tell you "Hi".

Thanks for the gum. Yes, I have the same electric current that you do. I expect a few of these darn bugs will come home with me. It will be a wonder if some don't crawl out of a package I send to you. You talk about having a good day at work and think you deserve it. I feel the same way about me and it looks like things are finally going to go my way.

Well, I'm going to quit for this time. Your typing was much better this time.

Lots of love,
Susie

0845

26 Oct 68

Dear Ruby,

I'm going to start a letter to you this morning. It probably won't be finished till tomorrow since I don't have yours here to answer. I'm off this afternoon and Ruthie and I are going to the monthly AG Company party. The new girl in the office, Camile Cardwell, wants to go with us. She and I get along great. She reminds me a little of Grace at Oakland.

My time of being left alone here sure went fast. First Camile came and then a day later we got a SGT in to replace Klunder. He has 12 years in the Army and was a SSG but he stayed out long enough to lose a stripe then came back.

My montegnard cross bow is on order now. The guy is supposed to be going out to the village tomorrow so he should be back Monday or Tuesday. It costs 300 P which is under $3.

Last night Ruthie and I watched "Combat" on TV and had our own back ground artillery. It was real close and even though we expected it after awhile we couldn't help but jump ever time it went off. Ruthie's mom finally sent her a package with some cookies and Halloween candy so we're eating that now.

One evening when I was working late the Cobra gunships (choppers) evidently had a good sized element of VC trapped down here by the river and they were really putting out the fire power with their mini guns and rockets. You could see a steady stream of fire shooting to the ground and part of it rebounded off something. That was the closest they've been to HQ while I was up here.

188

The last 2 days I've been using my lunch hour to lie in the sun. I can get a little bit pink in those 30 minutes. I want a good tan before I go on R&R. Usually when I'm off it's cloudy or raining all afternoon. I hope it won't be today.

I can't remember when I last mailed a letter to you. I hope it wasn't too long ago but I lost track of days this week. Monday morning at 0600 I have to be in formation to get a cholera shot. I think I'm going to need typhoid and typhus before I go on R&R. At 0730 Monday morning we have our first Unit Fund Council meeting. This afternoon I need to get some name tags made for the room doors in the barracks. I have 40 people living there now—7 of them E-6, one E-7 and the rest E-5s. Because I'm barracks SGT if we go on alert I have to get everybody out and take roll.

I think I'll close now and mail this. I'll have lots of time tomorrow to answer your letter.

Lots of love,
Susie

0930

27 October 1968

Dear Ruby,

This is the usual Sunday morning. I'm alone in the office right now and I'm sitting back at Bunnie's desk in the sun. I got a pretty good sunburn yesterday afternoon. My arms are tan this morning but my face is still red. I went to sleep for awhile lying on my back with my sunglasses on so I have white circles around my eyes. I know one guy who went to sleep without his sunglasses and he burned his eyelids. That would be pretty uncomfortable.

We went to the AG party last night. It was nice, better than usual because it was inside instead of the open tent. Every other time it has rained but since we were under cover last night it didn't. We actually wore civilian clothes, the first time in 3 months.

Tanya got back from Kuala Lumpur yesterday evening and she brought me two of the cutest things. One is a tiny stuffed koala bear and the other is a little pistol lighter. She knows I collect lighters and she thought I'd like this one. It's a butane one so the flame really shoots out. It should work for a long time. I brought it to work this morning and LTC Preuss scared a major in his office when he shot it at him.

It sounds like you really had a wonderful day at Forest Glen Park. How I would love to have been with you. I will be sometime. I always did want to be on that side of the river and look across. You must have been tired after walking so far.

I sure don't get tired of your long letters. The more you write the better. I'll close for now.

Lots of love,
Susie

30 Oct 68

Dear Ruby,

I guess I'd better get another letter written to you. I got a card for Carolyn and wrote her a note with it. It will take an awful long time for a fracture to heal for her.

Ruthie is in Hawaii on leave which you may already know when you get this. I gave her your phone number and she's supposed to call you. It's a common thing for anyone who is going near home to call somebody else's family for them. I'll be anxious to hear your comments if she gets through. When you would get the bill you could take the amount out of my petty cash fund. It's lonely here without her. An R&R to Hawaii or Australia is 7 days; others are 5 because those two take more flying time.

I got my walkie talkies today and Mr. Rynearson and me have been playing with them. They work but not as good as they would out in the open. Ruthie and I will sure have fun with them. I also got my flash gun and the rest of my Sears order.

Camile is trying to get herself, MAJ Warren and me each a bicycle. The shipment came in today so we're hoping to get them tomorrow. Pay call is tomorrow morning too.

I'm sure getting tired of the artillery. Every night just as I get to sleep it starts going off and wakes me up. I cover up my ears but it takes a while to go back to sleep when it's so close.

This picture I'm sending is the "Koala bear family" on the empty top bunk in my room. The big one is Tanya's and the other 2 are mine.

I just thought of another Christmas suggestion if you need any more—a jigsaw puzzle, one that isn't too big or complicated. These are all just ideas so don't think I expect everything I mention.

You sure did a beautiful job of typing on the envelope. It was in such perfect shape when it got here it looked like it hadn't even been mailed.

I sure hope we do get our bicycles. I'll believe it when I have mine with me.

I'll close for this time; it's almost time to go home.

Lots of love,
Susie

CHAPTER VIII

NOVEMBER 1968

3 November, 1968

Dear Ruby,

I'm going to start a letter to you now. MAJ Warren and I are the only ones at work this afternoon and it's real quiet. I just got through making new name plates for all the rooms in my barracks. A lot of new E-5s have moved in and the rain washes the names off too. I also made up the refrigerator detail roster for the rest of the month. While I'm on the subject, you wanted to know what I have to do as barracks sergeant. Mainly, my responsibility is to keep the building and outside area neat and orderly and make sure the girls conduct themselves as they should. It isn't much of a problem here because we have a pretty good group. I have to take up collections for parties and get ideas from the girls for them. The biggest thing would be a fire or an enemy attack. Then the barracks sergeant has to evacuate all occupants and check every room, latrine, etc. In case of incoming rounds, I would have to call roll at each bunker and make sure everybody was in the right one. At night now every time the artillery wakes me up I wonder if we're going to go on alert and lay there thinking about how much more I would have to do now. I guess those are the main things.

I am going up for E-6 this month but I don't want you to get excited about it because my hopes aren't too high with this other sergeant going up in the same MOS and there are probably others too. The board will be sometime in the middle of the month. I sure wish I had made it before they started having boards. I thought I might as well go ahead and tell you. It's hard to write to you without mentioning it.

I'm glad you liked the picture. Did I tell you I have a VC flag? One of the guys got it for me during one of their operations. I've wanted one since I got here. I bought a few Christmas presents yesterday. I have to send something to Barbara and Grace too. They must really be good friends because they never fail to write. I'm afraid you won't get the things from PACEX before Christmas. These little things aren't much but the PACEX order is where I got the nice things for each of you.

We never had any Halloween cards around here. I have already bought my Thanksgiving cards so I'd be sure to have them. Things disappear so fast once they go on sale. Oh yes, I got my tape recorder from PACEX Friday and it sure is a beautiful little thing and has perfect sound quality. I don't have anything on the way to me now.

No, I didn't know you would get a letter from CPT Murphy but some of the girls said the CO before her did that when she left. CPT J's name isn't hard to pronounce once you're used to it. She came here from White Sands. I think we're all going to like her real well.

I'm about at a loss as to what to suggest for you to get Ruthie. She loves nice poetry so about all I can think of would be a book such as an "Ideal" but not specifically that, would have some pretty pictures and poetry. She collects playing cards so if you could find a pack with pictures of Danville or any Illinois scene on them, that's an idea. I'm glad you have something in mind for me because I didn't have any more suggestions. I hope the tape comes in soon. This is the first time I went Christmas shopping in 90 degree weather. I went to a Vietnamese shop down at SP TRPS (Special Troops) and it's so hot and dusty down there. The rain is slowing down a lot. It still comes when we're watching a movie.

You can wear my suede coat all you want to. I was wondering the other day if you would keep that tan sweater for me and I guess you are. The article you sent is nice. I'm glad we like to read the same things. I'm going to church often now because I've been working every Sunday morning and can easily go. I have DNCO this coming Friday night. Tanya is taking Ready to Saigon and Tan Son Nhut to ship her home Saturday and I'd love to go with her if the orderly room would let me. I doubt it. I would be sleepy but I'll never miss an opportunity to get off this post.

Somebody left a '69 Chevrolet book lying by the mail room one day and I got it. It has a beautiful Chevelle in it. I didn't get the paper with the ad yet.

I guess I just want a general mixture of Christmas candy. I'd like to have some of that good fudge. Any of it that I can't keep in my room and don't want to put in the refrigerator, I can store in my desk. This office is the cleanest place I'm ever in. We possibly could be living in our new barracks by then but probably without air conditioning because they can't get parts for them. Just send some of the special kinds we've always had. I won't even get to smell a cedar tree this year much less a pine. Someway or other, bamboo shoots just wouldn't be the same and that's about all that is plentiful except some bigger trees.

Ruthie is supposed to be a stenographer. She went through school at Ft. Ben Harrison for it but she has never worked in it. Here she works in the AG division and just does general typing and administrative jobs much the same as mine. AG (Adjutant General) is primarily concerned with cutting orders for people coming and going from here and keeping each unit strength up.

I don't have much comment on the bombing halt. We have all been instructed not to discuss it with anybody. A secret message came down from DA and we got a briefing on it. I'm sure you know what I think about it anyway.

It's one year ago tomorrow since the rainy desolate Saturday night that I drove into Oakland. I never did feel as bad as that about this place mainly because I wanted to be here.

Well, I'd better close before I write a book. Thanks for the cute cards. I have them sitting on my dresser.

Lots of love,
Susie

7 Nov 68

Dear Ruby,

I think it's been quite awhile since I wrote to you so I'll write a short letter now. I'm sitting in Tanya's room using my two tape recorders to record some of her tapes that I want before she leaves. I'd rather be watching TV but I have to get this done before she goes and time is getting short.

If nothing happens I am going to Saigon with her Saturday. I hope we get to stay long enough to do some shopping. I should be able to get the rest of my Christmas presents if we can. Anyway, I'll get off Long Binh for awhile.

We're real busy at work now preparing this report that is due the 25th. Camille and I both typed almost all day and we haven't even started the final report so I'm not going to get much letter writing done at work for some time.

We had our weekly inspection with our new CO this morning for the first time. It went real good. I was afraid I would forget some of the commands since it's been 3 weeks since we had an inspection but I didn't.

Ruthie came back Tuesday evening. She didn't try to call you. She said there wasn't a phone where she was that she could call out on. She brought me a pretty Hawaiian shirt and a souvenir cup. I had given her money to get me a new bath robe and she got a real nice flowered one. All of them in Sears catalog were heavy material.

The PX has some artificial Christmas trees and a few lights but nothing else yet. If they get a variety of decorations I'll probably get some tinsel or something for my room.

I got a book about Thailand like the one I left there about RVN. It shows pictures of the River Kwai and its location. It looks like it will really be beautiful. Almost anything would I'm sure after all these months here.

We haven't had any rain for several days and it's getting dusty already and is it ever hot. Christmas decorations sure look out of place. Right now "The Green Green Grass of Home" is playing on this tape. It's one of our favorite songs over here.

Tomorrow night we're having a company party so it's a heck of a time to have DNCO.

Well I'm going to quit for this time.

Lots of love,
Susie

1530

10 Nov 68

Dear Ruby,

I'm sitting on the balcony where there is a breeze. This is a scorching day. I wrapped most of my Christmas packages this afternoon but it was so hot in my room even with the fan on that I quit and moved out here.

First I'll answer your two letters. I didn't think you would get anything from PACEX this soon. I'm curious as to what it is. I forgot to tell you it probably wouldn't all come at once. You'll be getting more packages till all of it gets there. The tape sounds like it will be good.

A few weeks ago I got a Petri camera. It's a good one with built in light meter, etc. I took a roll of color slides and got them back and they're all right. I didn't want to tell anybody I had it till I found out if it worked and it sure does. I'm going to use mostly slide film in it and get a slide projector before I leave here. Slides are so much cheaper and easier to store than prints. I took a whole bunch in Saigon yesterday.

I asked the CO about my chances to ever become a medic. The rank limit on the school for the basic medical course is E-4. The only way I could ever do it would be to go OJT as a medic long enough to get the MOS then go to the Clinical Specialist School. It's very unlikely that I could ever do it. That school does make a person equal to an LVN (Licensed Vocational Nurse). I sure wish I could get out of office work. Tanya said she would be a waitress before she would take a civilian typing job and I said I'd rather work in a factory.

· We have been having some bombing around here and every time we hear it we say it must be a figment of our imagination because the bombing has stopped. Of course the halt was only in the north but it makes a good joke anyway.

My night on DNCO was a quiet one and Tanya and I did go to Saigon yesterday. We took Ready to Tan Son Nhut and got her on the plane then the driver (a PFC) took us downtown to the USO. He let us out and left to find some place he wanted to go. We had a great time. We got several things. Among them, I got the pistol belt and holster I've been wanting and also a harmonica. We explored all the shops, took pictures and toured the USO. On the way home we went by a bicycle shop and I bought one for 2000 P, under $20. The other deal fell through and I thought I was never going to get one so when I saw it there I sure wanted it. It needs some adjustment on the seat and handlebars and I can get a wrench from MAJ Warren. It has hand brakes; otherwise it's a plain bike, bright green with red tires. We never paid much more than half what they were asking for the things we bought. They wanted 600: for the holster and I got it for 350P. The ride to and from Saigon scares me because there are so many accidents on that road the traffic is beyond anything you can imagine. The Vietnamese drive all over both sides of the road. We saw 2 accidents on the way down. I wasn't sleepy all day or yesterday evening. We got home at 1700 and 1SG Herney was waiting for us. I figured she would give me heck for buying the bike but she didn't. We're not supposed to spend much in piasters.

Well, I guess I'll quit for this time.

Lots of love,
Susie

13 Nov 68

Dear Ruby,

I don't really have a lot to say but I have to tell you a few things. Most important is that I got my R&R orders yesterday for the exact dates I wanted—7-12 December. My flight leaves TSN at 1010. It's only 24 days now till I go. I'm sure they will go by fast.

Tanya is going over to the 90th Replacement tonight and flies out for Oakland to be discharged and then home at 1155 tomorrow. I'll sure be glad when she writes and tells me how Ready came through the trip. I gave her a paper with Grace and Barbara's names on it and told her to try to see them. I'm sure she'll be there long enough. Just 5 ½ months and it will be me flying out of Bein Hoa. All stateside flights come and go from there and all R&R flights use TSN.

I go before the board at 0840 Friday morning but I won't know the outcome till late next week probably. If I don't make it this month, I'll try to get them to put me up as a 7lL next month. Ruthie's NCOIC didn't even put her paper work through while she was on leave so she's not going up. She works in a different section of AG now and she likes it a lot better.

I got what I wanted for you from Bangkok. A LTC down the hall went last week and I gave him the money and told him what I wanted so you will get it for Christmas. I think I'll mail this Christmas box to Aggie and let her take the customs label off so you won't see what's in it. Some of the stuff will be hers but she won't know which. I won't get it mailed before next week but that will give it plenty to time by SAM or PAL.

I don't think I told you that I got my Montegnard cross bow. It's real neat with arrows and all ready to shoot. Of course I can't shoot it here.

We finished typing our report this morning and sent it to AG to have 60 copies made. Tomorrow we'll have to put it together.

I'll close for now. I got a nice letter from Helen yesterday.

Lots of love,
Susie

16 November, 1968

Dear Ruby,

I got your letter at noon today but no package yet. I read all about your earth quake in the Stars and Stripes. I didn't think they ever happened except on a coast line. We wouldn't know it if we did have one here because the earth is always shaking anyway.

I'm glad you got another PACEX package. They are a lot faster than I thought they would be. I would like for you to send my Christmas package so I get it before I go on R&R because I get back the 12th and that would be a little late. I hate to get it so early but I sure want it to get here. I hope you can send me some pine. If it gets here in one piece I can put it in water.

You sure got a lot of money out of the beans. R&R will be hard on my bank account but since I have bought almost everything I want, when I get back I should be able to save a lot more each month. I wish you would get a new piano instead of just wanting to.

Well, the board is over and I'm sure I didn't make it. I didn't know the answer to one of the MOS questions and they just won't promote anybody who doesn't appear to know the MOS. The SGT that went up has worked in the MOS 8 years and he knew very few of the answers. I'm not too sure I could make it as a 71L either because I've never worked in that. As far as everything else goes, I would have made it. It's disgusting because I can't do a thing about the duty assignments I'm put in and as long as they put me in a different MOS everywhere I go I'll never really know one. Being a Sp5 over here isn't bad but I sure dread the thought of another stateside assignment as a Sp5. I wouldn't be making enough money to pay on a car and live off post and I don't want to live on post.

I guess you can understand why I won't go to church on Sunday whenever I manage to get off. My "dressing up" would be putting on fatigues but I still don't want to do it.

Camille (we call her "Georgie") is having a party at her hooch tonight and I'll have to go. Everybody in the office is supposed to be there. I don't know if I'll have to work all day tomorrow or what.

Starting on 1 Dec for 30 days, I have to work over in the "classified cage" of the admin office while they guy there is on his 30 day leave. It will mean filing and keeping track of all classified documents for Comptroller. I don't want to do it but I have no choice. At least I'll get out of a week of it on my R&R. 1SG Herney asked me who I'm going on R&R with and I told her my male friend. I didn't know what she would think but she said it's nice to be with a guy so it was OK.

I found a picture of a Plymouth Road Runner in a magazine. It's a sharp looking car and has the little bird all over the inside.

Well I think I'll close for this time. Don't freeze with your snow and cold weather. It was only 88 here yesterday.

Lots of love,
Susie

19 November 1968

Dear Ruby,

Once again, I don't think I'll have much to write but I'll start a letter anyway. I got yours yesterday. It's sure nice to see my account with you closed. Now I won't have $100 disappearing every payday. I won't have any more to put in the bank till December because I'll keep all my pay in cash this month for R&R. I'm sending you a copy of our pay scale. Mine may not be figured exactly right on the back but it's pretty close. I think you'll like the little comics I'm sending.

I still never got your package. The Christmas mail rush must be started. I wish it would hurry up and get here. It's just 18 days now till I fly out of here. It will sure be a great feeling to be airborne out of RVN. The only bad part is I know I'll wish I was going home instead of farther away. One of our girls just came back from Bangkok and she makes it sound even better than I had expected. She says it's clean and the people are friendly and it's hot there but not sticky like it is here. One thing I'll sure want to do is get outdoors and walk especially in the morning and evening because I can't do that here. It will be so great to go to sleep at night without the sound of artillery and not have to get up and stand reveille. I don't know why they even call it R&R because everybody tries to live for 6 months in that short week. When they get back they're worn out.

I got a cute kitten card from Aggie which you probably saw. I put it on the top of my desk. Helen was telling me about her cats. How I wish I could get a kitten from her next spring but I wouldn't have a civilian home to take it to right away and I'll more than likely be too far from there to come back for it. I haven't heard from Tanya yet so I still don't know how Ready is. Callie, the dog that I sent you the picture of as a pup, got run over and killed last week so all we had left was the cat. Now I think he got loose and ran away.

My countdown sure is looking a lot better. I want the end to come but not before I can make E-6. December will go fast.

I think I'll close for this time.

Lots of love,
Susie

25 Nov 68

Dear Ruby,

I didn't get a letter written to you yesterday so I'll do it now. First of all, my package finally got here Friday. It was in perfect shape. I love the tape. Ruthie and I played it through twice Friday night. It's a lot longer than most pre-recorded tapes. The kitten card is so cute. I have it and Aggie's both on my desk top. Anybody can sure tell I like cats. Boy when you say you're sending a bag of candy you really mean it. I have all of it here at work. It doesn't get sticky and it's a lot safer from bugs. We all share our "care" packages. Thanks a lot for all of it.

I have all but one Christmas present wrapped now so I hope to get them mailed tomorrow. I will put a sealed envelope in the box telling about the PACEX things so you'll know who belongs to what. I would rather have you open what I'm sending from here first. There will be some things for the neighbors in the box too. I'm anxious to get the package with my Christmas things. This coming weekend I will probably put up what Christmas things I have. I'll cover my tape recorder and table with wrapping paper and put the tree on the dresser. We are really going to have to decorate and use a lot of imagination to even know it is Christmas. I don't want to let it go by without anybody knowing the difference.

It's been half way cool the past few days because of this typhoon or whatever it is in the area. The wind has blown a lot but that's all that we got from it. I was off yesterday afternoon but it was cloudy so I couldn't sun myself. I put the cover on the ironing board and ironed some things, among them the Hawaiian shirt Ruthie brought me. It sure is pretty.

The SGT here in my office did make SSG. In December I may be on R&R when the board is held. I hope not but if I am there is nothing I can do about it. If I am here, LTC Preuss is going to put me up as a 71L considering that there are vacancies.

I guess I didn't tell you that I got a package from Mrs. Lockard (Barbara's mother). We write all the time but I sure didn't expect a package from her. I saw Lockard on it and thought it was Barbara then I looked closer and it was from New Jersey instead of Oakland.

Some of our girls who leave in December and January got their orders. Three are going to Oakland and two to McClellan. I dreamed the other night that I got orders for Ft. Knox. There and Ft. Dix are two places I sure don't want. I sure want to be home for Christmas next year.

Well I guess I'd better close for this time.

Lots of love,
Susie

26 Nov 68

Dear Ruby,

I got your letter last night so I'll write another one to you today. Your Thanksgiving cards will get there late because I didn't realize it was so close and just forgot to mail them. I got a nice long letter from SGT Hayes in Germany yesterday. He wants me to suggest something for him to send me for Christmas. I guess I'll tell him some kind of a souvenir of Germany. I want to get him something in Bangkok. He sure is a nice guy.

Boy did I have a surprise at mail call this morning—a great big package from Liberty Church. Evidently you know about it because they had my office address. They sure put a lot of nice things in it—boxes of snack crackers, a box of homemade fudge and a little box of cheese. These things weren't wrapped. The things that are, I'll keep till Christmas. I'm going to keep the fudge here because it won't get carried away by ants and everybody in the office likes it too. I have a letter written to them and I was trying to think how I could send them something so I decided I'll write a check to the church. I couldn't think of anything better. This box was mailed on 7 November.

Just think, when I get back from R&R I'll have only 4 ½ months to go.

27 Nov

I quit there and never did come back to it. I got your package mailed to Aggie yesterday. I used the box that I got from Liberty yesterday morning. It's the only one near the right size so I put everything from it in another box. When you get it, it will have traveled 21,000 miles.

Vietnamese is like no other language in the world. Even Chinese and Japanese aren't as bad. When you hear them talk it doesn't even sound like intelligent sounds. I don't want President Nixon to pull us out of here before my year is over. I need the money and I want to serve a full tour.

I hope we have a good dinner tomorrow. Our mess hall is getting terrible anymore. They almost never have fresh fruit for breakfast like they used to and the other meals aren't good at all like they used to be. Evidently one of the cooks left and the others are not as good.

I have been reading a lot about the Hong Kong flu and I sure hope none of you get it.

It's cloudy and fairly cool again today and from what I've heard there is another typhoon in the area. Yesterday it was boiling hot.

While I'm on R&R continue to write just as you would so I have mail waiting when I get back. I can't be sure I can write from Bangkok. I do want to mail postcards just for the sake of the Bangkok postmark.

I'm going to make the list of the PACEX things and enclose it in this letter. Open the packages first and then the list that tells who belongs to what. I can't say I love this way of Christmas shopping half way around the world but it's the only way.

I think I'll quit for now. Your package is coming by PAL so it shouldn't take too long unless it decides on the scenic route.

Lots of love,
Susie

30 Nov 68

Dear Ruby,

I don't have much to write but I want to tell you that I got one of your boxes yesterday. This was a big heavy one with nuts, fruit, etc., in it. LTC Preuss carried it into the office and immediately I had 3 vultures around my desk while I opened it. Bunnie and Georgie were practically in it before me. MAJ Warren got a package of his own but he was soon over to look in mine. I opened the one from you and the sack that said to open. I lit the candle and does it ever smell good. It is sitting on my desk now and Bunnie and I hung the mistletoe ball from the ceiling in front of my desk. We hung it on a paper clip chain and wrapped ribbon around it. I took a picture so I'm sending it. You can see the candle on my desk. I'll take it home before I go on R&R but the little elf would have gotten too dirty there. I see anything here a lot more anyway. I sorted out the food and put it with the food from Liberty in a box in the file cabinet and took the rest home. Boy you sure think I have will power by putting the list of what everything is in an unsealed envelope. I taped it shut so I wouldn't get tempted. I sure don't want to know what anything is in advance. Your other package should come soon. This one was sure fast—Saturday to Friday. Barbara has mailed me a package too. I got one off to her and Grace the same day I mailed yours.

I got your letter at noon today but I don't have it here and I don't know how much I can remember. You hadn't told me you were going to Smith's for Thanksgiving. I hope you did and had a nice time. It was just like any other day to us except the mess hall at noon. It was all decorated with lots of fruit and the full course meal. I'll send you a menu. We carried out all the fruit we could carry.

Yesterday was payday again. They sure never came this fast in the states. I got over 4 pay for half of last month and all of this month, $377 all together. I kept it all to take to Bangkok. I hope I can get you a diamond ring there but they may still cost too much. If so I'll probably get another stone that I think you would like. I really can't say till I get there and see everything for myself. 1SG Herney is back from there and she says it's really nice. The part I dread most is processing through the R&R center but maybe it won't be too bad.

I might try to call you anytime and maybe from somewhere other than Long Binh. They are setting up facilities to put calls through during the month of December so I hope to get a chance. It's not through MARS and it costs $22 for 5 minutes. If I do get it through I'll send the money but it would be worth $22 to talk to you.

I'm going to close for now.

Lots of love,
Susie

CHAPTER IX

DECEMBER 1968

3 December 1968

Dear Ruby,

I guess I'll start typing a letter to you and see how far I get. First of all, I got the second package yesterday along with one from Barbara. People around here are beginning to wonder what's going on because I keep getting big boxes. I got Barbara's at the barracks and yours here. It is my policy to open anything that isn't Christmas wrapped. I got the salt shaker which is certainly useful and the picture of JFK and RFK is so nice. I had seen it in the Family Weekly I think but hadn't said anything about it. I'll keep the salt shaker in the refrigerator and that way it shouldn't get clogged up. I have 2 boxes full of packages under my bed. Anything that was food is in the file cabinet here till I'm ready to eat it. I could have my own party with all this stuff. It's a good thing it will keep.

You say Maude wanted to know if there was anybody here who never gets packages. Well I don't know of a man but from the way it looks, Ruthie is not going to get anything from home. She is broke from trying to pay off her car. Her father had a heart attack and can't do anything now. She hasn't got a package since she's been here and she keeps looking at mine and saying she won't get any. I don't know if Maude would want to send her something or not but she is about the only one I know of.

I'm glad you sent the Christmas stamps and they sure are nice for once. I'm getting Christmas cards from people I never heard of. One is from a Westville Women's Club, and Alvin Church and a Mr. & Mrs. McCollum. I'll have my wall covered with them if they keep coming. Usually I don't get half as many as I send. I'm glad I got all my packages and know they won't come while I'm gone. I got a letter from Tanya yesterday and she and Ready got home all right. She stepped off the plane into a snow storm in Moab, Utah. She caught a cold and said she was freezing. I saw in the paper that El Paso had 4 inches of snow. They've had snow every year since I left.

This morning when I came out of the latrine door I heard a cat meowing and there was CPT Murphy's cat standing at my feet. Somebody else took her after CPT Murphy left and evidently she wandered back home. She is so sweet. I held her and she purred. One problem is I think she is going to have kittens and that's just what we need. I sure wish she were a he and I could keep her. The Supply SGT still has her kitten. Cats are so lovable.

Yes, our days are shorter now. It's barely daylight at 0630 when we leave and is just about dark at 1830 when we get off. It used to be light on both ends. Our office hours have had a slight alteration. Everything closes at 1830 now and just the on call NCO stays till 1930. I won't ever have to till I make SSG and then that is pulled about once every six weeks. On weekends we have to stay till 1830 too.

I saw in the paper where they are putting up the Christmas decorations. I sure wish I were there. Even if I did freeze it would be worth it. At Oakland at least I could go to stores and see Christmas things and hear the music and drive around at night looking at decorated houses. This is a lousy place to be. I sure want to be home next year.

Well just 2 more days to work and I'll get out of this place. I hope everything goes right. I don't think I'm going to have to come to work at all Friday and Saturday the 14th after I get back. I have DNCO so I'm going to be out of this office for quite awhile and that's fine with me. This typewriter isn't the best in the world and the letters and lines are uneven. About every office machine we have here should be in the junk yard.

LTC Preuss is in Hawaii now. His wife will join him this weekend for the second week. Mr. Rynearson is back from Hong Kong and will go home Monday if he gets his orders.

I think I'll quit for now. I should get a letter from you today I think. Again, thanks for all the packages. I hope you all are happy with what I send you. It will all be different if nothing else.

Lots of love,
Susie

5 December 1968

Dear Ruby,

I'll write a letter to you today because it will probably be the last one for awhile. I'm not doing a thing here and I wish I could go home because I have plenty to do there. I decided not to put any Christmas decorations up till I get back. I just came back from putting in a flight request for a chopper tomorrow afternoon. I'll have tomorrow morning to get everything together. I just can't believe that I'm really going.

My paperwork went in yesterday for E-6 again as a 71L40 this time. The board is Monday, 16 Dec. My first day back at work will be Friday the 13th. Saturday morning I have training and Saturday night I have DNCO so I can imagine I won't be too smart for the board. That Saturday night I might try to call you. It would probably be Saturday afternoon for you but I might not be able to get through.

They have decorated all the HQ buildings with trees, lights, etc. Of course the trees are artificial but at least they're green. I'm surprised at how good the place looks.

I had ordered a lock and light for my bike and one of the Christmas stockings from Sears and they came today. Sears sure does a booming business from people over here. They are fast and real good at filling the orders.

I didn't get a letter from you yet this week. It will probably come tomorrow after I'm gone. I hope not. I have a pretty good shopping list to get in Bangkok for different people but most of it is rings or little things. Mr. Rynearson gave me a card to a jewelry store that everybody likes and he said I should be able to get everything in 2 or 3 hours there.

I don't want to be obligated to do anything most of the time there—just be free.

Of course I can't be sure of anything till I'm in Bangkok but it looks as if everything will go as planned. Just so Charlie keeps out of it. Well I'll close for now. Don't worry about me.

Lots of love,
Susie

0940

6 Dec 68

Dear Ruby, I don't have much to say but wanted to tell you that I'm booked on a chopper that leaves USARV at 1335 and arrives at TSN at 1350. I have everything packed, have washed my hair and cleaned up the room. I went down and got my money conversion certificate and got 1SG Herney's order for what she wants. Mr. Rynearson gave me a list of bars, restaurants, etc. that are nice. Everybody has been so helpful.

Well, that's all for this time. The feeling I have right now must be something like the one a person gets when they're going home.

Lots of love,
Susie

PS I just got your letter. I don't have time to answer it but I'm glad I got it.

Bangkok, Thailand

9 Dec 68

Dear Ruby,

I'm going to start a letter to you. I don't really know where to start to tell you everything. Friday I got my chopper to TSN with no problem. There a CPT personally took my luggage and put it in his truck and took me to Camp Alpha. He stopped in front of the gate and Vic came out to meet me. He saluted the CPT of course and it looked almost like some kind of ceremony. I didn't have to process at all Friday so we walked all over TSN; PX, etc. We stayed together till about 2230 then went to our rooms. They have one room with 6 beds for any females that come in. A major came in later so I had company. She was real nice; a nurse from Pleiku going home on emergency leave. Saturday morning Vic reported one place and me another. We were together awhile then processed separately. I really got VIP treatment all the time at Camp Alpha. I had heard it was terrible but the guys were great. I had a personal escort everywhere I went. I was the first one to board the bus to go to the airfield, then E-7s and above came next so we got back together and have been since. Everything went so smoothly and easy. It took 1 hour 20 minutes to fly over here. We're staying at the Siam Inter-continental Hotel which is a huge place and beautiful. It's so quiet and clean and NO BUGS! The traffic is terrible and scares both of us every time we cross a street or ride in a taxi. The people are friendly. They give us VIP treatment all the time.

We signed up for some tours when we processed in at the R&R center. Sunday we went to the floating market which was about 3 hours riding in a wooden boat down rivers and canals to the boats where the people sell their goods. Today we went to some temples. Wednesday is an 8 hour tour that goes to the River Kwai. Thursday at 0945 we have to report to the R&R center to go home.

We've walked around a lot and done about all the shopping we want to do. I couldn't get you a diamond ring because they are too expensive. The diamond is not a native Thai stone. Anyway, I ordered you a star ruby with diamonds on each side. It's a beautiful stone and I sure hope you'll like it. I'm getting myself one too in a different design.

This is really great, I wish it could last longer but I really wouldn't want to stay here. We were both homesick the first day. I guess the jet made us think we were going home.

I'll write more after I get back.

Lots of love,
Susie

14 Dec 68

Dear Ruby,

This is my second day back and I'm just now writing but I haven't had time to write a letter. I don't know how I'll ever tell you everything. I think I wrote the letter to you in Bangkok on Monday night so I'll try to start from there. Tuesday morning we went to the APO so we could mail what we wanted to. I bought myself a couple of Thai swords and since they can't be mailed or brought into Vietnam I sent them to you. Vic got some wood carved elephants and mailed them home. I got some small wood carvings but brought them back here. The rest of that day we did various things, walked around and went to the zoo. We ate Thai food at noon. I wouldn't have touched it if he hadn't been brave enough to eat it. We ate with chop sticks as there was no other choice. It's not too hard but a slow process. He uses them fairly often so he knew what he was doing. The food wasn't bad, about like Chinese.

Wednesday was our River Kwai tour. The tourist agency picked us up at the hotel at 0700. The River Kwai is 73 miles from Bangkok almost on the Burma border so we really saw the country side of Thailand. We went to one temple on the way and stopped at a cemetery where soldiers from all over the world are buried. It was a beautiful place with all kinds of flowers and bushes in bloom. When we got to the Bridge on the River Kwai we stopped and they had box lunches for us to eat while looking out at the river. After that we got in boats and went down the river a long way to some caves up in the hills. We walked across the bridge and took a bunch of pictures of it. That was by far the best tour and the most interesting thing we saw. We were sure tired Wednesday night.

230 LINDA S. EARLS

You probably know Lynda Bird and Chuck were there. They stayed in the same hotel we were in and we saw them one evening. We met them and they were almost past before either of us woke up to who they were. There was only one guy with them. Thursday morning we had to report back to the R&R center at 0945 and finally flew out at 1200. It takes 1 hour and 15 minutes to come back but it sure didn't seem that long. There is a one hour time difference so we landed at TSN at about 1430. We were separated then and Vic got my uniform out of the laundry and brought it to me. After I got my money exchanged, I changed into fatigues and met him then we went to the heliport to get me booked on a chopper to come back here. We waited together till it came at about 1745. He called me that night. He had a flight back to his unit yesterday morning.

I went back to work yesterday, very tired and wishing I were still in Bangkok. This morning I had training and I'm off this afternoon. I have DNCO Monday night instead of tonight. As far as I know the board is still Monday. Ruthie is going up too. I'm trying to catch up on all the news. Of course President Nixon had to appoint his whole cabinet so they can ask us who they are. We may move to our new barracks tomorrow or at least very soon. I hope so because we can't put up Christmas decorations till we move.

Bangkok and all of Thailand looks a lot like Vietnam in terrain and vegetation. Parts of the city are dirty and smell like Saigon but the better areas are clean and look a lot like the states. They have a lot of modern stores and hundreds of little shops selling everything. The traffic was the worst. They drive on the wrong side of the road and I felt like we took our lives in our hands every time we crossed the street. Both of us jumped a foot every time there was a noise and when we were on the boat ride down the river Vic kept scanning the shores for VC. The temperature there was a few degrees higher than here, about 95 during the day and 75 at night but the humidity isn't quite as bad.

A lot of the radio stations there play American music and we heard so many songs. Some Christmas music was on. We took 2 rolls of slides on my Petri camera and I took some Polaroid pictures.

The night I got back I had a package from the Henebrys and 24 other pieces of mail with letters and Christmas cards. I'm getting a lot of cards and letters from kids in and around Danville. I want to answer them but it's going to take awhile. I didn't know Danville and Illinois people would react so good to a Christmas card list. It sure makes me happy.

I got each of us a star ruby ring. Both are specially made. Mine is yellow gold with the ruby and 6 tiny diamonds. Yours is white gold with a larger diamond on each side of the ruby. I hope it fits and you like it. A star ruby doesn't look anything like a plain ruby in color or texture so don't expect that. There is a definite star in it that moves with the light. The better quality stone it is, the sharper the star. They are beautiful. I don't know for sure when I'll get it mailed.

I was glad to have your 2 letters when I got back. I'm also glad you are enrolled in school for the winter. I think you'll like it and it should be interesting. My bike is waiting for repairs at the moment. I have everything to do it with but haven't done it yet.

Be sure to take pictures of your tree and all the Christmas activities for me. I hope you all get the box together for Ruthie. She opened my mail for me the night I got home and she couldn't believe I had so much. Neither could anyone else.

I'm not so tired today so I guess I'll recover. With 4 ½ months to go I can begin to see the end. Would you do some research on the Plymouth Roadrunner for me?

I'm going to close for now.

Lots of love,
Susie

18 Dec 68

Dear Ruby,

I finally got caught with DNCO so I'm trying to get some letters and all my Christmas cards written. The reason I'm so far behind is that we moved to our new barracks Sunday and since noon Saturday I haven't had a free moment between moving and trying to study for the board. You'd never believe what a mess of junk we all had to move over here. We started carrying things out at 0600 Sunday morning and the last truck unloaded at 1800. Of course beds, dressers and everything we owned had to come. A lot of men helped but we were still dead tired Sunday night and yesterday. As of now I have 3 roommates with Ruthie as one of them. The rooms are big so it isn't bad. I can finally have my Christmas decorations up. I have the tree on my dresser. I have 53 cards and letters so far. At every mail call I get a hand full. I'm sure going to be spoiled after this. I enjoy the letters from the kids but I don't know how I'll ever answer all of them.

I got a letter from Vic today which he wrote on the 13th after he got home. He says he had a wonderful time on R&R and I did too. It already seems like a dream and it was just last week.

I hope I get your ring mailed sometime soon. I just haven't had time. It's locked up so it's safe. Maybe now that the board is over I'll get something done. I did a lot better on this board. All the people were different to start with and the MOS made a big difference too. All I can do is hope I was good enough. A lot of people are going up so we probably won't know the outcome till next week.

I thought I would send you this invitation to our Christmas party just for fun. It will be over by the time you get this letter. Everything has been in such a mess it seems nowhere near Christmas. I'm afraid it's going to come and go without anyone knowing the difference.

Either it is hotter here than it was or it's because I was out of this humidity for a week because it sure seems boiling hot during the day now and it doesn't seem to cool off as much at night. The food and water here seem a lot worse since I came back. The water in Bangkok was so sparkling clear and good. Here it is always rusty looking.

There is a lot of action going on around here tonight and every night. Our alert condition is grey, just so it stays on that. There is supposed to be a major buildup going on around Saigon again so I suppose it will get like it was in May. This post was hit while I was on R&R. The peace talks and bombing halt are sure helping a lot, giving Charlie a big boost.

I'll sure be glad when tonight is over and I can go to bed. I don't think I'll ever get caught up on my sleep again. I'm no longer barracks sergeant. They all changed when we moved but it was time anyway because I had held it 3 months and that's the normal time. I guess I was really barracks SGT 2 months and assistant about 4. Anyway it was long enough.

Well, I'm going to close for now. In case I don't write again, have a nice Christmas. I hope you like your presents and I'll sure be thinking of you.

Lots of love,
Susie

19 Dec 68

Dear Ruby,

I'm at work and there's nothing to do so I'll start a letter. I got your letter and some more Christmas cards yesterday. I don't remember what I told you in my last letter because I was so tired and sleepy I didn't know what I was writing. I know several things I forgot to say. First I didn't mention the cards you sent. That blue jay one is so pretty. I think it's my favorite of all. Yesterday I counted them and put 2 strings of them up across my wall. I have over 60 cards and several letters. I think you are in for a joke on that last package. If it's a long narrow one and had a green sticker, it's not from PACEX, it's the one I mailed from Bangkok with the swords in it. I'm going to try to find a box to mail your ring in today. I want you to have it. I'm afraid it will be a little big but if it is too much you can have it cut down. When you get it I want you to put it on and keep it on through everything. It's a good ring and ordinary wear won't hurt it. Mine goes though more than yours probably ever would. It will come by registered mail because all jewelry has to. I have some wood carvings to mail too. I guess I never told you that my watch band broke just before I went on R&R. I kept it tied together till I could find one for it in Bangkok. Now I have a Seiko band on my Gruen watch. I had a hard time finding one to fit it.

I never told you that before I left on R&R, Mr. Rynearson told me about a Mexican restaurant in Bangkok. We went there and ate Mexican food one day. It was good but was far from being Mexican. It was hot anyway. Thai food is hot too so we both enjoyed that part. We had margueritas at the Mexican restaurant. There are many more things I'll think of to tell you.

We have several Christmas cards from other WAC companies. There is one from WBGH and one from Oakland. There aren't too many people that I know left at WBGH. Some that I knew as privates have gone up to E-6 now (medics) and others at Oakland have stayed the same or gone down.

Yesterday evening after I strung my Christmas cards up, I turned the lights on my tree on and the one in a little snow scene that I got in Bangkok and had my Christmas tape playing. It was nice even with the fan going. If this Christmas is remembered for only one thing that will surely be that it's the hottest one in my life. It could be hot besides weather wise too. The artillery was sure going out last night. It woke me up and I just knew we would go on alert but we didn't.

We're having our company Christmas party Saturday night and Martha Raye is going to be there. There are rumors that Bob Hope is coming Sunday. I sure hope I get to see him whenever he gets here. Monday night is the Comptroller Christmas party which I'm practically forced to go to.

It will take forever to get our new barracks and area cleaned up and put together the way it should be. I doubt very much if it will be done in 4 months. We are all still tired from that but I guess life will soon get back to normal. I really got hit with everything at once.

Well I'll quit now at the end of this page. Be sure you tell me everything about your Christmas.

Lots of love,
Susie

20 Dec 68

Dear Ruby,

I'm sitting on my bed listening to my Christmas tape and I just decided to write to you. I'll answer your letter now because I hadn't before. We are fairly well settled in our new home now. I have my little corner looking real nice with decorations and packages. Ruthie didn't get your package yet and I feel guilty having mine setting around. I hope it gets here soon so she will have something to look at and maybe be a little happier.

I'm pretty sure I'll get to see Bob Hope Sunday because I think they're going to close down all the offices. Billy Graham is going to have Christmas services all day Tuesday and the choir that Ruthie is in is going to sing for one of them so I intend to become a member of the choir for that day. You can't imagine how much it will mean to me to be able to see and hear him here and at Christmas. After all these years I'll finally catch up with him in VN of all places. I don't know yet when I'll open my presents. It depends on what we all do on Christmas Eve. Right now I have a background of artillery with my music and it's sure loud. They have really been going at it the past few nights.

If I make a word off the line it's because I jumped. It's a natural reflex to jump no matter how much I expect it. I bet this is the last time I ever volunteer for a combat zone. I'm never sorry that I did though.

I got your ring mailed yesterday so it's somewhere on its way. The stone is a genuine star ruby and the diamonds are real. I might as well tell you it cost $55 because you'll see it on the customs label anyway. You can consider that your birthday present.

I think about the things we used to do at Christmas too such as that manger scene. Those were good days. At the time we didn't especially think so but what I'd give to live just one week of that life again. I put this little sprig of tree that you sent in water and it has spread out and smells so good. We have one small real tree out on the patio and it smells so good. It's one of the kind we always liked.

I got a card from Senator and Mrs. Thomas Merrit from Hoopston and one from Mayor Al Gardner. I'm still getting some. I guess I'll have to write a letter to the Commercial News after this.

Well I'm going to close for now. You'll probably get this the day after Christmas. I love you and miss you all and I wish I were there.

Susie

24 Dec 68

Dear Ruby,

At 0900 I leave to go to the Billy Graham service so I'll write until then. First of all, Ruthie got her package Saturday night. She was so surprised and happy. She has the presents on her dresser and now we'll both have things to open. We're both trying to get tomorrow afternoon off so if we do we'll open them then. I think tonight and tomorrow will make us all feel even more in a different world because as we try to visualize what is going on at home we have to backtrack a day. Our Christmas party at the company Saturday night was nice. I did get to see Bob Hope Sunday from about a mile away but I was there anyway. I took my binoculars and watched everything through them. Three of us got down there at 1115 and the place was already full. The show didn't start till 1330. When it did we had to stand up to see and we stood there from 1330 to 1530. The sun was beating down and there was no shade. It's a wonder nobody got heat exhaustion or anything but I guess they didn't. We all got our faces and arms sunburned. The show itself wasn't really much for a girl to watch but of course the guys went wild over the 19 girls he had with him. It was so hard to believe that I was actually watching a Bob Hope show in person. It makes us all feel good to have these people give up their Christmas at home to come over here and be with us. Before the show started there was a jet making air strikes out in the valley in front of us. They had choppers patrolling the perimeter and armored tanks lined up along the road beside the amphitheater.

1430

I quit there and went down to the amphitheater. The choir was seated on the stage and when Billy got there he came out and sat down in the row of chairs in front of us. He talked to us and he was quite surprised to see girls in his audience. He had on a tan outfit and jungle boots. We all had him autograph our programs and I took 2 pictures of him. They aren't too good because there were too many people around him but they show I was close to him anyway. Before he got there the band played Christmas music. After the service started, Ted Smith played the piano for everything. The service lasted about an hour and he stayed about 20 minutes after that. His sermon was real good and he had the attention of everybody in the audience.

0730 26 Dec

Well I never got back to this letter and you'll soon know why. I had a lot of work to do in the afternoon and at 1500 1SG Herney called and wanted to know if I could get off early because the CO wanted to see me. We were all pretty sure of what it was for. I left work at 1700 and when I got to the company the clerk congratulated me, then I knew. At 1800 CPT J. called 3 of us in her office and promoted us—two to SSG and one to SP6.

She didn't even have orders to give to us but she said she couldn't think of a better time to give us the stripes than on Christmas Eve. I was so happy I was practically speechless. Ruthie didn't make it and the list isn't out yet so we don't know if she made it on there or not.

We went to midnight mass. I stayed with the 3 girls since we were the only WACs there so I was in the protestant choir. I felt rather strange in a protestant choir at a mass. We sang for a half hour before and during it. I sure got to sing Christmas songs this year. I forgot to tell you that at the Comptroller party Monday night they recruited me to play Christmas carols on the piano. I didn't want to very bad but I went out to the club in the afternoon and practiced. The piano was a mess and was dirty and didn't have any right pedal so I washed it off and went outside to find a stick to serve as a pedal. It worked and I rather enjoyed playing for them. There were about 40 people from full colonel on down. They all thought I did a good job.

Now for my Christmas Day. To start with, I didn't get to bed till 0330 Christmas morning. Four other E-6's invited me to their room for a promotion drink after I got back from mass and we didn't want to break up the party. Ruthie got me up at 0930 and started piling presents in bed with me. I sat there and unwrapped everything and had Ruthie take a picture of me in the midst of it. I'm very happy with everything I got but I think out of all of it the roadrunner coloring book was the best. That must be what you said I wanted when I first got here. I don't remember but it sure is cute. Where in the world did you find it? Everything is so nice. The popcorn popper is sure a nice thing to have. I don't have time now but I'll try to make a list of everything I got. After we opened presents we went to dinner then I decided we should try our luck at getting a chopper ride. We walked all over post and finally came to the USARV chopper pad. We asked the guy in the office if there was any chopper that we could ride on and a couple of pilots standing there said we could go with them. They took Arch Bishop Cook to Bien Hoa via a tour of Long Binh Post. He's the military vicar here and he held the Christmas Mass. We all got to shake hands with him and he gave us each a little card. We took the 3 priests to Bien Hoa then went to a place called Nha Be and picked up a LTC. We took him to TSN and landed at almost the same place my chopper took off when I came back from R&R. Then we came back to USARV. We had a great time flying everywhere that we're not supposed to be. We figured we at least started out safe with 3 priests and one of them a VIP. We took several pictures of each other and I'll send you at least one today. I had a real nice Christmas day but these SSG stripes on my sleeves sure helped a lot. There were 4 of us off and together all day yesterday; Ruthie and me and a SSG and a SP4.

I've answered the phone twice this morning and remembered to say "SGT Earls". I would have given anything to have called you when I made it but it was useless to try on Christmas Eve or day. Ruthie is happy with what was in her box. She knows how to play that game so she can show me.

Well I'm going to have to quit now. Thanks so much for everything you sent. I'm very happy with everything and Christmas in general.

Love from your Staff Sergeant,
Susie

28 December 1968

Dear Ruby,

I'm going to type you a letter this morning. I want to send you a copy of my orders which I finally got yesterday at noon. They sure look nice.

Yesterday afternoon I finally got to the dentist. My tooth was killing me so I told 1SG Herney and she told me to go to the dentist. They checked all my teeth and put a temporary filling in this one. The dentist said he thought the root was almost dead and he wants to watch it for a month and then either put a permanent filling in it or a root canal to save it. It doesn't hurt now but I'm afraid the filling will come out. I have a bunch of other cavities but none this big so I have an appointment the 30th to get some more filled. He was real good and didn't hurt me at all so I hope I get him again. He worked fast too. Now I can't chew very good on either side because the right side has that chipped tooth that is sensitive to anything that touches it. I'll have to save that bag of nuts till I get everything fixed. Ruthie had two packages of that dry soup and I got two in the box from Liberty so we've been having that for supper. It's real good besides not having to be chewed.

Tomorrow I have 4 months left. People are telling me I'm getting short. This time can go just as fast as it wants to now that I have my stripes. All I have to do is save money the next 4 months and I'll be ready to come back to the world. I've got to make up my mind about a car pretty soon so I can order it in about another month.

Your school sounds like it wouldn't be too bad. Of course you know my worst subject would be math and English would probably be my best. I think I would like history now but not science. I'm glad you're doing it. If your test would be the first week of May I'd say you should wait and take it because I don't intend to come home till at least the 11th if I can get the extension I want. I hope you have it and everything else over with by the time I get there. I'll really talk you all to death this time. We all have a language of our own around here and I don't even realize how much of it I use.

I can't wait to get your answer to the letter telling you I made my stripes. I have waited so long to be able to tell you that and our communication is so slow. I don't have to think about a promotion for several years now. I can at least relax somewhat. There are supposed to be more stripes coming out today or Monday so several others should get promoted. I don't know why they split them up but I'm sure glad I was in the first group. I'm wearing rank pins on my collar instead of stripes on the sleeves on all but one uniform. They sure look sharp and so does my hat with the stripes. I'm so proud of them. I'm anxious to hear what you think of your Christmas presents too. I haven't done anything with the jigsaw puzzles yet but they sure are pretty. Mrs. Lockard sent me a tube of Avon hand lotion, a bar of soap and can of bath powder, a six pack of gum and a can of hard candy. Barbara sent me a pink towel set and a picture of RFK and JFK. Grace sent me a yellow flowered towel set and a license plate with "Linda" and "USA" on it. In the box from Liberty there was a jar of lilac cream sachet, some crossword puzzle books and some other little books and a pen and book mark set that is real pretty. The Henebrys sent me a real pretty jigsaw puzzle. A girl that used to be here sent the company two great big boxes of Bazooka bubble gum. Everybody got enough to last about 4 months. I can't even chew mine now but I can keep it. I'm glad nobody else sent me any. I have about 3 cans of nuts that I can't eat now but they'll keep. Ruthie loves that little animal and I think he's cute too. She intends to write to you.

Well I'm going to quit for now. I hope you get that big envelope I sent soon because I know you'll like the pictures. You won't get this till next year but Happy New Year anyway. 1969 is the year that I'll come home (121 days today).

Lots of love,
Susie

CHAPTER X

JANUARY 1969

0750

1 January 1969

Dear Ruby,

Happy New Year! I'm at work and so far I'm the only one here. I would guess that MAJ Warren and LTC Preuss stayed out all night and they will soon come in.

Yesterday evening all the companies were ordered to have a party to try to keep everybody away from the clubs. I supposedly had company detail in the afternoon but all I really did was go with 4 others to buy and carry cases of soda and beer for the party. When we got back to the barracks we helped set up tables and chairs and set the food out. When Ruthie got home she wanted us to go to the Chinese restaurant that just opened so, since it's right down the street from us, we did go. I never thought I'd see anything like it on Long Binh. It's air-conditioned and really beautiful inside besides having a nice quiet atmosphere. They have a fork or chopsticks to eat with. I used the chop sticks. I'm getting pretty good with them and it's fun. The food I had was good, sweet and sour pork. I had wondered for a long time what it tasted like. We had a nice time there and then went back to the barracks. Marty and Marney had invited me over to their room earlier so I went over and they told me to go get Ruthie. When E-6's are drinking any liquor an E-5 isn't supposed to even be in the room but 1SG Herney said as long as she didn't see any E-5 drinking she didn't care so we felt fairly safe with Ruthie in there. There were 8 of us most of the time and we really had a good time just sitting there drinking and talking. At about 2345 we went out to the patio where the CO was entertaining 7 male officers. Several others were out there and we had a countdown to 2400. At that minute the sky was

245

yellow, red and green with flares. There was the noise of them being shot off and everybody yelling. Some people had noise makers and horns were blowing. The flares made quite a show. I've sure never seen that much celebration to bring in the new year before. As we were standing there watching one of the girls said that this will be one Christmas and New year's we will never forget and that is sure right.

I was sure glad to get your letter after you opened your presents. I thought you would like the watch because I remembered that you used to talk about wanting a new smaller one sometime and I also thought you'd want silver color so I got the ring in white gold to match it. You may not like the band on the watch. If you don't, feel free to get another one. It looks so neat with that one though. Everybody over here gets a Seiko watch. They are famous for being the best. If I needed one, I'd like to have one like yours. I hope you figured out how to set the date. I guess you know that as long as you don't stop wearing it for any long period of time you'll never have to wind it. I hope you've looked at the stone in the ring in different kinds of lighting so you can see how the star changes. Bright sunlight makes it so fine it sometimes gives you the feeling that the star stands up from the stone. Yes, the salad bowl set is wood. I thought Mom would like that rooster. Of course I haven't seen any of the things you got from PACEX so all I know is what they looked like in the catalog. I was just as happy when I opened my presents as you were when you saw yours. That coloring book still stands out over everything. I bought another roadrunner pin yesterday. I have this one on the back of my hat but probably won't get by wearing it there very long. When I made E-6 I started wearing a new hat and I'm going to keep the old one with the rank pin on it. It went through 8 months and to Bangkok with me.

Your red pen makes a pretty letter. I can't help but wish I was walking to the mailbox with you through the snow and cold air. I think it might feel pretty good once I got used to it. It's cloudy out today and I told Ruthie if it was 80 degrees cooler outside it would be like 1 January at home.

I hope you do get something for me on the Plymouth Roadrunner. I have talked to some people and part of them advise against ordering a car through the PX because sometimes people get cheated. Others say it's all right so I really don't know what to think. All I know is that I want a car at home waiting for me when I get there. I wouldn't want to get it at Oakland mainly because I'll be in too big of a hurry to get home and too tired to drive that far. Now I want to suggest something that you may not go for and if not just say so and I'll forget it. I wonder if you would be willing to order a car for me through a dealer there and have it delivered before I got there. I could tell you all the specific things just as I would the PX and write you a check for the down payment. Well that's enough of that, how nice it would be to say this instead of writing it.

I guess I had better compose a letter to the Commercial-News editor. You remember Mrs. Gray don't you? I got a Christmas card from her. She wants to know if I've seen "our boyfriend" yet. She hopes both of us will come back to WBGH.

Your Christmas dinner sure sounded good, especially the turkey, dressing and gravy. We never got a good piece of turkey in the mess hall. I'd like to have a leg all to myself.

When you were writing the letter on Christmas Eve you were hoping I was happy. Little did you know that I was being promoted. Tell Mrs. Johnson not to worry about not sending me anything. I just wanted her and Carolyn to have a souvenir from here. I knew the main thing Aggie got for you. You must have had a real nice Christmas and I'm glad you did.

Well I'd better close this chapter of my book and mail it. I'm so happy that you all liked what I sent you. Again, Happy New Year—this is the year I come home!

Lots of love,
Susie

4 January 1969

Dear Ruby,

I think I'll type you a letter this morning. I hope I get one from you soon but evidently the mail just isn't coming in even if I should be getting one because nobody is getting letters from anyone. It's sure a letdown after all that Christmas mail. Yesterday I got a bunch of newspapers and a thing from the National Wildlife Magazine telling me that Aggie sent me a subscription for it. Tell her thanks a lot. I will really enjoy it. I couldn't imagine why they were sending me something till I opened the envelope.

Boy I'm really getting a work over from the dentist. Every time I go they fill one tooth. They do that because they have so many patients and they want to get everybody in and out fast. It gets rather disgusting because I have to get Novocain every time and I have to walk up there and hitch a ride back to work. Anyway, I have a temporary filling in two teeth, one on each side. One of them is fine but the other one hurts if I get anything hot or cold or hard on it. He x-rayed it again yesterday and said the nerve is dying and there is an abscess starting so I got an appointment to get a root canal done on it. I don't know if you know what that is or not. I didn't so he explained it. They take the nerve completely out of the tooth and replace it with a filling so that the tooth is still there but is dead. He said sometimes they get brittle and start to break then they have to be capped. At least they are going to leave it in unless they discover something else. My appointment for that is 8 January. I kind of dread it. I've had so much Novocain this past 2 weeks on the same side that I don't think it works so good. They had better give me a good shot for that. I'm getting very tired of going to the dentist every other day.

I ordered myself some little things form a Spencer catalog. One is a gold plate with an adhesive back that has on it: "This car made especially for Linda S. Earls"

That will be nice in my new car because it will be true. Another thing is some English fern that grows without water or dirt. I have it on my desk. I don't have my name on my desk now because the guys in visual aids are too busy to make me one. I guess it doesn't matter. Sometime I want to order or get one of those real nice name plates with rank, name and branch on it.

We're getting ready for an IG inspection in the company so everybody is trying to clean everything. We already had it in the office. We have another little puppy for a mascot at the barracks. He's brown and so cute. I can't wait till I can have a cat again. It's been cloudy the past few days and not quite so hot. It even rained a tiny bit once. When you get this, you'll have Ruthie's letter. I didn't even know she was writing to you till after she had. She says you'll find out she can't write as good as me. We're still eating those cookies and they are still real good. We keep them in the refrigerator. My figs weren't dried out at all I didn't think. I keep them and the dates in my desk drawer and nibble on them. We just cut the fruitcake the other day and it is a lot better than any other we had here.

Ruthie and I had corn on the cob and fried chicken last night. We get the corn in cans and cook it. It is really good. I like the chicken that we cook but I sure hate it in the mess hall or at these parties because they never get it done. I know one thing I don't want to have for my first meal when I get home this time and that is chicken. Also I don't want hamburger or steak for awhile anyway. We get so tired of that and it's not very good and usually not done when we have it so we really hate the thought of it. Bunnie's boyfriend had been home on a 30 day leave and had promised to bring back some loaves of American bread. He brought me a giant loaf of Sunbeam sandwich bread. We are sure enjoying it. I just eat it plain with whatever else I'm eating or with apple butter. I never ate much bread at home but I have sure missed it in sandwiches here.

I don't remember if I told you that I got all 40 of my Bangkok slides back and they are perfect. There are some real good ones in them. Some I would like to have made into pictures if I could find the right kind of envelope to send them in. I can't wait to get home and show them to you and tell you everything that goes with them. I have a couple of tourist books too so they will help me remember everything.

I'm going to quit for now, maybe I'll add more later in the day.

1625

There really isn't much more to say. All I've done this afternoon is read a magazine. I just went over and visited Ruthie. I think we're going to eat at the Chinese restaurant tonight. Anything is good compared to snack bar hamburgers or mess hall food. It has seemed so much worse since I got back from Bangkok. I'm off all day tomorrow but I'll have to spend most of it getting my dresser drawers and wall locker in order for the inspection. I didn't want to have to get too organized because I know I'm going to move again but I don't have any choice now.

I didn't get caught with my roadrunner on my hat yet but it makes me nervous around the company so I guess I should take if off. Some others wear pins on their hats but they aren't career staff sergeants. Two pairs of my fatigues that I have alternated between this whole 8 months are real faded and old looking. The more faded they get the more I like them. I have one set I have never worn and 2 others are almost new. I sure hope I can get the new ones out of here.

Well, I'm going to close for now. I hope I get a letter from you soon so I can read your reaction to my promotion.

Lots of love,
Susie

7 January 1969

Dear Ruby,

I finally got some mail yesterday. None of us have been getting any for about a week and it came in all at once. I had two letters from you, one from Lucille Thomas and one from Tanya and another card from National Wildlife telling me I'm a member of their club and will receive a decal for my car, etc.

This typewriter ribbon is getting old and the keys don't hit even either. This is sure a lot easier than writing a long letter. I have all my Christmas things put away too. We're having that IG inspection in the barracks today so we had to get everything neat and clean. We have worked one puzzle, the fall scene and it sure is pretty. I hate to take it apart but there is sure no place to leave it set up. Maybe after I move it will be better.

The time in service to be promoted to SSG is technically 5 years but as long as the office and company are willing to waiver it, the minimum can be 3 years. I don't know how to explain how I became a SSG instead of Sp6, I'll try. After SP5, part of the MOS's are set up so those people of higher rank are in a supervisory position. Other MOS's in different fields never have that position, such as a draftsman or stenographer. All they will ever do is their one specific job. With 71L or 71H (Personnel) we are usually working in an office with lower ranking people and we act as supervisors or NCOIC. The admin and personnel fields are the best examples. In combat the platoon leaders and supply sergeants, etc., will be NCO's. As for my MOS change, 71L40 is just one step higher than 71L20. It's hard to tell what kind of a job I'll get in the states but what I'm supposed to be doing is acting as NCOIC of an admin branch or office. If I get on a big post I could be doing about anything, I just hope it's not typing. I hope I got that explanation half way clear. It's hard to write it out.

The SSG patch I sent you is a WAC one that we wear on all our uniforms. They are a lot smaller than the ones the men have. We wear their black stripes on our fatigues unless we wear rank pins. I wondered if you would see SSG on the outside of the letter before you read it. I still feel kind of strange calling myself "SGT". Now when I go someplace like to the dental clinic, the guys call me "Sarge". I rather like that. I have 16 years and two promotions to go now.

Choppers don't get shot down around here, at least not often. It's usually way out in the boonies. We did get pretty far out but with Arch Bishop Cooke with us and the LTC I think we were pretty safe. I hope I get to go up at least one more time because I want to take a roll of slide film up there.

I wrote a letter to the Commercial-News Editor. I'm sending you a copy. I hope they print it sometime. I'll be watching for your article. I got the 24 Dec paper yesterday. It had some pretty pictures in it. Just hang on to my income tax form. I don't know what to do with any of it but it's a lot safer with you right now, especially since I'm going to move again sometime. I'll find out what to do sometime later on.

I keep most of my candy here at work in a plastic container on my desk except what I want to keep for myself. This way it won't sit around and get old. I'm still eating the dates, have a few figs left and we're eating the cookies.

Boy I can't wait to get back to San Francisco. I'd like to leave here on Friday, 16 May and get there the same day then stay Saturday and Sunday and take off Monday.

Ruthie and I watched a Christmas presentation from San Diego to the servicemen and women in Vietnam the other evening. It was so good, showed the street lights, trees, people singing etc., it sure made us want to get back. I bet San Francisco will be the most beautiful place I ever saw when I see it again. It will be so great to be free again.

I don't care if your letters after this are short, I like them anyway. It took me a long time to read this one. Ruthie said she wouldn't know what to do if she ever got a letter that long.

Well I think I'd better sign off.

Lots of love,
Susie

9 January 1969

Dear Ruby,

I don't have much to tell you today but I want to send these two things and they make the envelope fat by themselves. One as you can see, is a page from the personnel roster for Comptroller. Since it has the whole Budget division and my new rank, I thought you might like to see it. The other is a copy of a set of orders that I typed.

Well I survived the dental appointment this morning. It wasn't bad at all, not much worse than having one filled except it took longer. He put a metal frame with a piece of rubber stretched across it in my mouth to separate the tooth and drilled out the temporary filling. He took some kind of little metal screw like things and put them up in the bone and each time asked if they hurt. They did but not a lot. He took another x-ray and sealed it up with another temporary filling. This has to stay 10 days to see if he got the bacteria out so it will be all right. I guess I have to go back two more times for this tooth. Boy I've never gone to the dentist this much before and hope I never do again. My next appointment is the 20th.

1SG Herney told me at noon that I can move anytime I want to over to the E-6 barracks. I'm going into the room I wanted and she didn't even know where I wanted to go. I like both of these girls but they both leave either this month or next month. They are both young SSG's. I'm hoping Ruthie will make it this month then she can move in when one of them leaves. I think 1SG Herney has that in mind too. She is sure good to us and we like her.

I have DNCO on the 17th. It seems like I shouldn't have it so soon but I guess it's because a lot of people are going on R&R now and quite a few are leaving too. I don't mind having it at all.

Well I'm coming to the end of the paper and my "short" letter so I'll close.

Lots of love,
Susie

PS I keep forgetting to tell you that Bob Hope's Christmas show is supposed to be on TV on 16 January. I'd like for you to watch it if it is. Maybe some of the Long Binh show would be in it.

11 January 1969

Dear Ruby,

I'm using a different typewriter today because another office borrowed mine. This one looks better but it feels strange. Before I get on the car subject I'll talk about everything else. First of all, I'm going to have a kitty cat for a week. Our supply sergeant goes on R&R Sunday and she knows I love cats so she asked me to keep her cat while she's gone. Since I'm moving out of the building where she lives tomorrow, she said to take him over to my new room but if he didn't get along with my roommates or wouldn't stay there, to move into her room for the week. I went up to get acquainted with him last night and he made friends right away, played with my boot laces and laid on my lap. She said he usually runs under the bed when somebody walks in the room. She's a real nice person, a SSG with 12 years in service. She was in the band at Ft. McClellan for 7 years but got out of it because she could never get anymore rank. She bought a trailer there and had it parked on about 5 acres of land just outside the post.

I was going to tell you to take and wear any of my clothes that you find that you want. When I get back I'm going to want new clothes anyway.

Usually I write a letter to you in the morning and mail it at noon or write in the afternoon and mail it in the evening. If I get it in the box before 1700 it goes out that evening.

I sure would love to see some snow. It would feel so good to put on a coat and go out in the snow and feel that crisp cold air on my face. I'm sure no matter what kind of weather you're having in May I'll think it's cold. The more I look at the pictures of the Roadrunner and think about it, the more anxious I am to come home. Last night after I went to bed I visualized myself with a beautiful Roadrunner running around at home.

Well now I'll hit my favorite subject—cars. That picture of the red one is beautiful. I'm getting pretty sure that it is what I want. I think a Chevelle is too small and I don't care for the Impala. It looks to me like the Roadrunner already has a lot of the extras I want as standard equipment. On the list I made if all of that runs the price too high I can knock off the vinyl top or bucket seats. I don't care what anybody says about a 4 speed, that's all I want. You know how I love to shift those gears—that's half the fun of driving. I know an automatic would have better trade-in value but I just don't want one. It looks like a car I would love. As for how I'm going to get it, you didn't have my letter yet where I was asking if you would be willing to order it for me. I would like to get it through Eddie. Does he mean they could give me a 10% discount without anything to do with the PX ordering? I want to put $2000 down on it but I won't be able to do that till in April. I don't know when it would have to be ordered. As for the insurance, I want Criterion and the closest office is in Champaign. I don't want any other and probably couldn't get it anyway because I'm under 25. I typed all the information from under that one picture and am underlining the things I want to be sure the car has. I can't tell what is standard and what is optional. As I said before, I don't think I can go over 3600 dollars and of course I'd like to have it under that if possible. I would like to have the color be that beautiful bright blue with black stripes. It would be great to have it there waiting for me.

I'm off all day tomorrow so I'll move then. SSG Hollowell never cares if he's off tomorrow so he takes Saturday afternoon most of the time and I get all day Sunday. I guess he gets bored at the barracks because he comes to the office when he is off.

Well I'm going to close this time.

Lots of love,
Susie

13 January 1969

Dear Ruby,

The typewriter I'm using should have been considered a combat loss long ago but I'll see how good a mechanic I am. I just put it back together and decided to use the red side of the ribbon. I don't know what will happen when I erase. Well I just found out.

I got your letter with the pictures today. That one of the snow is beautiful. I'm showing it to everybody and we all wish we were in it. The one of you and Mom is good, she is actually smiling, about the first picture that she ever was. I see the watch and ring on you. The one at the table is good too. I could see the tea pot in that one.

I wish I was there to shovel your snow. That part about the school bus sure was history repeating itself. Thank goodness those days are over. That was the worst part of living out there by far. I wish you and Aggie would learn to ride a bike before I get back there but if you ever do attempt it, don't get on one with a high seat whatever you do because when you try to stop you'll go off every time. I think that old one of mine would be best to learn on because it's slow and has big tires. Just be sure your feet touch the ground easily.

Today it's hotter than the devil and at noon I read your letter about all the clothes you had on and looked at the snow picture but I still couldn't imagine it. It must be at least 100 here today. It's been in the 90's in Saigon so it should be 100 here. We just about boiled at noon when we were waiting for the bus.

Just think, at the end of this week I'll break 100 in my countdown. I guess next month I'd better put my papers in for my 2 week extension so I know they will get through.

You sure got further word on the car in my last letter. You'll be so tired of it you won't even want to see it. I guess we might as well say the Roadrunner is it. I don't think I'm going to see anything better suited to me. I can't possibly make a down payment big enough to prevent financing. If I would stay here another 3 months even I could but I want to come home. I couldn't tell if the 4 speed was standard or not. At first I thought so then I changed my mind.

They don't postmark my letters and I don't remember when I mailed them to tell you. I never know for sure when I seal it if I'll get it in the box for the next pick up or not. Our mail is coming in pretty good now.

I don't really know what I'll want to eat when I get home. I seem to want any kind of pork more than anything else because we almost never get any. Pork chops and ribs sound real good, also that ham you always cook. I guess the thing I'll appreciate most is the clear sparkling water. That was so nice in Bangkok.

I got moved yesterday and I'm very happy with my new room. The way it is set up now we have the 3 beds on one side with the 6 wall lockers in the middle for a divider and the kitchen and bar and living room on the other side. The two girls who are leaving soon are leaving their kitchen equipment, a few chairs and some tables so we'll gain a lot. I only hope Ruthie can make E-6 in time to move in with me.

I fed the cat last night and left him in his own room. He's OK today and he comes to me already. He was purring and playing with my hands last night. He's so cute. I think I'll take him over to my room tonight if he's home when I get home. He is free to come and go as he pleases.

My teeth feel real good now but little pieces of the temporary fillings keep falling out. I sure did let them go too long but it was so hard to get to the dental clinic and I didn't know for sure where it was. I don't really hate going as bad as I used to and the more I go the more routine it gets. I still don't like the shots though.

I forgot to mention your paper that you typed that other letter on. It was government paper but I don't know where you got it unless it was at school or maybe you dug it out of some of my stuff. Boy I'm going to have the most fun going through my junk when I get back. I don't remember half of it now and I'm sure a lot will go out. It will have to so

I'll have room for my RVN things. The way it sounds I should be able to get out of here with 2 sets of fatigues and 2 pairs of boots.

I got a nice long letter from Aggie the other day and a congratulations card from Jim. When she finally writes she writes a book. I'll let Ruthie read the part of your letter about her.

Well, I'm going to quit for now and I'll mail your birthday card with this in it this evening so it will go out in the mail at 1700. I hope you have a happy birthday.

Lots of love,
Susie

16 January 1969

Dear Ruby,

It's 1240 and I'm just sitting here so I'll start typing a letter to you. I went to early chow today because Hollowell is off since he had CQ last night. This makes the afternoon so much longer. Georgie has some shorthand books and she's going to bring one to me and I'll fool around with it in my spare time. At least it will be something to do. I haven't forgotten all of it but an awful lot. It probably wouldn't take long for it all to come back but I never want a job where I have to use it. I should have been taking a correspondence course these last 6 months here.

The more I look at these two color pictures you sent me the more little details I see in them. I have them on my desk top so I sit here and look at them all the time. I can tell what was in the bowls and dishes on the table without looking up your letter telling me what you had. I can almost taste the mashed potatoes and giblet gravy. Those are sure good pictures. You all look so natural in them. While I'm thinking of it, how come the Sheets family was so split up? I was surprised to hear that they were with you. Where was Elias, in Ohio? I wish I could put myself in that picture.

One of my roommates leaves tonight. Right now I intend to put my extension up to 15 May. That way 1SG Herney, Ruthie and I would fly to Travis together. It would be great to have the three of us together. The flight would go a lot faster and we would have a good time. That would give me Friday and whatever part of the weekend I wanted to stay at Oakland. Nora from Oakland is supposed to get here next month.

I wrote a long letter to Aggie yesterday. I haven't heard from Barb or Grace for ages. I don't know what has become of them.

Marney got some pork chops at the commissary today so I hope we'll eat them tonight. I'd like to have sauerkraut with mine. Nobody else especially likes it. I can't wait till I can get home and go in a grocery store. You never know how much the simple little things mean till you don't have them—things like clear water and a clean smelling towel. Well this year has sure given me an appreciation for my life and my home. I really have something to look forward to when I return.

I'll give you fair warning that TET starts officially on 17 February so we don't know what to expect. It sounds like they are planning another TET offensive like last year but since we'll know it's coming they shouldn't get away with it like they did last year. Anyway, you'll know if you don't get mail for too long that it's probably grounded. You never know when or what will happen around here. Just remember that if Long Binh post would receive even a couple of enemy rounds the stupid newspapers and newscasters will make it sound like the whole post was destroyed. One time I read in the Commercial-News where Long Binh had been hit and I didn't even know it till then.

I hope I get a letter from you tomorrow or Saturday. I'm going to close for now. I probably won't mail this in time for the evening mail.

Lots of love,
Susie

17 January 1969

Dear Ruby,

I started to type you a letter but the typewriter decided not to work. I took the ribbon off and still couldn't get it fixed so I got mad at it and quit. Maybe you'd rather I didn't type all of them anyway but when I write long ones it's so much easier.

I got your letter with the pictures today. The one of you would have been good if he had got all of you. I love these pictures but they sure make me want to come home. The salad bowl set looks like I thought it would. Aggie looks natural in her red sweater. The jokes are cute. I finally got the newspaper with my promotion article in it. I'm glad my letter to the editor was printed so soon and I hope everybody saw it.

You must look like a Dr. Zhivago character in all your clothes walking through the snow. You're wearing the same GI socks that I'm wearing. They keep your feet warm and mine cool.

Yes, I moved again because of my rank. I live in Building B room 4 of the NCO barracks now—E-6s and above. That B-4 came real close to being B-3, my basic training platoon. I bet very few if any of those girls stayed in. I'd like to know but I never will unless I run into one sometime.

No it won't take me two weeks to clear out of here. I'll only get about 2 days. There isn't much to it. Our hold baggage can be shipped as soon as we have orders. I sure hope I can ship it home instead of my new duty station because some of the stuff, especially the tape recorder I want at home. You had better believe Cannon street will look good to me.

I'm positive I want a Roadrunner now. I really want a bigger car. I think the RR will fit me perfectly.

No, I can't imagine you staying up till 2230. That's the time I go to bed most of the time and I get up at 0630 now. I don't think anybody over here is ever really awake. We're always ready to sleep every chance we get and they all say when they get home they want to sleep for a week. I doubt if they do but it's a nice thought. I hope I wake up when I get home. The times I'm most wide awake are when I get to bed and the artillery or mortar fire sounds close, then I want to go out and try to see it. Wednesday night we really had a war going in the ammo dump area. We all came out to watch it for about ½ hour. They never do it till after we go to bed.

My tooth with the root canal is fine but the one on the other side lost part of its temporary filling so I can't chew much on it. Monday I go back to have something done to this other one. We have flu and colds going around here too. I sure hope I escape it.

By now you have my long letter about the car.

Well it's 1625 now and in 25 minutes I leave to go on DNCO at 1830 so I think I'll quit and go mail this.

Lots of love,
Susie

24 January 1969

Dear Ruby,

It's typing time again. I've been pretty busy all day but maybe I'll have a break now. I got your letter at noon. Before I forget, our APO at the WAC DET has changed to 96384 as of yesterday. We will still get anything that comes to 375 but start using this one now. I don't know why it changed. The one here at the office is still the same.

Yesterday afternoon I went over to AG reassignment branch and asked about my assignment. The SFC in there wrote down all the information, name, rank, etc., and where I want to go. He said he will check it and tell Ruthie what he finds out. Maybe if I start now I can run a better chance getting what I want. Ft. Sam is big enough that surely they would have a slot open.

Marney leaves here this afternoon and flies out either tonight or tomorrow. She has your phone number and she's going to call you sometime. She said she would like to talk to you. She is so nice and we had so many good times together. Ruthie, she and I were one group of 3 people that got along perfectly. Usually 3 don't. We have been together almost every evening the past month.

I'm sure glad to know you got your flowers all right and on the day I asked for them to be delivered. MAJ Warren had the order blanks because he had sent some to his wife so I used one and got the orchids for you. There was a picture of them and they looked pretty so I thought you would probably like a real orchid corsage in the middle of your snow. I also knew you would be quite surprised. They have a lot of convenient ways for us over here to send things to somebody in the states.

I'm so glad to hear that you bought a turkey. I sure would like to have oysters with it. I'll love that. With all these people that mean a lot to me leaving, it's kind of getting to me and do I ever want to follow. I'm glad Ruthie is still here for as long as I am. I just dream and dream of the day when I board that freedom bird.

The supply sergeant, SSG Calcio, the one I kept the cat for, is getting out of her supply job into a different one in a few weeks and since cadre has private rooms, she will have to move. She's going to try to get 1SG Herney to hold the space in my room where Marney moved out for her. I sure hope she can because I like her and I'd love to have the cat living in my room. My other roommate, SSG Doris Lewis is seldom home because she sings with a band at the clubs every night. Ruthie didn't make E-6 this month. Only 2 people did but she went up to number 2 on the list so maybe next month. She's so afraid she won't get to move into my room. Doris leaves next month so if Ruthie makes it she should be able to get in my room. We are getting several new girls in now, E-4s and E-5s. I'll probably never know them because I don't live in their barracks and I'll never be around them.

I hope you do have something on the car for me soon. Naturally Vic thinks I should order it and have it sent to San Antonio so I could come there, register it in Texas and then drive it home. I can't do that because I won't know I'm going to be stationed in Texas soon enough and I don't want to use the PX system anyway. It was a good idea otherwise. If I can only get to San Antonio, I will be in my glory, deep in the heart of Texas, 200 miles from Laredo and not too far from Houston. Don't you think that sounds good?

I got this tooth checked yesterday. He took out the temporary filling, irrigated and drilled it and put another one in. He has to be sure the abscess is gone before he fills it permanently. I'm going back Monday for that then I'll be through I hope. The big filling on the other side seems to be all right.

I think this is enough from me for now.

Lots of love,
Susie

27 January 1969

Dear Ruby,

We're pretty busy today so I don't know how much I'll get written. I'm on call NCO in the office this week and we're going to be having practice alerts which means I'll have to come to the office if they send a car down for me. I hope it's at a decent hour. The one last week was at 2030.

Well, our friend Marney is still with us. She went out to the 90ᵗʰ Replacement Company Friday afternoon and they were going to try to get her out that night. The plane was already full so Saturday afternoon she called Ruthie and asked her if we cared if she came back to the barracks. Of course we didn't except it meant saying good-bye again. She came and we sat and talked and played Yahtzee and Marney and I drank bourbon and Coke. She kept telling us she had to see the CO and 1SG. We hoped like everything that she was trying to extend and sure enough after a few conferences with them she came back and said she was coming back. So now whenever they can get her paperwork processed, she'll go home for a 30 day leave then come back. I still have her for a roommate. We're both so happy to have her back. We couldn't believe it. Of course she shipped almost everything she had to Ft. McNair so they'll have to get that back. There has only been one other girl that got that far and decided to extend. Sometimes there is just no way to know till you're ready to go. I can't have that chance because once you order that car for me I'll have to come home to stay whether I want to or not. The way things are right now if I would get a different job I probably would extend. Marney, Ruthie and I have such a good time together and I like my room now. Of course 1SG Herney will leave so things could change. Marney said her mother will probably shoot her when she gets home and tells her. She will leave in August now. We have more fun playing Yahtzee. Something funny always happens and usually everybody wins about the same number of games. Last night I won all but one. It's so nice to go home in the evening, fix our own food and sit in our little lounge and do what we want. Ruthie is never in her room anymore except to sleep.

Believe it or not, I got a nice letter from Darla the other day. She saw my letter in the paper. She didn't even know I was here till then. I wrote back and I hope we can keep writing. I also got a letter from Edie. She is at her husband's parents house while he is over here.

I want to know how far ahead you'll have to order the car. Somehow being over here changes everybody and none of us can be absolutely sure of what we're going to do till we do it. You know I'll be home in May no matter what I do.

It's too bad all of you can't be in "sunny South Vietnam" for a few days to soak up our beautiful sun. The only time you could stand it would be in the morning because it boils everything by noon. The mornings are sure beautiful and I'd love to go for a long walk.

I'm going to close now and mail this on my out to the bus. I'm leaving at 1130 and have my dental appointment at 1300.

Lots of love,
Susie

28 January 1969

Dear Ruby,

I just got back from chow and getting your second letter in two days so I'll attempt to type you one. I was sure surprised to get another one today. I'm so happy that you got all the car information and also that the price is no higher than it is. I was just about ready to say forget the bucket seats then I looked at this picture showing the seats and it looks to me as if plain seats would make one solid front seat. If they were two separate seats like my other car had it would be all right but I don't want one solid front seat. I sure do want that blue exterior and I think a white interior would be best with a black vinyl top. I don't want the sport paint stripe, just the hood paint. I had a pretty good idea of what the air grabbers were for. I knew they were more than decoration although they do add a lot to the looks. Yes, I know the wheel covers are extra. It looks like that list is just what I want except the paint stripe. The price isn't really as bad as I thought it would be with all this on it. I'd say this discount is probably more than I would have through the PX. I'll make up a separate list when I finish this letter.

I wish it didn't have to be ordered so soon because I hate to commit myself that far ahead. I doubt very much if I'll know where I'm being assigned by then so once you have ordered the car I'm going to be stuck with whatever I get. I just hate to know that I have to take what they give me. I really do want to come home this spring and stay in the states but I'm still in a stage of indecision. If I don't have orders by the first of March I'll tell you to go ahead with the car. If they will really order it with only $100 on it, you could get that from my account at American

Savings and Loan. One thing is for sure, once you order that car, I'll come and get it. I think it will be a real beauty. It sure is a lot of money but it's what I want and I feel that I deserve it after this year.

Just 91 days now. Tomorrow I'll be considered what we call a 90 day loss. This is for purposes of job transfer or anything. After a person gets under 90 days, they are usually put on an excess list and left where they are. Since I'm not in a slot for my MOS here I need to be under 90 to be sure they don't try to move me. No, I'm not extending into May to get the combat pay although I will. My main object is just to be home on Memorial Day and if I left here on 29 April, I would have to be at my new duty station on 28 May. I will get the tax exemption for that month too. I know I don't have to file my income tax for 180 days after I get back.

Last night we had another alert and tonight the whole post is supposed to go on a practice alert. Very likely I'll have to come to the office. I didn't last night. Boy I hate going home every evening and knowing all I'll get to do is stay in uniform and wait for an alert then go sit in or stand around the bunkers. They usually start around 2030 and last about an hour and a half or longer. I wouldn't even mind it so much if it was real. Marney is getting so bored sitting around here she doesn't know what to do. She thinks she will get out of here on the 31st now.

If you ever want a pleasant feeling, try stepping out of your bed at 0630 in the dark and putting your foot in the middle of about 10,000 ants. That happened to me the other morning. I felt them crawling and couldn't imagine what in the heck was going on. I had to grab the bug spray and let them have it and that's just a grand way to start the day because that stuff stinks. I finally got them killed off and swept out. Boy am I ever sick of bugs and ants. I was still half asleep anyway and in no mood to battle a battalion of ants. What a life.

I think this is all for this time.

Lots of love,
Susie

CHAPTER XI

FEBRUARY 1969

2 February 1969

Dear Ruby,

It's 1800 Sunday evening and I'm home after working the whole weekend till 1630 today. We had a 45 page Command Operating Budget for FY70 to put together and type on mats for reproduction so that's what I've been doing. We finally got it finished. Obviously I haven't had time to write to you at work. I don't even remember when I last wrote or what I haven't told you.

First of all, Marney finally got out of here Friday. When she gets back I'll have about 2 months left. I am beginning to feel somewhat like a "short timer" now and it's sure nice. The new major in my office, Major Cratty, keeps telling me how short I am. Friday was payday and I got my E-6 pay for 8 days last month and this month—$422. I guess I'll get about $410 after this.

Boy we had a war going on all around all day today. When I had time I watched the bombs falling with my binoculars. They were hitting 3 different areas. Usually it's all in one place. Through my binoculars I can see the dirt and pieces of trees fly up with the fire flash when the bomb hits. Last night just after I went to bed a bunch of artillery went off real loud and I got up and went outside but I couldn't see anything so I went back to bed. I don't know what you saw in the paper about Long Binh and Bien Hoa being in danger. I haven't heard or seen anything new so I'm anxious to see the paper. Of course anything over here is in danger but evidently some news man decided to write a story about it. Nobody knows what will happen in the next few weeks so there's no use to worry about it. I'm not half as scared here as you are there reading the paper and hearing the news. As I've said before, I worry more about everything I have here than I do about me because I can move but everything I have would just have to stay here. Ruthie is opposite. She says everything she has can be replaced but she can't. I suppose Vic is somewhere in Texas, haven't heard from him yet.

I don't imagine I would be much help with your school work except maybe in English. I've probably forgotten most of that. It would be fun to try anyway. I might like it myself now, especially history. No wonder you need new glasses after that factory and the school work too. It's a good thing I've always had good eyes with all the typing I do, especially numbers. I'm going to try to send you a copy of this thing I just typed since I did all of it.

I would love to go to Brooke but my chances of getting there would be small. More than likely I would be in 4th Army headquarters. I sure would like to know where I'm going before 1 March but I doubt if I can. I would only be about 1,000 miles from home there.

I don't know if I told you about the finishing of my tooth or not but I don't think so. He put a little piece of metal, about like a needle, up in the bone and cemented it in then I went back 2 days later and got the permanent filling. It's a little sensitive but not bad. When he was putting that needle thing up in there I thought it was going to come out the top of my head. I didn't know he would leave it in. All this would cost a fortune, 7 trips and at least 4 x-rays on one tooth. I don't trust the big filling on the other side. I just hope it lasts till I get out of here.

I'll close for now. I marked off 87 today; I think you're still a day behind.

Lots of love,
Susie

4 February 1969

Dear Ruby,

I guess I'll start typing you a letter while I'm not doing anything. We got the Command operating Budget (COB) put together and printed and then put 60 copies together yesterday afternoon so I have one for you. One page is missing but that won't matter. I should wrap it and one of the VC flags into a package and mail them. I have to mail those flags home because somebody in customs might take them away from me if I try to hand carry them and I'd sure be ready to shoot somebody if they did. LTC Preuss leaves here Friday and then I'm the shortest one in the office and next to go. We're getting a civilian replacement for him, Mr. Sears from USARPAC in Hawaii. He won't be here long with me so I don't care who comes.

1SG Herney borrowed my jigsaw puzzles and is putting them together. She finished the snow scene yesterday. It's hard to do because the pieces don't all fit into each other, part of them are just plain edges. It sure is pretty when it's together. Ruthie and I were helping part of the time. I think Ruthie is going to extend and take her 30 day leave on 1 April. Her dad is getting worse instead of improving from the heart attack he had last year and she wants to get home and find out what is going on. If she does Marney will just get back before she leaves then when Ruthie gets back I'll have about 2 weeks left.

I just got through processing the sub vouchers for a CPT from the Regional Communications Group near Saigon. He said he'd sure like to have me in his office as his Admin NCO. He said it's an E-7 slot. It's sure too bad I couldn't go but of course no WACs can be there. I couldn't get promoted for 3 more years anyway. It's nice to have somebody say things like that. He's a real nice guy. He always sits and talks while he's here.

On the 9th Ruthie leaves for R&R in Penang for 5 days and Doris, my roommate leaves to go to MACV. Of course Marney is gone so that will leave me alone in my room with nobody around. It will be strange. I have one more girl I could invite over to spend some evenings and eat with me. She's the SP4 who was with us all on Christmas day.

You should have seen me tearing around this morning. Evidently I turned my alarm off at 0630 and went back to sleep. When I woke up and looked at my watch is was 0700 and the bus comes at 0710. I jumped out of bed and into my uniform in 7 minutes—even got my face washed. I didn't know I could even lace my boots that fast. Anyway, I was out waiting for the bus when it came. I probably broke the sound barrier. That was one time I needed the roadrunner on my hat. By the way, I left him on there and 1SG Herney saw it and thought it was cute so I'm cleared to wear it now. I sure hope I never wake up that late again. I think the main reason is because I haven't had a chance to sleep late for almost a month. I go to bed early enough but I just need that chance to sleep late.

I think Ruthie and I are going to have pork chops tonight. The Commissary usually keeps them now and they are so good. We cook them in the electric skillet and eat them with our fingers and they are delicious. They are supposed to be closing the commissaries to all military and civilian personnel who have access to a messing facility so if they do, after 15 March we won't be able to get much. We really have it made now by fixing our own meals at night. Some of them are really good. We buy a lot of Stokely's corn on the cob in cans and I love it. We also make instant mashed potatoes and those 2 things with pork chops are my favorite meals.

It's raining this afternoon, lightly, and it's almost a decent temperature outside. In the evening when we sit outside and watch the movie sometimes there is a breeze blowing and we actually get cold out there. Without that break we would smother in the heat. Everything is dry as a bone now. Even a little rain is gone the minute it hits. The trees are losing their leaves like it's fall and I noticed the ones around the barracks have new little leaves coming out like spring before the old ones are completely off. It's strange to think about fall and spring meeting on the same branch of a tree. Everything looks like you would expect fall to look. Maybe it is but there won't be much difference. The grass is dried up too except the few places where it is watered. We don't have one bit around the barracks, just nice thick dust or gravel. We do have some sidewalks but not everywhere. I'd like to walk barefoot in some of the deep thick dust along the road. It would be soft. I sure wish I would ever get some time off so I could get some more sun.

Well, I'm going to close for now because I've run out of anything to say and Major Cratty keeps giving me things to type.

Lots of love,
Susie

6 February 1969

Dear Ruby,

I got your letter yesterday so I'll start one to you now. It's 0830 and I just got to work after our monthly Unit Fund Council Meeting. They are boring but at least they keep us out of work for awhile. I'd rather do anything than come to work.

I told 1SG Herney to type up the paper for my 2 week extension today so as soon as it goes through, I'm going to have 15 more days added to my calendar. I guess the best thing would be to quit marking them off for 15 days because I have to know the real number of days I have to go. Of course 1SG Herney will keep me well informed. She tells everybody I'm extending 2 weeks so I can go back with her.

If your one tooth cost $11, I can imagine how much I have in all of mine. It's a good thing I don't have to pay for my teeth or I could never own a car.

I finally got to go to the USARV main PX yesterday. They had pre-recorded tapes in and I got two by Ray Conniff. One has "Honey" and a lot of other good ones and the other has "It Must Be Him", "Impossible Dream", "Yesterday" and others. They cost $4.75 each here. I also got a bottle of Jim Beam to restock our bar. That costs $2.00 for a fifth here and in Oakland it was $6.50. Ruthie still hasn't heard anything about her promotion but I think it's too soon yet because the board was only 2 days ago. She's No. 2 on the list but the board has to be over and have the orders cut on them first before the ones on the list find out anything.

Last night we went to the Chinese restaurant and then came home and played Yahtzee and listened to my tapes. I love to play that game. It's more fun with 3 of us but it isn't bad with just two. I'm sure glad you sent it. I'm getting so good with chop sticks. I'm going to bring another set home and we're going to eat Chinese food with them sometime. I can never say I haven't learned a lot of various new things while I've been here.

You can send the rest of my income tax forms now if you want to. I got my W-2 form. I only paid about $120 this year so I probably won't get anything back. I might as well send it in and get it over with.

Boy I wish I were going on R&R with Ruthie next week. I wish I could take another one to break up these next 3 months but I can't. Even a trip to Saigon would help but I don't foresee that very soon either. I have to get there once more before I leave. LTC Preuss leaves here today for Cam Ranh Bay to fly out of there to Ft. Lewis. Washington. He's sure glad to be going.

Well, I can't think of anymore to say right now so I'll quit.

Lots of love,
Susie

9 February 1969

Dear Ruby,

At the moment everyone is out of the office so I'll try to write you a letter. MAJ Warren is in a meeting so he will probably come out of it with something for me to type. I'm working through my second weekend. I'll have to be off next Saturday morning because I have training. I'll take advantage of anything now to get out of here. I had MAJ Warren sign my paper for my 17 day extension yesterday. I said if I didn't want to be home on Memorial Day awful bad I never would do that. I don't mind staying over here but I hate 2 more weeks in this office. This paper has to be approved in Special Troops then my DEROS will be 15 May.

Last night Ruthie went to an office party and there was a party going on in the company area. After I got home I popped a big bag of popcorn and listened to tapes. Later Nancy Young come over and then Ruthie. I had such a nice relaxing evening. I don't think I've mentioned what beautiful corn that popper makes. It's so big and fluffy and so easy to do.

I'm glad you're sending me a Valentine package. I hadn't thought about it but I sure remember that beautiful yellow rose on that heart last year. We didn't have much choice of Valentines in the PX but I found some pretty nice ones.

Do you know the story you sent me about goddess Athena is about Palace Athena, the WAC goddess? I have never read that story but it's got to be the same one. Ours is always in gold armor. Boy what a story.

I got a card from PACEX last week telling me my order should be filled in about 20 days so you are going to get them. I'm sure you'll enjoy the binoculars.

I do get all my newspapers even though they sometimes take forever to get here. I'm glad the reserve center finally got a new flag. The old one had been dingy for as long as I can remember.

It's fine with me for the days to fly past. The faster these next three months go the happier I'll be. Being on a stateside post for a year without going home would seem like forever or at least it would have before, but being here has made it a short year.

Nora from Oakland got here the other day so I've been brought up to date on the happenings there. She used to go places with Barb, Grace and me sometimes. She's a SP4. Barb is on the list to make Sp5. Ruthie still hasn't heard anything and it looks like the stripes will come out while she's on R&R so she's going to have to wonder for another week. I wish she would make it before they have to move somebody else in my room. 1SG Herney won't unless she has to. I've never had a 1SG as good as her before and probably never will again. She's so friendly and nice to have around but yet she never loses any of her status as 1SG.

Well I guess I'll close for now since I had such good luck writing this without getting interrupted once.

Lots of love,
Susie

12 Feb 69

Dear Ruby,

This won't be long but it's been awhile since I've written and since TET is coming and a VC element was spotted close last night, I'd better write a little so when it comes out in the paper you won't have to wonder about it so long. The post didn't get hit or anything but we saw and heard all the action all night. I'll send you the USARV news release about it.

We have been so busy at work I haven't had a chance to do anything. I think we're about to get through the mess and maybe I'll get some time off, I hope. I did get 2 hours off at noon today so I had time to put on my bathing suit and go to the pool and get a nice sunburn.

Ruthie is on R&R now and we're hoping very strongly that when she gets back she'll get promoted. 1SG Herney is holding my room for her so I'm still living alone. This is sure a big empty room. MAJ Warren is putting in my papers for my award, a bronze star. I sure hope it doesn't get downgraded because they are given only in a combat zone and I don't intend to be in another one very soon. I feel like I'm really getting "short." Boy I can't wait for 15 May, especially after a week like this one.

I hope I get a chance to write a long letter to you tomorrow. We aren't getting any mail, evidently it's being held up some place. You can tell by the writing that I'm in a hurry so I'm going to quit.

Lots of love,
Susie

13 February 1969

Dear Ruby,

It looks like I have a good chance to type you a letter so I'll start. I brought my little tape recorder to work today because the band is having a concert up here from 1200-1300 and I want to record it. I hope they play their good songs.

My arms are sure a nice copper color this morning but my back and legs are red and I suppose they will peel because it has been too long since they had any sun. I have DNCO Monday night, 17 Feb, the day TET officially starts, so Tuesday I can lay in the sun again. That's sure a great night for me to have it. I hope they don't blow the place up that night if they ever do. This is my 19th day to work without even an afternoon off. I don't know if I'll ever get one or not. I have training Saturday morning and I'll be free most of the morning then off Tuesday after duty so that will be a little break. I'm sure glad the end is in sight. We've had so many visiting generals here to be briefed and that's what has caused all the mess. Three months and two days and 1SG Herney and I will be on our way out of here. She reminds me a lot of Aggie with the things she says and does. She's always stopping by my room to talk and sometimes watches TV with us.

We had a lot of booming going on in that same area last night and when I got ready to go to bed it was really getting loud but nothing else happened. That area is a lot closer than other places have been. On that news report they said the azimuth of the rockets wasn't reported. That's probably because they were facing Long Binh.

14 February 1969

I got interrupted yesterday and never came back. I listened to the whole band concert and recorded it. It turned out perfect on tape except you can hear some sparrows chattering in the background but they don't really hurt it.

As of tomorrow, everyone is restricted to this post till after TET. The curfew for everybody to be in their barracks area is 2200 and we can't wear civilian clothes except in the company area. They are really putting up tight security everywhere. I don't know how much good it will do. I hope nothing happens before Ruthie gets back because I don't want her stuck at TSN for a week.

If we don't have a disaster in the next 30 minutes, I'm off this afternoon. I can't believe it. Tomorrow morning I'll have training so I'm finally going to get a little time out of here. The worst should be over now. MAJ Warren left for 2 weeks in Hawaii this morning so there are only 5 of us left all together.

Yesterday I got a package from Aggie and Jim but I still don't have one from you. I haven't gotten a letter from you for ages. I got another one from Darla yesterday. I'm going to close and start getting ready to leave now.

Lots of love,
PS

I have the vase and flowers Jim sent on my desk and they add a lot to brighten the office. I didn't give the mouse to the cat yet. I couldn't imagine what it was for till I read on the back "for the cat." Tell Aggie and Jim thanks.

I had a real mouse in my room when I got up this morning but he was dead. He was real tiny with a pointed nose and ears.

16 February 1969

Dear Ruby,

I'm typing on an old battered typewriter again because my other one fell apart. The chain that runs the ribbon broke for the second time. It's Sunday morning, 0800 and there are only 3 of us in the office. I did have Friday afternoon off and yesterday morning except for the one hour of training. Yesterday afternoon wasn't bad and today shouldn't be either. At noon yesterday I was talking to 1SG Herney and she said she got some orders. Of course I wanted to know for who and what. She said "If I tell you will you blab it all over the company?" I told her she knew I wouldn't so she said she got orders promoting Ruthie to SSG. I'm so glad. She's held that space in my room open for over a week and it worked. I think Ruthie is due back today. I hope 1SG Herney sees her before I do because the first thing she'll ask me is if I've heard anything. I had wondered if 1SG Herney would tell me if the orders came while Ruthie was gone.

I got all your valentines and the package Friday. That heart is beautiful and it is in perfect shape, the rose isn't even smashed and you can't tell the chocolates were ever moved from the store. Nobody can figure out how they got here in such perfect shape. Everybody else that has chocolate mailed to them gets it after it's half melted. This package took 9 days to get here but it must have been in the states maybe snowbound part of that time because I sure don't think it was over here. I never thought about you getting me one with a yellow rose again. It seems like this one is prettier than last year's but maybe it's because I appreciate it more. I love the red hots too. Thanks so much for the valentines and the candy.

The card Mom sent is so sweet. I can't wait to have my own furry little kitten again. I have cat pictures all over my desk and room because every time somebody sends me a card with a cat on it I want to put it up where I can see it. I like what your card says "Wish I could see you on Valentine's Day". I wish so too.

You should get your binoculars soon. I sure hope you never have any bombing to watch. Yes, 1,000 miles would be just a walk away from home after this. I dream about being there and having my car sometimes. I bet it's going to be strange to be behind the wheel of a car again but wonderful too.

Our trees are all leafed out again now, at least the ones I was watching around the company are. They are such a bright pretty green. Of course the grass will stay dried up till the monsoons come again. Do you ever see the moon anymore? I sure do. Last week it was full and so pretty. Sometime I'm going to take a picture when there are a lot of flares up and see if it works. There was a lot of noise last night but I guess nothing big happened. They are building some bunkers up here around headquarters. The VC and NVA and SVN are supposed to be in a holiday truce now but our bombers are sure letting them have it and so was the artillery last night. Our hour of training yesterday was on the code of conduct and of course part of it is about being a prisoner of war and that we can't tell them anything but name, rank, and service number and date of birth. If we tell them more than that we're likely to be court martialed when we get released. If we won't tell them more we may be held for a long time or killed. That's really quite a choice. I just hope I never have to make that decision. It doesn't seem likely but I guess you never know. If they ever overpowered Long Binh enough to capture the WACs this war would be over and won by the communists.

I'm sending you a drawing so you can see where Penang is. Boy, I couldn't believe the long letter I got from Aggie the other day. I'll answer it soon, maybe today if I don't get buried under typing. I used Bunnie's book to figure out how much income tax I should get back and it's $102. That will sure be nice.

Well I'm going to close for this time. Thanks again for everything you sent on Valentine's Day. You are wonderful people and I'm lucky to have you. Three months from today I should be in Oakland. I can't wait.

Lots of Love,
Susie

1530

18 Feb 69

Dear Ruby,

I'm off today since I had DNCO. It was a very quiet night except for some small arms fire early around 2200. Everybody is so sure something is going to happen. I don't really think it will till after TET. We keep getting briefings on what to do in case of attack at work and here. We're going to have a practice red alert here in the company tonight.

Well Ruthie has her stripes. She got back Sunday and she practically knew she had made it by the way 1SG Herney and I acted. Sunday 1SG Herney said she needed someone to take formation for her Monday morning. Her excuse was that she didn't want to be in uniform that morning and neither would any of the other cadre because they were getting ready for the IG inspection.

Of course I said I'd be glad to. I knew why she wanted me. After Ruthie was out of the room, 1SG Herney told me what to do in the morning. For about 10 minutes I was acting 1SG. Everything went beautifully. I took the reports from the platoon sergeants then said "Specialist McKenney front and center." She came up in front of me and we exchanged salutes then the CO came out and Ruthie and I stood side by side while the CO read her orders and put her strips on. After Ruthie went back to her platoon I had to tell all of them a few things then turned the platoons over to the platoon sergeants. It was really great of 1SG Herney to do that so I could have a part in Ruthie's promotion. 1SG Herney stood and watched and after it was over she said I did such a good job she'd like to have me do it all the time. She has to do it every day. That sure started our week off good. Ruthie moved into my room last night. We never dreamed the 3 of us would get to live here together. Tonight Ruthie, 1SG Herney and I are going to the Chinese restaurant and then come back and have a celebration drink. Tomorrow Ruthie and I are supposed to get new ID cards made. Everybody who makes E-6 has to have that rank on their ID cards. Our pictures on these will be in fatigues. That will sure be nice when we get back to the states.

I got a nice long letter from Barb yesterday. She's sure making plans for when I get back there. She even has a car lined up for us to use. I don't love the idea of driving somebody else's car around there after not driving for a year but I guess we can go around in Oakland till I get used to it again. I sure hope she can get it because so many places I want to go back to we need a car for. She's sure she can get off for the days I'm there. Also on 24 May she's going on leave and riding to Iowa with another girl and her mother.

I turned the TV on today and when they signed on at 1415 with the 2 national anthems, I recorded them. The RVN one is really pretty. I didn't have ours till now. Ruthie and I both stand up every time we hear it. She's as patriotic as I am, the first person I've met who is.

I may get a letter from you this evening but I thought I'd write and tell you everything this afternoon.

I'm sending you a sweet picture of Otto that Ruthie took. You can keep it and be sure Aggie sees it. He's so cute. He's our company dog.

Well, I guess I'll close now. I had to iron 3 sets of fatigues this afternoon because the maids are off all week for TET. The starch is about all that is holding 2 sets of them together.

Lots of love,
Susie

20 February 1969

Dear Ruby,

I'll start typing you a letter on this nice black ribbon. I just finished writing one to Grace. I have several others to answer; maybe I'll get caught up someday. We're not so busy in the office now. I fixed up my income tax and mailed it yesterday. The envelope was made to send to Austin, Texas but the back of the booklet said to send it to Kansas City, Missouri for a refund so that's where mine is going.

I have ordered my slide projector and screen so sometime you will get them. I ordered them from an Army/Air force exchange service in Fort Worth. It's really made to send gifts so I made it look like they're a gift to you so they wouldn't question it. All I need now is my speakers and I think Bunnie and her friend can get them in Hong Kong when they go in March. I'm going to have things from all over the world by the time I get back. When you get this, you'll have my wood carvings that I finally mailed. I don't know who gets what yet except the cats are mine. The little vase is one somebody brought to me from Singapore. I hope it gets there all right.

Only 8 more days of this month and payday will be here and the beginning of another month. I don't know for sure when my driver's license expires but I think it's 1970. We had a great time with 1SG Herney the other night. We had our drinks and played Yahtzee. That game was the best one you could have sent. We were running out of score cards fast so 1SG Herney suggested covering them with acetate and using grease pencils to write then erase them. It works just fine. I won't be going to Saigon very soon because nobody can. I hope to go there and to Vung Tau once more. The Vung Tau trip would serve as my last chopper ride. I could get some beautiful pictures with the camera I have now. Last May all I had was that little cheap one. I got Mom's Valentine card a day later than yours.

Yes, they have school in Saigon just like anywhere else. The kids all dress alike and they do the same in Bangkok. I have some pictures of a Saigon school when the kids were out. I don't think most of them are very old when they get out or quit. The very upper class families are the only ones that go to high school or universities even in Bangkok. This is a pretty uncivilized world over here but sometimes I wonder if it's really that much worse than ours. We have everything compared to these people but we're no safer from war than they are considering that other big countries have the same military power that we have.

We got our ID cards all fixed yesterday but they had to laminate them in plastic so we're going to pick them up today. I'll send you these two pictures that were extras from the ones on the card. We have 2 women, an SFC and a MSG leaving here tomorrow who are going to Ft. Ben Harrison. They are friends and wanted to go to the same place and they got it.

If I'm lucky I might get this afternoon off. I'll sure be glad when the TET holiday is over and our maids come back. It takes forever to iron these fatigues. I guess they should come back Friday.

By now it is beginning to be spring in San Francisco and should be soon in El Paso. I guess you have at least another month to wait but it won't be too long. I guess there's no better time to leave here than in the spring because everything will be so fresh and clean at home.

I'm going to close for now. I never think I have much to say till I get to the end of the letter and read back over it.

Lots of love,
Susie

and arrived around 0730 to see a pig hanging on a hook . . . .

23 Feb 69

Dear Ruby,

This may not be much of a letter but I have to write something. This morning at 0200 all hell broke loose here. I was blasted out of bed by incoming rounds and grabbed my field gear and headed for the door to go to the bunker. Just as I got in the doorway another round came in and hit the finance building right across the street from my room. I saw the fire flash and shrapnel fly into the air and I took off for my bunker. Of course I was in my pajamas but I grabbed my field gear on the way out. I had my tape recorder set up but there was no time to grab it. We stayed in the bunker while rounds came in all around till about 0430 then went out and since the firing had slacked off some most of us went and put our fatigues on. A little while after that, they said a major ground attack was expected so we went back to the bunkers. We stayed about an hour and a half and around 0730 we got to go back to our rooms. Needless to say we had been on red alert all this time. Ruthie and I with the help of some donated food, fixed breakfast of an egg omelet, bacon, bread and jelly and coffee for ourselves and 4 other NCOs. At 1100 buses came and got the ones of us that had to come to work and we came with our helmets on. The buildings here at USARV weren't hit but 1st Log Command across the street was torn up. All day Cobra gunships have been pouring rocket fire into a couple of hills on the perimeter below USARV. I've been watching all of it and I have my tape recorder here now. I talked on it about what all has happened and I've left it setting in the window recording all the noise. A stray round (JS type) came into our G-1 section about an hour ago so Bunnie said I'd better not stand in the window with my recorder. So far there are casualty reports of approximately 80 wounded and 7 killed. One of them was the Commanding Officer of Special Troops, LTC Dickey. He was president of the board that promoted me and seemed like a nice guy. His jeep was hit. A CPT and LT were killed in a bunker and several other colonels have been wounded. Also, the VC infiltrated the post in 3 places and are evidently running loose somewhere. None of us can really believe this is happening. The girls were great this morning. Everybody went right to their bunkers and nobody panicked or did anything wrong. Last night was the first time I have really had a fear of either being hit or captured. If the round that hit finance had been a few hundred feet to the right it would have been in the middle of 2 of our buildings. We're just darn lucky. This is very hard on the nerves and the worst part is that we feel completely helpless being unarmed. Every girl over here should at least be weapons qualified. I'd feel a whole lot safer if I had something to fight with. It's hard to tell what will happen tonight. I know this will hit all the papers and scare you to death but I thought I'd better tell you all the details myself. They are trying to keep it out of the news right now because they don't want everybody to know how bad we were hit. We are certainly earning our combat pay this month. For several days we had been getting reports that Long Binh was going to be hit that night but we didn't think much about it because nothing every happened before. Last night we got another warning and MAJ Cratty and I were joking about it as I was leaving. He said he'd see me in the morning and I said "Yes, if we're not under attack." I never dreamed we would be. I only got about 2 ½ hours sleep last night but I'm not sleepy. I'm nervous but not actually aware of being scared. We all have a strange feeling that I can't describe. It's hard to tell when this letter will get out but I hope this mess is over by then.

I have your letter here to answer. I'm sure glad I got it yesterday. Unless this offensive is a long one, I should know my assignment within the next couple of weeks. I sure hope I get Ft. Sam on the first try. Yes, I got a nice letter from Maude, I thought I told you. I should write to her but haven't yet.

You should see the beautiful tan I have. I helped clean out the swimming pool in the company Thursday afternoon and my face arms and legs got so brown.

Yesterday I got a call from a SGM Johnson out at Bearcat (about 5 miles from here). He used to live in Danville (raised there) on Griffin

Street. He's been overseas 4 years but he gets the Commercial-News and somebody wrote and asked him if he knew me because they saw my picture in the paper. Neither of us have the paper yet but he traced me down some way. We had a nice talk.

I sure hate to appear so stupid again but I just can't recall anybody named Ewania. It sounds like she knows me and makes me feel dumb.

So you've seen the first signs of spring. I'm glad you have, it won't be too long now.

You wished me a quiet TET and that's what we had. TET is over now and look what happened. About all I've done today is watch the war. It's still going strong. I've stopped this letter several times to look. This is one time I hate to see night come. Those sneaky little devils might do anything. You can't imagine what it's like to go through this. We're going to be so jumpy we can't stay still for a long time. I'll have some of the sound effects on tape for you to hear but not those incoming whistling rounds last night. If we get them tonight I intend to record them of course depending on the circumstances.

1SG Herney played Yahtzee with us again last night. We have such a good time with her in the game too.

I sure need to wash my hair if I get a chance. We had to stay in those horrible dirty bunkers so much last night that we were filthy this morning. They have men all around the company area guarding it and it's all fenced in with a tall wooden picket fence and concertina wire outside that. I feel much safer in the barracks than up here alone.

Well, I'm going to close now. I'll mail this on my way home this evening but it may not go anyplace for awhile.

Lots of love,
Susie

PS By the time you read this the worst will have to be over so don't worry.

24 February 1969

Dear Ruby,

Well, we got through another night of sleeping in the bunker, on the ground, etc. They continued the rocket and mini gun fire out here by USARV till about 1630 yesterday evening. I went home and Ruthie and I fixed ourselves something to eat. We were going to watch the news at 1930 but at 1920 we had to go out to the bunkers. Nothing happened for a few minutes then we went on red alert. I'm getting so I can grab my tape recorder along with my field gear now. We stayed around the bunkers that time till about 2300 and went to our rooms and laid down leaving everything but the field gear on. I had just gone to sleep and a loud bang woke me up. I went outside and looked but nothing was happening. I went back to bed and finally went back to sleep. At 1220 I woke up when somebody (one of the reactionary force men) yelled "INCOMING ROUNDS!" I flew out of that bed, snatched everything off the chair where I had purposely left it and took off for the bunker. It's getting so I feel it's almost a hopeless cause to try to go to sleep. Every time I do something happens to wake me up. That time we stayed in the bunkers the rest of the night or else sat outside by them. I finally went in and laid down and did sleep a little. The seats are about 8 inches off the ground and very narrow. Two by fours stick out here and there and the walls are curved steel. Doesn't that sound like a comfortable bed? That along with all the noise makes sleeping a little difficult and most of us are so tired now we can't sleep. I have slept about 5 hours out of the past 48 and some haven't had that much. Of course we have to come to work just as usual. We got out of the bunkers at 0700 this morning. The incoming rounds weren't real close this time. I tried to record the sirens as they went off but didn't get a chance to listen to it yet so I don't know if they are on it or not. I got a lot of the background noise and talked quite a bit about what was going on. What a life! I don't know if I told you yesterday that a stray round came into our G-1 building. Well, I later found out that it came through the wall and bounced off the head of a WAC. She had a headache and a slight bruise and they sent her to the hospital to be checked but she was all right. Can you imagine that? That's the closest a girl has come to being hurt here. She was sure lucky because one WAC getting hurt over here could end this tour for the rest of us. Other than that and one girl who stumbled over her own feet and broke her toe on the way to the bunker, everyone is fine. We're in good spirits and feeling very confident in our fellow soldiers. There's nothing to equal these Cobra gunships. It if wasn't for them there wouldn't be any war. The element of VC that attacked us was North Vietnamese Regular soldiers, just over from Cambodia. There were about 430 of them to start with and they estimate about 150 are left. I guess they have killed the ones that infiltrated the post. Our new casualty count is 7 killed and 30 wounded here on Long Binh post. Considering there are almost 35,000 people here and 80 rockets were fired in, that isn't bad. The VC don't aim their rockets. They set them in the ground or rest them on 2 sticks of wood and fire them and wherever they land that's fine. I found out last night that we had tanks with gas out on those hills where they were firing yesterday to try to gas them out. Evidently it didn't work.

The stateside papers will mess this report up even more than our own rumors do. Things happen so fast and everybody wants to be first to know everything. I even found myself getting carried away at times when I was talking on that tape. I sure hope this ends pretty soon. I don't know how long we can go through days and nights with so little sleep. I guess we can do whatever we have to. I'll tell you more details about this after I get home. I've probably told you far too much but as long as I'm writing you know I'm all right. I just hope these letters go out sometime. The mail room is closed this morning because all the guys are out on the perimeter. COL Metts, ACofS, Comptroller and CPT Jurgevich both keep telling us to write home every day. At least whenever they do get out maybe you'll get more than one at a time and can follow the action blow by blow. We're all remaining very calm outwardly and company morale is high, probably higher than it's been for a long time. We have been put to the test and passed it beautifully. We're jumpy at every sound and tense but no more than the men are.

Well you're going to get tired of reading my war stories but that's just all there is to tell for now so I'll quit. Now remember don't be scared for us, we're fine and the guys are taking good care of us.

Lots of love,
Susie

25 February 1969

Dear Ruby,

We had a pretty good night last night. We all took our field gear out and watched the movie. We were afraid to go to bed before we found out what was going to happen if anything and the movie gave us something to think about. It was over at 2145 and we went in and went to bed. I did take my boots off but that's all. You'd be surprised how comfortable fatigues are to sleep in. There were several bangs during the night that woke me up but other than that it was quiet. We all wake up at the slightest sound now because we are constantly ready to take off. Last night when we were watching the movie our own jets started making air strikes real close. The first one hit and we didn't know who was doing it so the CO said "Hit the bunkers!" and we did. There are about 6 of us NCO's that can get in that bunker in at least 1 minute from anywhere in the detachment area. CPT J. thinks everything she hears in incoming so she's always ready to head for the bunker. I can pretty well tell which way it's going now at least if it's coming in close there's no question. We all felt terrible when we got up this morning. It will be a long time before we get caught up on our sleep and get settled down to normal again. We did get to come to work on time although we still have to carry our helmets with us. We feel like we've really been through a war now. It may not be over yet but we have all done a great job all through it. They captured two VC on post yesterday in a jungle area behind the civilian and officer quarters. I'm sure glad they cleared all that perimeter this morning. They use jets close around here because if the B-52's dropped them like they do farther away, everything would fall apart in the buildings. We can hear the B-52s farther away at night. They just rain bombs down on a place. I wonder what you have read in the news and heard on the radio by now. They are using choppers to deliver our mail both ways and it's gong and coming from TSN so mine should be getting out to you. I got your letter yesterday.

You would love to get the suntan I have but I don't think you would enjoy being here to get it right now. I hope I can get an afternoon off every week to keep it up. It should be warm when I'm home but I probably will freeze half the time because it's always cool in the morning. We get so cold outside at night when we have to stay out there. I have some pictures of 1SG Herney but they aren't good ones for you to see what she looks like. They were taken at the party we had when CPT Murphy left. I'll see if I can find one at noon and send it to you. Marney will be here for about 3 months after I'm gone. Ruthie will be here till January of 1970 because her DEROS was the end of June this year and she has already extended for 6 more months after that.

Our guys sure are protecting the place. They have done a great job and our air fire power is unbelievable. This is an experience I wouldn't miss for anything but while it's happening it's not too comfortable. I have always wondered how I would act under fire and this has shown me that I can stay calm and do anything I have to do. It gives me much more confidence in my ability to handle any situation and that's a good thing for an NCO to have. I went over this morning and saw the hole in the wall in G-1 where the round came in. It's a pretty big hole for one round, about 5 inches around with splintered wood all around it. They have it circled with the date and time in the circle. One guy got shot in the leg in the bus sitting in the parking lot Sunday. It was a long range bullet that strayed. We had lead flying all over the place. None of us even realized at the time just how dangerous it was. If we had, we wouldn't have been standing outside watching it.

Thank goodness our maids are still coming so we don't have to worry about our uniforms. When you wear them 24 hours a day you need somebody to iron them. I hope we get a chance to relax pretty soon but when we get home all we can do is sit there and say "I wonder if they'll hit?" I washed and trimmed my hair during my lunch hour yesterday because I knew I might not get to do it last night. We have to take our showers in the morning or at noon because it isn't safe to risk being in there at night. We all have to be back in the detachment area at 1900 now. You're going to have something not too many people do when I get back—a daughter who has gone through combat. Out of all the women in the world a very small number ever get in the Army and out of them even a smaller number ever come over here and from that group, only about 90 of us are going through this. That was a good process of elimination.

I'm going to quit for now. I'm not quite so sleepy today since I've finally got going. All of us are sore from trying to sleep in those horrible bunkers.

Lots of love,
Susie

PS I couldn't find a picture of 1SG Herney at all. I can't find much of anything now. We've been rushing around throwing things every direction so much.

27 February 1969

Dear Ruby,

I didn't write to you yesterday so I will today. The war is still raging although they haven't bothered us for a couple of nights. Tuesday night we went to bed at 2100 and couldn't go to sleep. At 2200 the booming got so loud we got up and stayed up for about an hour then went back to bed. Last night was the first half way normal night we've had since this started. We had wieners and sauerkraut for supper and 1SG Herney ate with us then we went out and watched the movie. We decided to take a chance on taking a shower before we went to bed and we slept in our pajama tops and fatigue pants. That's the first night since Saturday that we haven't slept in full uniform. It felt good to go to bed clean between sheets again. I woke up once and heard a lot of banging but it didn't get any louder so I went back to sleep. We had muster formation this morning so Ruthie and I walked to breakfast after it. They have cleared almost all the jungle around here now and they are burning some places off because the VC are hiding on post in the jungle and they have found some tunnels. Anyway, this morning when we were walking to breakfast, there is a garbage burner along the way and it was burning something. Whatever it was popped when we went by and we both almost jumped off the road. Every time there is a noise, we get the strangest feeling inside, like we're ready to take off. Yesterday sometime in the early morning hours, a VC was captured between the WAC DET and commissary. There is a wooded area there that we use for a short cut to the commissary and that's where they found him. I guess it's not safe to walk anywhere but on the road now. Yesterday afternoon they found a tunnel that came out in the BOQ area. Evidently that's how some of them have been getting in. They have captured 3 or 4 down there. Bien Hoa was under attack all day yesterday till early this morning. I guess that's why they left us alone. We'll probably get it again soon. They have finally officially declared this another offensive so we should get another campaign star for our Vietnam Service Medals. At least we get something out of it. Our guys are really bombing close this morning, everything in the building is shaking but we can't see them.

I was glad to get your letter yesterday but I'm anxious to get one after the full story of the war broke. In your Sunday paper you evidently just got the first news release because you would have said more than you did if the whole thing had been there. I'm not getting any newspapers now; the boat mail must not be getting in. I never even got the one with my picture in it yet.

I'm really going to have war stories to tell when I get home now along with everything else. I always have a lot to say but I've gone through so many more experiences and it's been longer this time. As of tomorrow I have a full tour here completed for record purposes. Ten months is the minimum for credit for an overseas short tour. This month has been the most harassing and nerve wracking of all but it's worth it. I guess we'll all get over being so jumpy after we're away for awhile.

Yes, Barb lives in New Jersey. Marney is due back in about 5 days. I should try to fly home on the 2/3 military fare. That way it's a reserved seat but still cheaper. I could do it all right from San Francisco but I don't know about Chicago to Danville. I'll probably get to O'Hare at an hour when there is no flight to Danville. I won't make any plans for when I'll leave SF till I get there and see how I feel and what I'm doing. I'll have to call you collect from there; I won't be able to collect enough change for a long time unless Barb has some saved up. I keep dreaming about the day I get off the plane at home in my green uniform with SSG stripes and all these ribbons. I'll be in my glory then and I hope you will too. Right now everyone is wearing fatigues back to Travis and changing there.

One night when we were out on alert, there was some kind of a bird chirping. He didn't sound too happy; I guess he got woke up from his sleep. I feel sorry for the birds and animals and I suppose even the people to have to live their whole lives in war and never know peace and quiet and the chance to relax and not worry about being shot at. That would be terrible. I don't really like these people but they are humans just as the VC are too and they have families up north waiting for them that will never know what happened to them because they are buried down here and nobody even knows who half of them were. I don't trust any of them now. One woman who works in the USARV Officer's mess hall was carrying a plastic explosive charge under her blouse and was going to stick it in the tray holder but they caught her. That would have blown up when the guys were going through the chow line. There are no Vietnamese working in the officer's mess now. I even wonder about our maids. The ones that are here during the day could very well be shooting at us at night.

Georgie has her radio on this morning and they played "On the Dock of the Bay". I can't wait to get home and hear all my music again. The only way I'm positive I won't extend is if I get Ft. Sam on the first try. If I get it I can't turn it down. Otherwise, I don't know. After this offensive everything should be quiet for another 6 months.

Well I think that's all the news this time. I hope I put enough variety in it to make it interesting.

Lots of love,
Susie

28 February 1969

Dear Ruby,

You're going to wonder what in the heck is going on when you get these money orders so I'll explain. There is no way that the orderly room or anybody else can get money over to the Bien Hoa bank because they're completely blocked off from the fighting. Last month's pay never got there either and it was being kept in the orderly room safe but $700 is just too much to have in a safe where it could obviously be destroyed anytime. The only way I could send it to you was with these money orders from the bank here on post. It wasn't open when I first got here or my money would all be in it. They don't have such a thing as bank drafts or cashier's checks. It's run by Vietnamese so that's no wonder. Anyway, I also decided that you might as well put this in my account there and it will be that much less that I have to worry about bringing home. After you put it in, tell me exactly how much I have there. I hope this isn't too much trouble for you but it's the safest thing I could find to do with it. I'll have to keep my checking account at Bein Hoa even if I could get it all out because I may want to write some more checks before I leave. I owed PACEX 16 cents on Tanya's binoculars and didn't know how I was going to pay it till I found a girl who was lucky enough to have a nickel and a dime. She gave them to me and I have a penny.

We got hit again last night but nothing big, just 3 rounds into the ammo dump area. We went to bed at 2200 and there was enough noise to keep me awake till almost 2300 then we went on yellow alert and the sirens went off and we had to get in gear and go out to the bunkers. We stayed in them till about 0045 then went back to bed. Boy that is sure getting disgusting. I guess we'll never be able to put on pajamas and go to bed right again. I like to never went back to sleep because I could still hear firing and every time it was loud I almost jumped out of bed. It's natural reflexes for all of us now to start to move when we hear it. I'm not too tired today. At least we had one decent night's rest. Fatigues are getting pretty comfortable to sleep in. I was off yesterday afternoon and got some more sun.

I bet you're practically eating the newspapers now to see what is going on. I sure hope all my letters are getting to you on time. I still haven't got any newspapers since about the issue for the 14th. I hope they come since there is something in them for me to see.

Well I'd better sign off so I can go get this in the mail and hope it doesn't get lost this time.

Lots of love,
Susie

CHAPTER XII

MARCH 1969

2 March 1969

Dear Ruby,

I guess this is a good time to start a letter to you. I'm really going to have you spoiled after writing one almost every day this past week. Most of the excitement seems to be over. We have some banging around every night but nothing bad. Last night we had a real good time. 1SG Herney invited Ruthie and me and some others up to her room for supper of spaghetti. There were the 3 of us, 2 E-7s and 1 E-5, a new girl who just got in yesterday. Ruthie went through basic with her. We ate and the one SFC, we call her "Ski" because her last name is Brozowski, played the tape she recorded in the bunker the other night. After that we all started talking on the tape and had a lot of fun doing that. We stayed up there till about 2200. There was a small war going on but we went to bed anyway. Nothing happened all night and I didn't even wake up all night for the first time in a week. We're still sleeping in our fatigue pants because as sure as we don't we'll have to hit the bunker. I told the others I could just imagine us in bed at home and a car backfires on the street and we go looking for a bunker.

Well it's 2 March now. It doesn't seem to me like a different month. In fact they all seem just the same because there is no change in the weather or anything else. This is like having the month of July go on for a year. I sure feel good when I see all these new girls coming in with 364 days to go. I wish I would get my orders. Some that leave next month don't have theirs so I'm getting very much afraid I'm going to have to give up waiting but I won't till the last possible day that you can order the car. You did say it could be the first of April if it had to didn't you?

I want to see Marney's reaction to coming back here too. She should be back in a few days. This new girl who came knew Lilia at Ft. McClellan. I guess I won't ever hear from Lilia again. I'd like to know if she did get married. You were wondering once what became of Tom and I never did say anything. He extended and took a 30 day leave over Christmas. He's back now and I see him around sometimes.

There isn't much to do here today but the other offices or comptroller will probably bring me some typing before the day is over. I hate that because if I have to work every Sunday then their typists could too. If I had a decent job, this would be a pretty good place to be.

I wish I knew what to tell you to send me for my birthday but I don't. All I can say is that I don't need cosmetics. Ruthie asked me to see if you would get a couple of boxes of pancake mix to send us. I guess all you have to put in it would be milk or butter and we have that. I don't love them but she does. Come to think of it, if you sent them with my birthday package, she would be almost ready to go on leave so maybe we should let her get her own. I liked that birthday box you sent last year. Just put together any little thing you think I would like. I would like anything you sent anyway. Ski got her birthday package yesterday. Her birthday was in November and her mother mailed the package on 13 November by PAL and it just now got here. Everything in cans was all right but the boxes of candy and cookies were ruined. I don't see how anything can take that long to get here unless the post office buries it and never digs it out. Sometime before I leave here I'd like for you to send me that white nylon jacket so I can have it to wear at Oakland. I'm sure I'll freeze there especially at night. How glad I'll be when the next 72 days are over and I'll be at Oakland.

Well I'm going to close for now. I won't mail this in case I get a letter from you today but I doubt if I will.

Lots of love,
Susie

4 March 1969

Dear Ruby,

I hope you don't get tired of me typing my letters but it's so much easier. It's 0850 and nothing is going on this morning so I suppose they'll find something for me to do now. I got your letter yesterday and I'm surprised you hadn't heard anymore about the war than that. It looks as if they didn't let it get out but I'll never know how they kept it from leaking out to everybody. I guess it's a good thing the whole report didn't come out in Monday's paper after it happened. Most of the girls are getting letters that mention it now but none of the mothers sound concerned or even say much about it so the only thing we can figure is that none of you know much about it. As you know by now, we didn't sleep very well for quite awhile. We have started sleeping in pajamas again now but we still leave our fatigues right by the bed ready to jump into. Everything is quiet now but they are still out there and nobody knows what they will do next.

I still didn't get any newspapers. I wonder where they are. Maybe the ship they were on sank. Yes, I remember that LCA changed its name but I didn't mention it in a letter because I couldn't spell it. I wish they hadn't moved their boarding place though. At least it sounds like I have a better chance of not hanging around O'Hare for hours. It won't be too terribly long till I'm in Chicago. I used to start planning for an ordinary leave 2 months ahead of time and that's about all that's left now. There is still nothing on my assignment. 1SG Herney didn't get hers yet either so I shouldn't even expect mine. There is no spring here because everything is still hot and dirty all year so I'm really going to love getting back when everything is fresh and green. Oakland will be beautiful, especially around the lake. I wish I could just skip the next few weeks and get back there.

It is foggy here early in the morning now but by the time I go to work, it's gone. The moon was full last night and so pretty. During those nights in the bunkers when we could get outside, the moon and stars were shining so brightly and I thought about all the times we used to look at them and I used to be so fascinated by them. I saw the big dipper and the thing we called the little dipper. That's all I could recognize. One night I saw what I guess was a shooting star and I thought it was a rocket till I realized it was too far away and burned out too fast.

Everybody on the post and I guess just about everybody in RVN is getting Hong Kong flu shots this week. We get ours tomorrow afternoon. Next month I'll be due for 2 more shots before I leave. I'd hate to see anybody who couldn't stand shots get over here.

Oh how I wish my orders for Ft. Sam would come and I could tell you to order the car. I dream about being there and driving it.

I guess that's all for this time. The daily paper just came in so I'll read it.

Lots of love,
Susie

0845

5 March, 1969

Dear Ruby,

I got your letter yesterday so I'll write another one to you today. I'm glad you got my letters about the war so fast. At least they didn't get the mail stopped. Nobody knows exactly how the VC get up so close to US installations. The only explanation is the jungle being so thick and the people are so small that they dig tunnels and sneak around through the bushes. One guy that was captured down here had carried a rocket all the way from Hanoi down here on his back. These rockets are over 6 feet long and I'm sure they are not light. Most of the infiltration now is from Cambodia but it's still a long way over to this area. Everything is quiet now but they are still around and there's a good chance they're getting built up and reorganized to hit again.

When we go to the bunkers, whoever has Otto takes him too. Usually he's one of the first ones there. The first night we were out he lost his dog tag and they never got him another one yet. He needs a helmet because he's getting too big to fit under one of ours but I don't know where we'd get one his size. Yesterday evening they were blowing charges at the ammo dump and I was playing with Otto. Every time there was a boom he jumped and perked up his ears and looked in that direction. He acted like he was ready to go for the bunker. The cats all play in the bunkers half the time. 1SG Herney is always out looking for Otto to be sure he got in a bunker. Speaking of her, she got her orders yesterday for Presidio of San Francisco as a Master Sergeant. That's exactly what she wanted. She wanted the 6th Army Area and she didn't want to be a 1SG. I wish I could be so lucky.

I'm glad the carvings got there in good shape. How I wish I could go back to Bangkok or go anyplace. Most of all I want my orders. Remember when Elias used to bring back things to Aunt Gertie and us from foreign countries and we thought they were really something? They were then but now it's me bringing and sending things back and to me they aren't nearly as great now. It sure makes a difference when you do it yourself than just to hear somebody else talk about being in all these places. I sure do want to go to Europe sometime so I can travel to all those countries. You can drive all over the place there. What I've heard of all that over there, it sounds like a story book. The plans far in the back of my mind now are to come back to the states for the rest of this enlistment then re-enlist for Germany. That's a 3 year tour over there. I thought it was 2 but you can go back to the states during that time without spending a fortune. Most career soldiers are in Germany sometime.

I never told you that on the Valentine's package that Aggie and Jim sent me the $1.24 in postage wasn't canceled at all so I rescued the $1 stamp and the 4 cent one. The 20 cent one was kind of dirty and looked used. I hope you like your typing classes and do good in them. I guess I could be a typing instructor by now but I'm not sure I'd ever want to be. I sometimes think I would kind of like to be an instructor in something at McClellan but maybe not.

When I start typing a letter I just keep going on and on. I think you like longer letters but maybe they get ridiculous after awhile. It's so much easier to type and my hands don't get tired so I keep saying everything I think of. I'm going to quit now.

Lots of love,
Susie

7 March 1969

Dear Ruby,

I guess I'll write you a letter this morning. I have a lot of time so I'll write instead of typing.

Well at 2200 last night I had just gone to bed and Ruthie was asleep and there came 1SG Herney in asking if anyone was awake. I was and she said "Marney is out at the 90th". With that Ruthie jumped up and in about 10 minutes Marney came in. I stayed up till 2400 and they stayed up about an hour after that. Marney had quite a time on leave. An uncle died, an aunt had a car accident and she was making talks at schools. She said she's glad to be back.

I don't know much more about my orders except I'm one of the few with an original DEROS in April that is still indefinite. Of course the orders have to come from DA. I figure I have to know by the 24th of this month to give you the word on the car. That isn't very far from now.

I was off yesterday afternoon and got some sun. I'm so nice and brown now if I can keep it. The water in the pool was too dirty to get in and besides that, we didn't have water to take showers in yesterday. Somebody did something to our water lines. Anyway, they had an emergency supply turned on but there wasn't enough for showers.

There hasn't been a lot of action around lately. Of course after what we went through the routine noise seems like nothing. We're supposed to be hit again but that's a rumor like they had going for 2 weeks before the other hit. Marney wishes she hadn't missed it and I know I'd hate to have now that it's over.

If you want to, you could send something for Easter in my birthday package. I'd like some big Easter eggs especially. I still have a few of the Valentine chocolates left at home in the refrigerator. They are sure good. Remember my little white and blue rabbit? She looks terrible now, even the blue is dirty. My koala bears are brown except one has white ears so they don't show dirt.

Our movie last night was "The Bible". I wanted to see it at Oakland but couldn't afford it. 1SG Herney showed it and someway she managed to get the last 2 reels on first so it was rather mixed up but it would be a beautiful movie. If you ever get a chance you should see it. The scenery and music are great and so is the story.

Well, I'm going to close for this time.

Lots of love,
Susie

8 March 1969

Dear Ruby,

I may not get to finish this letter today but I'll start it. I got yours yesterday with the gum. I could smell it through the envelope and it smelled like Kool-Aid. It's good gum. I have really hit the jack pot for mail yesterday and today—letters from you, SSG Hayes, Barb and Edie. Hayes finally made SFC. He's been in the Army since 1942 and could never make it because he wasn't in a slot. He's a postal NCO. I finally got him a plaque to send with the wood carvings I got him in Bangkok and mailed them last week. He says he's sending me something. He's sure a good guy. He even sent me his home address (Pine Bluff, Arkansas) so I'll never have an excuse not to write him. Edie is worrying about Dave and wanting him home. He's up in the DMZ. Barb is falling for some civilian construction worker and she wants my advice on what to do. Edie wants me to tell her how to get Dave back. They all think I know everything I guess. Too bad I don't, I could make a fortune.

This morning Ruthie and I thought we had 1 hour of training and we were going to take the rest of the morning off but we found out we didn't have even that one hour because it had been canceled. We were already up and dressed so we invited Ski down and we all ate breakfast of bacon and eggs. We took the whole morning off.

I don't need fizzies or Kool-Aid when you send my package. A few packs of fruit flavored gum would be good. I'll make a little list of the underwear with this letter. I don't need very many of anything, just enough to get home on. I don't know if things will be quiet by the time you mail it or not. They keep threatening another attack on Long Binh and I suppose they will sometime. I'm getting too short to have this going on, I know that. I never used to care so much what happened but I have the same feeling everybody else gets now. When we get close to going home we start getting a little more careful or thinking a lot more about it at least. Oh, the commissary got the pancake mix in so you can forget that. I guess it will be strange for you to see me get off a plane again. It will be the same for me to do it because it has been 3 years since I flew in from anywhere. I would like for you to take a picture as I get off the plane. No, it doesn't seem possible that ten months have gone by and neither does it seem possible that I'm getting so close to coming home.

We were going to celebrate Marney's homecoming last night but that sure got messed up. There's a little SP4 who follows Marney like a shadow and she came in just as we finished eating and sat there and talked to Marney for 1 ½ hours. Ruthie and I read books and looked as bored and disgusted as we could but she didn't take the hint. Finally I went outside with another girl and played with the cats. I told 1SG Herney today what happened because she had expected to be invited. She said we should have gone to bed and turned the lights out. I said the girl would have talked in the dark. I think tonight we're going to 1SG Herney's room.

I've looked for St Pat's day cards but can't find any. I already bought Easter cards while the supply was fresh. I guess Easter this year will sure be a less significant day from last year when I was driving down the coast of California and spent the night in Yuma, Arizona. I'm sure glad I've traveled as much as I have. It's nice to know more about the states and know where a lot of towns are.

Well I think I'm going to quit for now. I have 4 other letters to answer today and tomorrow so it should keep me busy.

Lots of love,
Susie

11 March 1969

Dear Ruby,

I have 2 of your letters to answer so I'd better get busy. I would have written yesterday afternoon but I got tied up typing a 6 page letter and by the time I got finished I didn't want to write. First of all, I can't figure what the 2 dimes and penny are for. I have needed dimes before now to send to somebody but I don't know why you put them in a letter. I'm glad you did. They may come in handy and if I don't use them here, I'll use one to call you when I get to SF. We can use pennies in the post office or commissary. It's nice to see American dimes again. I'm sure glad you got my $700 all right. I may just send you all the rest of my pay from here. Yes, I'm getting all your letters on time but my newspapers are sure messed up. So far all I have since 10 Feb is the one for the 23rd. They seem to have my APO wrong on them now and they're being sent to a couple of places before they get to me. The last two have both had a strange APO and mine has been put over it. I doubt very much if I'll ever get all the ones in between so I hope you saved everything I was supposed to see.

I'm sure glad you did so well on the tests. That's practically equal to me getting promoted. I know you sure did a lot better in math than I ever would. You should go on into something else now with those scores. You never thought you would be ready to take the tests in March and just look what you did. I thought you were pretty smart but you never had a chance to prove it.

I never thought about you getting the projector and screen so soon. The place I sent the order to was in Fort Worth. I'm going to have so much stuff at home when I get there. I don't have too many slides but I want to take several more around here before I go. I'm sure going to love showing these slides and explaining them. Oh I hope I get Ft. Sam so I can leave here and get my car and a home and a cat. Last night SGT Calcio's cat, Caesar, came into my room and nosed around. I put him on the bed with his mouse and he played with it. I keep it there for him because she moved into my building now and he comes down to visit. He's so big and pretty and just purrs when he's playing. I don't know how he stays so white. He's the only thing around that does.

That was an RC in front of me in that picture. I have to be terribly thirsty with nothing else around before I'll drink beer. The Thai beer in Bangkok was so strong. I have 2 more of those sweatshirts ordered and if they don't come before I leave I guess Ruthie will send them to me. They will look real sharp when I'm away from here. Everybody here wears one.

I might like parsnips by now although I doubt it. One thing I sure want you to have some of when I get there is ribs and I want to fix barbecue sauce on them. I love them that way. I'm getting to be a pretty good cook over here considering the circumstances. I can fry real good chicken and pork chops. I always remember to salt everything and the other 2 don't. We've had so much spaghetti that we're tired of it. We had bacon and pancakes for supper last night. They were pretty good.

I think we should start bombing NVN again and just forget the stupid peace talks. We get intelligence reports every night to expect an attack and a lot of other places are getting hit. The standard joke around here now is "Tonight's the night". I suppose sometime it won't be a joke. Charlie is definitely out there and when he decides the time is right he will hit again. There are a few things we want left alone—our barracks, finance, the PO and the commissary. All of these things are real close together and they are the most essential. Our water lines are repaired now and nothing else has happened to them.

It's just 64 days now. A year ago tomorrow was the day 1SG Spyker called me and told me I was on alert to come over. I will sure never forget that day because I was so happy.

I'd better close now before I run out of paper.

Lots of love,
Susie

12 March, 1969

Dear Ruby,

I just told you that this day last year I was so happy because I found out I was coming over here. Well, this afternoon Ruthie got the DA message on my assignment and guess what? It's Ft. Sam Houston, Texas and not only that but BAMC (Brooke Army Medical Center). Isn't that great? Talk about luck, I never dared wish for BAMC. They have me as an E-5 on the message but as long as I don't request reassignment because of rank they won't change it. When I get to BAMC if they couldn't use me they would probably reassign me to 4th Army HQ. I think it's very likely the promotion won't make any difference though. When they see how bad I want to be there they'll probably let me stay. I just can't believe this. Everybody says I must be living right and I agree I must do something good sometimes. So, I can have my Roadrunner now but I want you to wait until you get another letter before you order it. I want to hear 1SG Herney say they won't change my orders and then everything is "GO!!!" Boy I'm so happy. As soon as 1SG Herney says they're safe, I'm going to put a big sign on the front of my desk that says "Deep in the Heart of Texas." I'm thinking that song all the time now. All my waiting paid off. I'll never know how I escaped Ft. McClellan because I'm in a perfect position to go there. I should celebrate tonight. We're playing volleyball about 3 nights a week now right after work. It stays light a lot longer than it did.

1SG Herney is getting as anxious to go as I am. Just last night we were talking about it. She invited the 3 of us up to her room for a drink.

I called her to tell her about my assignment but she wasn't there so I'll tell her tonight if she hasn't already heard by then.

Next week we all have to go through the gas chamber. They never had it over here before but I guess they figure we need practice. I think I'll go Thursday. Saturday night I have DNCO so by golly I'll get a Sunday off.

I think I'll close for now. I just had to tell you this and remember, wait for one more letter before you order the Roadrunner.

Lots of love,
Susie

13 March 1969

Dear Ruby,

I'll start another letter to you now. 1SG Herney was so happy to hear where I'm going. She said the promotion won't affect the orders at all so the condition is GREEN for GO now. Order that ROADRUNNER!!!! I thought I would never get to tell you that. I bet you're as happy as I am because I know you sure didn't want me to stay over here and I very likely would have if I had got anyplace but Ft. Sam. If you question whether or not I want bucket seats, I do even if that makes the price $100 higher like it was on the list you sent me. I can't have a sporty car like that without bucket seats. I guess money is no problem now that I have that much there. I'm sure there is no way I could get a temporary license or anything so I could register it and get the license in Texas. I definitely will want it registered there but I guess I'll have to wait till next year and then change it. I'm making a sign for the front of my desk. You'll see it sometime. I have 2 little maps of Texas on a piece of paper with "Deep in the Heart of Texas" centered, a roadrunner on one side and a Texas flag on the other. I don't have it finished yet but it should be real pretty. How far is San Antonio from Chicago or Danville? This will be the closest I've ever been at least with a car. Won't I have a great time exploring all of east Texas? The first thing I want to see is the Alamo.

Bunnie is going to Hong Kong on the 22nd and she's going to get my speakers for me and mail them home. During the next 2 months you may be getting all kinds of packages in the mail, things I send or somebody else gets for me. I'll address everything like that to myself and you can just store it someplace. It's going to be like Christmas when I get there.

Last night we had a practice yellow alert. They blew the siren and of course we thought it was real so we grabbed our gear and took off to the bunkers. We stayed there about 40 minutes-till 2300. They're making sure we take our gas masks with us now because the intelligence report yesterday said that Charlie does have gas in this area and might very likely throw some in on us. Also, starting Monday we have to take a white malaria pill everyday along with the pink ones because the second kind of malaria (I can't spell it) that the pink pills are no good for is spreading in the Saigon area. When I come home all I'll get done is take a bunch of pills for eight weeks. The one a week was bad enough. We should never catch anything the rest of our lives after being immunized here for a year.

I think I'll be wearing my surgeon general's patch at BAMC instead of the 4th Army one. I hope so because I sure did like that patch.

I'm going to close at the bottom of this page because I don't have any more to say.

Lots of love,
Susie

15 March 1969

Dear Ruby,

It's 1510 Saturday afternoon and I'll see if I can get a letter typed. I got yours yesterday evening. I'm sure glad you finally got your binoculars. Aggie's jewel chest will come sometime because I got the receipt saying it had been mailed. You don't need directions to do anything with them. The only adjustments are the space between the eyes which you correct by pulling them apart and making them fit your eyes which is the right eye piece. The knob with 70-80 on it has something to do with the angle you have them at to get them to fit your eyes but I don't know what. You don't have to know anything about the numbers to use them. You will find that when you're looking at something fairly close then want to look far away you have to readjust the right eye piece. That takes care of both sides. I have never tried mine at night because they are always here in the office. You've always wanted some good ones and now you sure have them. OK, I'll try not to get anything else for you before I come home. I guess you've done real well during my year here and I get my big prize when I get home.

I sure would have loved your snow. I remember in March of 1967 when we had a snow in El Paso how beautiful it was. I don't know if it snows in San Antonio or not. It gets pretty cool because I've been watching the temperature all winter. I still can hardly believe I'm really going there. During this past year everything has gone my way-coming here, making E-6, my R&R and now San Antonio.

I got one more newspaper yesterday and it still had the wrong APO. There wasn't anything special in this one. It was sometime in February. I'm missing almost a month of them now.

Everybody notices my Texas sign on the front of my desk. Tomorrow I'll have 59 to go. I feel like I'm really getting close to the end now. Before I got my orders I didn't know whether I could feel short or not because I wasn't sure how long I would be but now I know I won't be coming back. I think it's for the best too because a year over here gives a person just enough of combat and experiences but 18 months is just a little too much. Right now we have the radio on and Glen Campbell is singing a song called "Galveston". I guess I won't be too far from there when I'm in San Antonio. I hope not because I sure want to see the Gulf of Mexico. I can go that way to see water and toward Austin or Laredo to see desert. I think it's very likely that I'll be in San Antonio the next 2 ½ years but I can't tell for sure.

Say, while I'm looking at the rip, my fatigue pants are falling apart and I would like for you to get some iron on olive drab patches for me. These are my favorite pair. They are so faded they're almost gray but I love them now. I have one brand new set that I'll probably wear a few times just before I leave. These may get beyond wear before you can send me any patches but I'll patch them up the best I can and wear them to the end. At least the shirt ripped out in a seam so I could sew it up.

I got a letter from Mrs. J. and Carolyn yesterday too.

Well I'm going to quit for now. Did you order the Roadrunner yet?

Lots of love,
Susie

18 March 1969

Dear Ruby,

Thanks for the pretty St. Pat's cards. I left all of them out on my dresser. I bet nobody else around here got one. They all think I'm Irish because I did. I wish I could have got some for you but there just weren't any to be found. I sure didn't have any problem wearing green.

I don't know what those crazy papers were saying but as you'll know from my letters, we haven't been having a war real close. We know they're out there but they haven't tried to hit Long Binh again. They were supposed to last weekend and didn't. They'll probably wait till this weekend when I'm on DNCO. I'll be glad to hear your reaction to my assignment. I don't have orders yet and probably won't for some time. The DA message comes to AG and then goes to our personnel section where they cut the orders on a stencil and have copies run. They'll come to me through distribution. I hope I get them reasonably ahead of time so I can ship my hold baggage and have it get there so I won't have to wait forever for it. 1SG Herney says I can ship it home instead of to Ft. Sam so I'll ship just about everything I can. Our room is sure going to be empty with a TV, tape recorder and other various things all gone. After I ship that I'll be ready to go. Remember how I wanted to go back to San Francisco as soon as I sold Junior? Well this will be about the same. I won't have anything left here except the people. I'm sure going to hate to leave Marney and Ruthie. Marney put a map of the world up on her wall and put map tacks in each of our home towns and connected them with Long Binh with red string. It looks real neat but makes it look farther across the ocean than ever.

You should enjoy your typing classes with an IBM typewriter. I would hardly know what to do with one of them by now after a year on these horrible old things that are falling apart. That's nice that your diploma is fixed up in a book.

When I leave here I'm not going to have hardly any clothes that are fit for anything. I hope I can buy a bunch of new things and for once have them be what I want. I should leave practically all of these things here but I suppose I won't. It won't be any cost or trouble to me to ship them anyway. When I get home I want everything white I can find. Also, if I ever smell a soured towel I'll swear I'm still here.

Yes, I remember the mission pictures you took in El Paso. I guess you never looked in the right place for the name of the mission. I'd like to go back there and take pictures of everything with my Petri camera so I'd have slides of all of it. I figure San Antonio would be only 800 miles at the most from El Paso so I should be able to get back there fairly easy sometime. I sure want to.

We aren't getting the Stars and Stripes on time now because of the snow in Japan. I haven't got any more of my newspapers. Aggie sure wrote me a nice long letter. I took two pictures of Caesar I should send to you but they're at home. He came in the room one night and I asked Ruthie or Marney to get my Polaroid out while I had him lying on the bed. Ruthie got it and set up and shot the picture with no flash. I think it would have worked but she didn't have it focused either. She left after that. Marney kept sneezing and scaring him half to death so she went outside and I was left alone to handle the camera and keep him on the bed. I gave him his mouse and he pulled the tail and one eye off it but it kept him entertained long enough for me to get a good picture. Then I put him on the dresser because he kept trying to jump up there and I got another one. He sure is getting big and he's so sweet. The two kittens, Joanne and Murphy are sweet too. Joanne was in the room with me at noon yesterday and she played and crawled all over me. Otto is always sticking his nose in something. He twists his little tail around and thinks he's so smart.

We got a nice cabinet made at the stockade to put our food in. We have a real stock but that's it because they closed the commissary to us on the 15th. We can do pretty good getting bread and milk from the mess hall as long as Ruthie is here to scrounge it but when she goes on leave I don't know where we'll get it. I guess I can live a month without bread since I'll only have one month left. When Ruthie gets back I should have about 10 days left. Somebody sent Marney some games, Parcheesi and some others. We played it one night and had more fun. They kind of wanted to keep the Yahtzee game and I said I didn't really want to leave it because it was a Christmas present so Ruthie is supposed to bring one back from the states for them. I'm going to be looking for my birthday box. I love to get packages and not know what is in them. I told Ruthie you were sending me one and she said "It must be nice to have somebody like that". It sure is. The older I get the more I realize how lucky I am to have the wonderful family and friends that I do.

I'm off this afternoon and Bunnie wants me to go get her a sandwich so I'll close for now.

Lots of love,
Susie

22 March 1969

Dear Ruby,

I guess I might as well start a letter. It's 0845 so I'll leave it open till noon and see if I get one from you. I think I should pretty soon. Thursday we did go through the gas chamber and we got to fire afterwards. For the gas they had us all standing in a group (two companies of men and about half of our company) and they had us test our masks then put them back in the carrier. In a minute they threw gas grenades in among us and we had to mask and stand there in it. One landed beside me and I sure got that mask on. It made our skin burn terribly but my mask fit so perfectly that I didn't get a bit on my face or in my eyes till I took it off and the gas came off my clothes into my eyes. That's by far the strongest I ever went through. It sure gives a person confidence in that mask. I pity anybody that gets in there and finds out their mask leaks. We're supposed to check them before but half the people don't bother. After that, the bus took most of the girls back but some of us, among them, Ski, Sgt Gold, Ruthie and I and others stayed to fire weapons. The only one I fired was a .38 Cal pistol. I loved it. It's easy to fire and real neat, loads like a six-shooter. We talked to a LT from SP TRPS and he's going to try to get a training class for any of us who want weapons familiarization starting next month. I sure hope they do in time for me to go. I kept the bullets that were the first ones I fired. We had a good time out there even if we did have to get gassed. It was way out in the boondocks on top of a hill where they said Charlie was last week. Of course they had guards watching the valley below the whole time we were there.

I'm keeping the kittens now. SGT Gold left yesterday morning. The kittens have a room of their own on the second floor of my barracks so I keep them in there at night with their food. They're so cute and playful but I can't very well keep them in my room because in the first place Marney and Ruthie don't especially like cats and second, they jump on everything and knock it down. Boy last night was sure a party night. There were a lot going on all over post and the ones of us that stayed home had our own going. For some reason everybody wanted to get drunk or as near as possible. I've never seen so many people do that in one night. The NCO barracks was the worst of course because we can all drink at home but the others were stumbling in from the clubs. The intelligence report yesterday said we were going to get hit last night and it's sure a good thing we didn't. I drank but I didn't get to the place where I was floating on air like the rest of them. I figured somebody better watch them. We all stayed up till about 2400. I sat outside with 3 others holding Caesar on my lap. Artillery zoomed over the detachment almost all night so nobody got much sleep. They are firing from someplace close behind the detachment because we can hear the whistle when it goes over. It's easy enough to tell outgoing from incoming. When it's outgoing you hear the bang of it being fired then the whistle when it goes over. If it's incoming you hear the whistle of it coming down then the explosion. Even though I know it's outgoing, I just can't go to sleep with it whistling overhead.

I've sure been having some dreams lately. One night I dreamed that I was at home and the VC were there too and after us and I was trying to get you and Mom away. Another time I dreamed my birthday package came and some other girl got it and opened it and had eaten something when I caught her. I guess I would be pretty mad if somebody ever took anything you sent me because it means so much but I can't imagine why I dreamed some stupid thing like that because nobody else could get my mail.

Bunnie leaves for Hong Kong today so sometime this coming week she should mail my speakers. I have given her $100 to get me speakers, stereo headphones and a telephoto lens for my camera. MAJ Warren goes to Bangkok next month and I'll have him buy Barb's ring so that should be about all. Of course she'll pay me for it.

Well just 53 days now and I can't wait. I'm so glad I didn't have to extend. I'm going to close for now and hold this till this afternoon.

1240

I did get a letter from you just as I thought I should. It's a nice long one too. Thanks for the gum. I'm sending you a typed copy of another poem from the Stars and Stripes. I think this one really hits home. Are you still going to let me paint the kitchen? I want to. I think mail from here to Germany and vice versa goes through New York all the way across the long way but there is no way to know for sure. I suppose it could go around the other way through both APO's. It doesn't take it too long. I wish I would hurry up and get a letter from after you found out I'm going to Ft. Sam. Brooke is a whole lot bigger than WBGH and Ft Sam is a huge post. It's known as one of the most beautiful in the world too. I got one more newspaper from 2 March. I'm glad Aggie finally got her jewel box. I have never seen one and will probably wish I had one or something in lacquer ware for myself. As long as Ruthie is here maybe I could get her to order something for me later. It won't be too long till you can see a Vietnam soldier in our own yard and will I ever be glad when that time comes.

Well I'm going to quit now.

Lots of love,
Susie

24 March 1969

Dear Ruby,

I got your letter yesterday and I'm glad you're happy with my assignment but I knew you would be. What I sent you I think I explained later was not my orders, just the DA message. I don't have the orders yet but it doesn't make much difference when I get them except then I can ship my hold baggage. I sure hope you got the car ordered Thursday. I figured you wouldn't waste any time. The Roadrunner is the car of the year in Motor Trend magazine. Boy I just can't wait to get behind the wheel of that hot car. I wish I had some idea of what the insurance would cost though. I'm going to see if I could get it financed with NCOA (the paper I'm enclosing). It should be a lot lower rate. I'll look into it before I leave. Also, I don't know exactly how I'll go about getting the insurance since the closest office is in Champaign but I have to have Criterion. San Antonio isn't too far away, in fact I could drive that distance straight because I've gone around a thousand miles in a day before and quit only because I had about 1500 total. I couldn't get any farther away than I am now so I had to come closer to home. I don't know much about the terrain around San Antonio. It isn't dry there but it is known for heat and high humidity in the summer. I'll have the time of my life in my Roadrunner exploring the place. Three months from today I'll be there but 2 months from today I'll be at home driving my Roadrunner.

I'm glad you're finally having some nice weather although by the time you get this you may have winter again. This crazy place is sure messed up. You remember me telling you about the trees leafing out fresh, well now they're all dried up and losing their leaves again. I don't see why they leafed out in the first place with no rain. The monsoons should begin the end of next month or at least just before I leave. We had one short rain last month and that's all since a few showers in December. It sounds like you are sending me quite a box. I will get the girls together and send a card or something to Aggie and Maude. I don't think I can find a thank you card here. When I get this package I don't think I'll open it at the office because some things (namely the underwear) I don't want everybody to see and they just go wild. My old APO goes on the HQ address. Ruthie will be almost ready to go home when the box comes considering it gets here in a decent length of time. She got a port call for 31 March but she's trying to get it changed to 1 or 2 April so she doesn't lose a month's combat pay and tax exemption. Maybe we will have a party when I get it—my birthday party. We have a growing group of people who are in our social group at least part of the time. Mainly they are 1SG Herney, Ski, Nancy Young and Kathy Oatman. Kathy came here from Hawaii about 3 weeks ago and is a SP5.

Well I got through DNCO without anything exciting. We had artillery going out over the barracks all night but nothing else happened. Last night everybody was pretty peaceful and we all went to bed fairly early and went to sleep. At about ten till one I woke up hearing a blast and I thought to myself that it sure didn't sound like it was outgoing so I got up and was just to the door to investigate when the guard yelled "Incoming" so I woke up my roommates and we got into our fatigues and took off. I don't know how many rounds came in, we haven't' gotten an intelligence report yet today but evidently this one came in pretty close to our barracks. The way it looks they are either trying to knock off Finance or the WAC Det and I sure hope it's finance. Every time I hear this now my first thought is "They can't hit us now. I want to go home". We have one girl who leaves in about 11 days and she's so nervous she stays in the orderly room all night almost every night. I don't know how she does it when she has to work every day. We stayed in the bunkers till 0230 then went back to bed and I guess nothing else happened. I felt rather proud of myself because even waking up I knew the round was incoming. I guess Charlie just wants to let us know he's still there.

Yesterday afternoon after I got up, Marney and I and some other onlookers tried to fix my bike. The tires were both flat and had Vietnamese valves which an American pump won't fit so we got some others and changed them. We did a beautiful job on that and had no trouble with the chain or anything but we tried to put a new seat on and we can't get it on solid for anything. It flips up and won't stay in one place. Otherwise the bike is in great shape considering that we had it completely apart. It's disgusting that I can't figure out anything to do to get the seat to fit. Marney and I had a good time messing with it. She's a good mechanic and enjoys it too.

I'm getting along fine keeping the cats. They're so sweet and loveable. Even Marney likes to play with them now but Ruthie still won't touch them. They were tearing around the room yesterday. When SGT Gold gets back they are supposed to go to a major who has a trailer. I hope they do because they're so sweet and they would be a lot better off.

Tell Aggie I finally got my February-March National Wildlife. I wondered if I ever would but maybe it's just now time for it. I still don't have any newspapers.

Well I'm going to close for now. It's 1215 and I'll mail this on my way to chow. Only 51 days to go—short, short, short.

Lots of love,
Susie

26 March 1969

Dear Ruby,

It's needless to say how happy I was to get your letter yesterday and know my Roadrunner is on its way. Also, I'm very pleased with the final price. It's about $200 less than I thought it would be. By the time I put $2000 down on that there won't be too much left and I can get those payments down. Almost everybody I talk to thinks the RR is the best looking '69 car. It is an awful lot of money but I can do it and want it more than anything else so why not. Marni is trying to get me an order form to fill out to get some information on how the NCOA can finance it. I don't see how it can be done with me here, the car there and NCOA HQS is in San Antonio. If I could get a loan through something military and pay cash for the car then pay off the loan I would be ahead. It sure is something to be able to order a car costing that much with only $100. I know the tires have the red band. White walls don't belong on a car like that.

It's sure a good thing I got those patches yesterday because that one pair of pants was getting a little too much air conditioned. I ironed one on yesterday afternoon. The maid came in while I was doing it and she couldn't figure out what in the world it was. I hope she doesn't beat it off washing them. I sure hope my birthday package comes in a reasonable length of time.

We never did start taking the white malaria pills. I don't know what happened to them. I have to go get a plague and cholera shot this week and that's all I have to get before leaving here. Tanya sent me the prettiest picture of Ready. She looks like a queen sitting in front of the

Christmas tree. Last night the B-52s were bombing and shaking the earth. I thought I was going to have to get up and set our mirrors on the floor but I didn't.

One time during the night I woke up and thought I heard a scream. I didn't know if I was dreaming or it was real. Marni got up and went outside but she came back in a minute so I went back to sleep. This morning I found out it was Kathy Oatman and she saw a man looking in the window of her room. She thinks it was a security guard and I wouldn't doubt it because with all the fence and wire around the area it would be next to impossible for any other man to get inside. Of course it scared her to death and she's already scared of the war. From now on we'll be sleeping with our doors locked. The E-5s and below can't because of bed check at 2400. We have enough disturbances at night without the men trying to get in.

My cats are so cute. They come in my room and play around. They love that poor little mouse. They have his tail and eyes off now. They are so limp and floppy when I pick them up and just have their little motors going full force. They are being raised on PUP-O horsemeat dog food. It must be good for them because I think they've grown a lot since I've been keeping them. Sometimes all three cats and Otto come into my room especially if I'm there alone trying to cook supper. That's quite a contest between me and them.

I think I'll quit now.

Lots of love,
Susie

27 Mar 69

Dear Ruby,

I don't have a thing to say this morning but I want to send you my art work. You'll probably get it late but I guess it doesn't matter. It's a pretty wild looking drawing. Now and then I get to use these pens for real, making charts or something.

After we got home from work yesterday some of us played volleyball for about an hour then we had spaghetti for supper and Kathy came over. Ruthie went to bed early and the other 3 of us played Yahtzee till about 2200. SGT Calcio moved into the room where the cats were living yesterday and since she wanted to leave the door open for Caesar to come and go all night, I took the kittens to my room for the night. They started out sleeping with me and they were so soft and cuddly but they didn't stay long. Of course they had to bother Ruthie since she doesn't like them. They really behaved better than I thought they would.

We got another civilian GS-12 in the office yesterday. She's from Ft. Worth, Texas and worked in El Paso from '62 to '67. We seem to hit it off real good because we both love Texas. She's 44, 6 feet tall and slim and very quiet. We have 9 people in this office now, 5 women and 4 men. Bunnie is due back from Hong Kong today. I hope she got everything for me.

Awhile ago I answered the phone and a guy said "I just wanted to hear you say good morning. Good bye" and hung up. I don't know who in the heck he could have been.

Well, I'm going to quit for now.

Lots of love,
Susie

340

30 March 1969

Dear Ruby,

What better day could there be to use this pretty stationary for the first time? While I was still on the Unit Fund Council we ordered it and it finally came. We only got 9 sheets and I'd like to have enough to write on it till I leave. I got your letter and birthday card yesterday but still no package.

Last night we had a sort of birthday party for me. We invited 7 people to the room and had chicken, potatoes, corn and salad. We had all our favorite NCO's and the two lower graders. We had a good time. I got to bed at about 2400. We had to have it last night because Ruthie reports to the 90th Replacement today and she may not be back. Besides, our movie tonight is "The Graduate" and I've wanted to see it since I left the states. This morning I got a pleasant surprise. The SMAJ brought me a letter birthday greeting from our top boss, Colonel Metts. I'm enclosing a thermo-fax copy. Also yesterday I got a package of information from the San Antonio Chamber of Commerce. It seems like only about a week ago that I wrote to them. It is called "The Alamo City". I'm sending you one little thing that was with it. They sent a map of the city and several other things. It looks more wonderful all the time, so much to see and do. The Gulf Coast is 150 miles from there and Houston is 200.

I like the Roadrunner ad. I put it on my desk top and colored the car blue and black. No matter how much I try to picture that car as blue, I keep coming up with red. I don't even want another red car but that's all I can visualize. Somehow or other, it seems so hard to believe that in such a short time I really will be there and that the car will be there waiting for me. I guess I think this place will go on forever. Thank goodness it won't. Forty five days isn't long I keep telling myself but will it ever be over? You say the grass is starting to get green. I keep thinking how fresh and beautiful everything will be for me. I couldn't be coming back at a better time of year. One of these things about San Antonio says it has a tropical climate.

I can't ship everything to Ft. Sam because there isn't that much that I want to go straight there and I don't want to carry hardly anything with me. The problem of knowing what to take with me from home will be that a lot of that stuff I won't want till I get a place off post and I can't have it all with me before, dishes, bicycle, etc. I will have to have it moved by somebody because I don't want to have my Roadrunner loaded down to start out its life. I'm going to try to leave almost all the clothes I brought here behind because if they aren't Vietnam dirt color by now they are just plain old.

Our cats behaved very well for the whole week till yesterday and all three of them got shut in the room during the morning and tore around and knocked over several things but no serious damage. I guess SGT Gold took them back last night; at least they weren't around when I went to bed. She got back from Hawaii Friday.

No we, at least I, don't ever eat in the mess hall. Ruthie does whenever she needs to scrounge something for us. We have everything except bread and milk stocked up and we're doing pretty good getting that. I'll never start eating in that mess hall again. I've been in there about 3 times since I got back from R&R.

I was thinking last night that so many people don't really get anxious to go home from here because they just don't have anything that special to go back to. I have everything anybody could ever want—a wonderful family and friends, so many material things, and I'm going exactly where I want. You'll have to admit this has been quite a good year for me. Of course when I get home and jump out of my shoes at a noise or look for a bunker when I hear a fire truck you'll wonder but that won't last too long.

Tomorrow is pay day so I guess I'll go get it put into money orders for you again. I still didn't go get my shots and I intend to again tomorrow. I wish my package would come tonight. Ruthie won't get to even see it I don't think.

I don't pay any attention to when I mail letters to you anymore. I think I write enough so I don't think it matters when. It's much easier to just sit down and write when the opportunity comes than to have a certain day.

I'm going to quit for this time. I'm another year older now, in more ways than on the calendar.

Lots of love,
Susie

CHAPTER XIII

APRIL 1969

2 April 1969

Dear Ruby,

This has been quite a day. I'm in the Admin office sitting here for this last hour so I'll write to you. Our newest civilian, Mary Bracker, the one from Fort Worth, was moving into her permanent room today and she asked Mr. Sears if I could help her. He said I could so we left at 0845 and spent almost the whole day—till 1600. I helped her unpack everything and did she ever bring a lot of stuff with her. She has a bunch of Texas flags and gave me one and also a bright yellow orange sweatshirt and a black banlon turtle neck which she says she would look terrible in. Of course we talked about Texas and she told me she owned 8 acres out in Ysleta not far from Horizon City. She had a trailer on it and a bunch of animals, even chickens. That would be great. Anyway, she says rent is low around San Antonio and it isn't far to go from town to get out in wide open country. She loves cats too and she has some at home.

My package didn't come yet and since I know the wrong APO is on it, I can't even guess when it will come. I'm going to check at the PO tomorrow and see if there's any way they can put a tracer out for it. I sure hope so. 96384 is about 3 other big units and it may go through all of the companies within each of them. I should have had you send it to the WAC DET.

If I ever don't write for very long now you'll sure wonder why because I've been writing a lot more recently than I used to. Won't it be great when our letters only take 2 days again?

No, our star rubies aren't natural. As far as I know a natural one would be the chunk of stone before it's cut or polished. I have no idea what it would look like. I read in a book that a good star will have 6 separate stars in it when it's under artificial light and mine does. The light has to be just right but they are there.

Yes, I knew all that about Otis Redding. He was killed when I was at Oakland. Ruthie will be home 30 days now. She got out of here all right.

The lens for my camera will be for taking close ups of birds, flowers, etc., and the wide angle one enables you to get a lot more in a picture at a closer distance. I don't have it yet but I know 2 people who are going to Hong Kong so one of them will get it for me, either the colonel or the WAC E-5.

After this week which will be gone when you get this letter I'll have 5 ½ and the last ½ week doesn't amount to much for me at least because I won't be working more than one day of it. I can't say how long I'll stay in San Francisco. I'll probably be ready to leave on Sunday but that's a bad day for flights. If I'd get to Chicago and be grounded I'd probably rent a car and drive the rest of the way. Marni did and she got a military discount. When I get that close nothing can stop me. But I want to fly because I want all the glory of stepping off that plane and having you there to see me. Also it's a wonderful feeling to watch the airport come into view. It's so close but yet so far.

Oh, while I'm thinking about it, my Bronze Star Medal was downgraded to an Army Commendation Medal. That's a good one to get too but I sure wanted that BSM. Oh well, I got everything else I wanted and SSG and San Antonio are a lot more important. I'll have a colorful bunch of ribbons anyway.

I cut my hair yesterday and I guess I'll let it grow till I get home now. I got a nice sunburn too. I went to sleep out at the pool and really got my back red.

Marni has started school 4 nights a week now from 1900-2130 so she's not going to be around too much. A bunch of us went to the NCOA meeting last night. It wasn't too bad. We rode in the back of a truck.

Well I'm going to quit now, my hand is tired. I hope I can get that package traced down because I sure do want it. It's terrible to know it's over here and I can't get it.

Lots of love,
Susie

3 April 1969

Dear Ruby,

I'll have to write something to you today because we got hit last night again and this time they did get one USARV HQ building. Of all things they hit the post office and completely tore it out-there is nothing left but an empty shell with debris all over. It went in the outside wall and blew out the ceiling all the way across that end of the building and splintered the doors. It looks like it was aimed to go in there. I don't know for sure but it seems to have been a mortar not a rocket. I wanted to take a picture as did everybody else but for some silly reason they won't let us. Two officers were killed last night; one was the R&R officer. It looks almost like they had the whole thing planned as psychological warfare-hit the PO and kill the R&R officer. A rocket hit the BOQ that Mr. Sears lives in and that's where the two officers were killed. Four of us were upstairs in 1SG Herney's room watching the movie at 2230 when we started hearing noise. We thought it sounded very strange and just as Ski started to look out the door one hit down the street and then we didn't have any questions. I think that's the fastest yet that everybody got in the bunkers. I was in my pajamas and robe and got down to my room and put my fatigues on over my pajamas. I don't even remember getting the robe unbuttoned or off. I got everything but my boots. After we had been in the bunker for awhile, I decided it was safe to go back for my boots and Marni's dog tags which she was worried about not having on. We stayed out in the bunker till about 0030 and then went in and went to bed. It's almost unbelievable to see something as completely demolished as the PO is when just yesterday it was standing

349

there in perfect shape. The same thing happened to the room in the BOQ. Nobody can ever know where they're going to hit and there is no warning except the whistle just seconds before it hits. Otto goes to the bunker all by himself every time he hears a siren or a loud boom now. The kittens were in SGT Gold's room huddled down in a corner. When I went in to get my boots I stayed in the room to put my feet in them and as I did my ankle cracked like it always has and scared me half to death. I guess I sure won't get to do anything about my package today. I'm sure it wasn't in the PO because this morning's mail wouldn't have been in yet at 2230 last night. I have my picture and VC flag ready to mail to you but I don't think I'd better today unless I take it to the PO across from the barracks. I am just too short for this kind of carrying on. We got a new MSG in one day ago and she sure got an initiation.

I'm wearing my new uniform that has never been worn before today. It's one that I brought over here from OAB and just put away and never got it out. It is stiff and feels so funny after the old thin ones. It looks like I just got in-country. It's the one I want to make sure I get home with.

We had an NCO get together last night to welcome the new MSG. We had steaks (real good for once) and wine, salad and beans. That's kind of nice.

Soon I'll be down in the 30's. I'd only have 26 if I hadn't extended. Oh well, I guess the last 17 days won't be too bad. I'm going to close for now and see if I can find a place to mail this.

Lots of love,
Susie

5 April 1969

Dear Ruby,

I want to mail a letter with these money orders so I'll get busy typing it now. I was glad to get your letter yesterday. You say I won't have to write so often when I get back to the states. There just won't be that much to say after I get settled.

Yes, I'm acquainted with Hanover House. I got one of the catalogs and ordered that jacket sent to me there. The ad said any sports car emblem could be on it. After I ordered it I was afraid they might just put a plain Plymouth emblem on it and I'm glad you opened it and saw the Roadrunner. I thought that bright red would be beautiful beside my bright blue car. There were supposed to be a couple of other small things in it. I told you that there might be packages coming to me from now till I come home. I had never seen a jacket like that before either and I just had to get it.

I was telling SGT Gold about my package yesterday and she said she had just gotten her birthday package which was mailed airmail in February the other day. I don't feel so bad about mine now. Maybe it isn't the APO that is holding it up. Marni is sure getting a lot and they are on time but I guess some just get delayed someplace. I don't know why it had to be mine.

When I typed that budget I didn't figure out the settings in the correct way. I just used my eye to get the columns even and once I had the tabs set they were the same on almost every page. I don't ever figure them out right now because it's too much bother. It's easier just to set them by sight. I can imagine the fun you have trying to figure it out. I don't really know how I get them even, just luck I guess.

I bet the sun there will be cool to me. Did you keep any of the cake you made for my birthday? I'd love to be able to put the flag up on Carolyn's flag pole. No you hadn't told me you are going to get the piano tuned. You know, I don't know why but I thought for some reason that you already had my income tax return. You said I had $905 there and the $100 went for the car so I thought the $102 was already in that. If not, I'm a lot better off than I thought. The car cost less and so did my speakers, etc. If I knew how much the insurance was going to cost I could figure how much I'm going to have left. It was $127 on the Rambler but it is going to be an awful lot more on this one. If I had the address of the Criterion I might write to them and see what I could find out. I'll get credit for 5 months here on next year's tax.

I don't know what I'll want to do when I get home. I may be so tired I don't want to do anything but when I think about it now, I think I'll be full of energy and wanting to do everything. I hope if that's the way I feel I can wear some of it off in San Francisco. I should be able to. Of course that car is going to pull me like a magnet. I'll probably almost want to sleep in it. You just can't imagine how it is to know what all I've got waiting for me when I get back. It's really great and that alone almost would make the year worthwhile.

As you know by my previous letter, I didn't get to do anything special on my birthday. I had such a perfect day last year so I guess I couldn't expect much this year. It doesn't even register with me that tomorrow is Easter Sunday. Easter Sunday last year was special but only because I was on my way home. My holidays are sure messed up but I hope next year they can be better. I remember that one Easter so long ago when we were going to Sunrise Service and that bob-tailed cat, Smoky was shut in the old house overnight. I went out there after we got up and let him out. Isn't that a silly thing to remember? Yes, I remember how old 23 used to seem. I don't ever want to get old and I think fewer women in the Army get old than ones on the outside. What do you remember from when you were 23?

Tell me exactly how much money I have there now after you get this $350.

We haven't had any more activity. We had a practice yellow alert last night but didn't have to do anything. Well, 5 days of this month will be gone after today and I have 39 left now. That sure sounds good. Each letter we write is getting on nearer the end. I wish there was something I could do to get these 39 days to just be gone or at least 30 of them.

Well, I think that's all for now. This turned out to be a long letter and I hope it's got enough variety. I enjoyed the Norman Vincent Peale column. I don't get many newspapers even though they put the right APO on them.

Lots of love,
Susie

7 April 1969

Dear Ruby,

I guess I'll write you another letter today. I have a few things to tell you. First, thanks for the pretty Easter cards. I got all of them yesterday. I'll sure be glad when I can see the flowers and birds for real.

I was talking to a girl who works in personnel today and she said I should get my orders when I have about 30 days left and that is next week. Also, the hold baggage we ship usually takes around 3 weeks to get where it is going. I sure hate to ship everything away but I'll have to. I'd like to have it already there when I get there or shortly after. I guess before we know it I'm going to be shipping myself back.

Can you plant your garden early, especially lettuce, so it will be big enough to eat while I'm there? I love that kind of lettuce and I haven't had any since May 1966 I guess. I know it's been a long time.

We are going to get our firing instruction. I thought the CO had stopped it but this Friday and Saturday we have classes and next week we go out to the firing range. We'll probably use only the .45 cal pistol and the M-16 rifle because they're the standard Army weapons but that's fine. This is a strictly volunteer basis but I think there will be several go. I know I would feel much better just knowing that I could fire and load a weapon if I had to. The way it's getting around here we never know what we might have to do. Nothing more has happened but last night it sure sounded like it was going to.

I think you must still have money in my account so if you do, I found something I would like for you to order for me. It's a tape by Dean Martin and he's singing Latin songs. The ones listed are "South of the Border" and "Rancho Grande". I've been trying to find "Rancho Grande" since I heard a guy sing it when I was in Oakland. I'll type up the information on a little piece of paper. I'm going to have a good bunch of tapes by the time I get out of here. Bunnie has recorded some for me and Major Warren loaned me two of his that came from the American Airlines group that they have taped throughout the jets to listen to. They are both beautiful and Bunnie is going to record them for me.

No package yet. I've almost given up looking for it. When it comes it does and until then there's no use worrying about it like I did at first. I'll sure be happy if I ever do get it though. It will have to come sometime but it could have been a week ago. I'm glad this didn't happen to any of my Christmas packages.

I'm going to quit now because I don't have enough to start a new sheet of paper. Only 37 days till I put my feet down on the good old USA!!!

Lots of love,
Susie

9 April 1969

Dear Ruby,

I just cleaned the typewriter keys so they should look good. A new ribbon sure collects bad on the keys. I didn't have time to write yesterday so I suppose you won't get this on Saturday and I'd like for you to but I really can't do much about it. I still didn't get the package. I got a letter from Ruthie yesterday. She sounded lonely, she was writing it at 0200 and she couldn't sleep. Marni said when she was on leave she always thought about this place at night.

I wrote to the NCOA and told them everything I could about the car and asked them to let me know if I could finance it through them and how. Of course they wanted the addresses of a bunch of references and I didn't know the street number on any of them. I did remember the streets. Did you take the $100 for the car out of my money? I don't think you did because I have too much there. I'm going to come out of this with a lot more than I thought I would. I should have quite a bit left after taking care of the car. I had thought I'd be almost down to nothing again. I have my car payment now. The rest of what I get here is extra and for insurance.

Yes, I have enough patching. The maids speak a little English and I can speak a few words of Vietnamese and together with hand signs we can do pretty good. When I ship my hold baggage I'll ship my two best pairs of fatigues so I'll be wearing my oldest ones the rest of the time. I want to be sure I get out of here with the good ones so I'll have to ship them and the best pair of boots. NDSM is National Defense Service Medal. That jacket is just going to be beautiful with all the ribbons and stripes. I hope I can get new winter uniforms and the overcoat issued while I'm at Oakland. I think Vietnam returnees are supposed to get the overcoat (new green one) and if I can get the Supply Sergeant to take the winter uniforms off my clothing record, I can get them too. I'll need them soon and they cost an awful lot.

This office is overrun with people and I can't wait till I'm not in the running anymore. They took the slot I was in for a guy across the hall so I don't think I'll be replaced.

My US map is shrinking too. When I started it on the East coast, I thought I'd never work my way over. You can believe I will put some life in the place when I get home. I always do and it should be more this time than ever. I hope I have more energy then than I do now. None of us are getting nearly enough sleep but we never want to go to bed. Once we give in and go to bed it's morning so soon and time to come back to work. Marni is always wound up and ready to talk after she gets back from school at 2130 and we stay up till about 2400. I guess I'll make it for 35 days. I think you'll love my Roadrunner too. Everybody thinks it's great.

I'm going to quit now because I don't have anything more to say. All I think now is how many days.

Lots of love,
Susie

11 April 1969

Dear Ruby,

I guess I won't type this letter. I got one from you at noon today. That patch looks so bright and pretty. I can't wait to have my green uniform on. I want out of here more everyday and they are going by pretty good. When I get under 30 which will be Wednesday or maybe the day you get this letter, they should go even better. I have training and the weapons class tomorrow to take care of most of the day. The last time I had a whole day off without DNCO the night before was in early January. Thank goodness I'll have DNCO once more.

The CO announced a party that a unit is having on 4 May at Phu Loi. That's a place northwest of Tan Son Nhut and Cu Chi. It isn't too far from here. Anybody that can get off can go by chopper and spend the day. I'm determined I will get off. That would be a chance for that last chopper ride I wanted. Also, Major Warren has promised to take me to Saigon. I got film for my camera which I had to have to go there. I don't know when we can go but I won't let him forget. I wish we could go next week. I know I'm too short to go to Saigon but nothing much happens there in the day time and it would get me out of here. I really do want more pictures too. It's been so darn long since I've been off this lousy post.

You make me want to be home more than ever with your talk about robins and frogs. You'll get plenty of walks while I'm there so get in shape. That bicycle seat can be lowered with little trouble, just take the seat off and hammer the rod down.

At times I have wondered if being here is worth all I get from it too but I know it is. Of course the risk wasn't quite so real till a few weeks ago. The thing that I have thought about most through all these attacks is that is isn't fair to you for me to be here risking my neck because I volunteered myself into it and even though I believe I should be here and would or I should say am willing to risk my life for my country. That still doesn't make it any more fair to you. But I'm almost out of here now and when I am we can all relax.

Mary was in Okinawa before she came here. She left El Paso in 1966. DAC's (Dept of Army Civilians) travel around about as much as we do. She was on leave in Fort Worth before coming here though. I sure look good in the black sweater she gave me when I have my black slacks and it on.

I'm glad you had such a beautiful Easter day. I bet you love warm sunshine. I'm going to try to be real dark by the time I get there. I'll have to start lying in the sun during my lunch hour every day as soon as I'm under 30 days. It's a nuisance to change clothes in that short time but I'll have to.

I still didn't get the box. As long as the cookies don't mold we'll eat them no matter how old they are. You wouldn't believe some of the things we eat and think they are good. When somebody has a big plate or dish of something we all dip in and at DEROS parties everybody drinks champaign out of the same glass. We don't think anything about it. If food comes around we grab.

I'm going to close for now.

Lots of love,
Susie

13 April 1969

Dear Ruby,

I'm sitting here as I usually do on Sunday so I'll start writing. I was glad to get your letter today. It seems like I don't get much mail now. I guess I've been here so long everybody has either decided I should be back home or I like it here.

We haven't had any more war since the last time we were hit. There's still a lot of noise at night and we're ready to take off sometimes but nothing real has happened. I'm glad that flag got there all right. I have one more to mail. I also have a set of jungle (camouflage) fatigues and my poncho liner to mail. None of them are supposed to be mailed but a lot of people do and get by with it. Just so nobody opens the package to inspect it. I don't know what I'm going to do with that switchblade knife but I decided since it's not even a good one; I won't take the chance of carrying it out. I'll be so excited I might forget to hide it.

I know a little about the wooden fruit. It comes in a wooden bowl so I assume one bowl full will do. Major Warren will get it and Barb's ring. LTC L. is going to Hong Kong Thursday and he said he would get my camera lens. I can't wait to try it out but film is so hard to get here I probably won't use a roll and get it developed before I leave by the time he gets back with the lens. The last two times I sent a roll in I ordered another roll of film. That's about the only way to be sure I can get it. I've had a terrible time trying to get color Polaroid too but finally found two packs at noon today at the 24th Evac.

Oh what I'd give to be in that spring weather you're having. I know I will be soon but I want to be there now. It's a year ago tomorrow since I left Oakland. Boy has that year gone fast. I went across all that beautiful blooming desert. At night we hear crickets or some kind of bugs singing and rats squeaking outside. We have rat poison all over the place and the cats catch them but they still survive. I saw one run in the bunker one night. We have very few mice now with the cats running around.

I was getting my newspapers real good for awhile but they've slowed down again now. I wonder if that subscription expires before I leave. I'm glad you got your typewriter fixed. You planted your garden before you got my letter asking you about it I think. I know what the thing from Spencer gifts is. It was broken when it got here so I sent it back and asked them to send another to me there. Also, the WAC band has put out a record of the Army song, Colonel Bogey and the WAC song so I ordered it to be sent there. I have wanted our song (Pallas Athena) for so long and can finally get it. I hope the grass is thick when I get home. Don't mow the lawn just before I get there. I want lots of grass to walk barefoot in and I will mow it. Very likely no matter what I do I'm going to catch a cold when I get back. Very few people don't. I haven't had one here since last June I think. I finally got over all the symptoms that all people have over here. After 11 months nothing bothers me.

I bet we're practically crawling with germs when we leave here. I know when I handled the records of the guys at Oakland that had come back from here I felt like they were so dirty and terrible. We don't feel so bad here but I bet when we get to the states and everything is clean we will feel awful. We still didn't start taking the white malaria pills but Monday we have to start taking the orange ones that the men have been taking all the time. Ours were pink before. The orange ones are a lot stronger—chloroquine and primaquine combined. Those words may not be spelled right.

Yes, I have to pay for the stamps and registering anything the same as you do. I hope to have about $2,500 all together when I leave here, maybe more, depending on if I get all my May pay and how much travel pay I get. It's pretty far from Travis to San Antonio so I should get quite a bit. Do you know what PCS means? If you don't, it's permanent change of station. That's when the Army moves you from one place to another. That's the only time we get travel pay. This will be my fourth PCS.

Next week we're having 1SG Herney's DEROS party and I guess the one for the rest of us in the first half of May too. They combine the last half of one month with the first half of another. Very few people leave in May. I'll have over three weeks left and that's too long to have a DEROS

party. 1SG Herney said we'd have our own about three days before we
leave.

Our weapons class yesterday was great. It lasted 3 hours and we all
loved it. They showed us how to take the .45 cal pistol and M-14 rifle
apart and put them back together and we each got to do our own. The
.45 is fairly easy and I feel very confident that I can load and shoot it now.
The M-14 is a little more complicated. I wish they had demonstrated
the .38 because that's what I want to buy but it's not an official US Army
weapon although a lot of guys have them here. That was about the best
class I've ever had in anything. They also showed us how to fire the M-60
machine gun and an M-70 grenade launcher. When we go to the range
next week we'll fire the .45, M-14, and M-60 and they will demonstrate
the grenade launcher. The guys said we learn faster than the men do. I
sure hope I can follow up on this at Ft Sam and maybe qualify in one of
them to get a sharpshooter badge. Ft Sam should be a big enough place
to have a rifle and gun club.

This would be a day to really get a sunburn if I wasn't stuck here. I'm
going to close for now. This is a pretty long letter.

Lots of love,
Susie

1400

15 Apr 69

Dear Ruby,

I guess I should have written yesterday but I just didn't. Georgie has been out sick for days so I still don't get off at all. Just 28 more days now and I figure 24 to come in here. That's really sounding good. A month from today I'll be in San Francisco.

We got hit again Monday night, that's why I said I should have written yesterday because I usually do the day after we're hit but I don't think you hear about it anyway till I tell you. This was only 10 rounds of 107mm rockets and none of them hit close around us. Some hit in an Ordinance Company over the hill from USARV and some at II Field Forces which is back behind the WAC DET. We were out on the patio watching the movie and they were changing the reels so it was quiet and the siren went off. It was only 2130 so we sure weren't expecting it. We all took off for our rooms to get our gear and then head back to the bunkers. We were in them about 40 minutes. Nothing else happened the rest of the night. Every time it happens now I hope it will be the last time I'm in the bunkers. Every time we get a new NCO in we get a trip to the bunker to initiate her. Otto is listed on one of the rosters in a bunker now and 1SG Herney makes sure he gets there.

Tomorrow we go out to fire. Major Warren brought his .45 in yesterday and I practiced taking it apart and putting it together all day. I'm real good now. It feels strange to be able to handle a real gun like that. I can even load the clips that go in it, 7 rounds in each one.

The females in Comptroller are having a party this afternoon. It's a combination birthday going away party and they're having it in Colonel

Metts' house. We all get off work to go at 1500 so I'm sure going. We would practically be forced to anyway.

Just 28 more days till I touch that "Green Green Grass of Home", home being San Francisco or anywhere in the states. I have DNCO next Tuesday night so that will get me a day off if I don't get one any other way. Then when I get back I'll only have 20 to go. At that point, I think I can just coast down the hill. I hope it's a steep hill.

Well I'm going to close now because it's time to go to lunch and I probably won't have time to finish this later so I'll mail it on my way out.

Lots of love,
Susie

18 April 1969

Dear Ruby,

This day last year I arrived at home after my cross country journey. I hope Mom gets her flowers all right today. I just had to do something for her birthday too although I don't plan to get either of you anything for Mothers Day, I'll be there soon after that.

We went out to the firing range yesterday afternoon. Believe it or not I managed to get the morning off since Georgie finally came back and at 1300 we left to go to the range. We wore our helmets and took our cameras. The first thing we did was pair off in twos to have a firer and assistant firer. Marni and I were together and she fired the M-14 first. They had us lie on the ground to fire. After the first 8 fired we went to see a demonstration on the M-79 grenade launder and to fire the M-60 machine gun. I love to fire that machine gun. The range on it is about 2 miles and it fires 100 rounds without a break if you want it to. That's sure quite a feeling to pull that trigger and watch the bullets fly. We were shooting at old tanks with it. After that we went back and I fired the M-14. I didn't do too bad and toward the end of the 38 rounds I felt like I was getting pretty good control. I hit the center of the target twice. I bet I'd be good if I had a chance. After that we fired the .45. Our ears were stopped up so bad we could hardly hear yesterday evening and they still aren't right today. The worst thing that happened to anybody was skinned elbows from the ground. Mine got very little because when I fired I had my sleeves rolled down and pieces of cardboard under my elbows. The ones without it got their elbows shoved into the ground from the kick of the rifle. The M-14 has a small kick but not much if it's held solid against the shoulder and jaw. Marni and Ski had skinned elbows. I have sore spots here and there but not much. It was really great and we all enjoyed it so much. I took a lot of pictures, I hope they are all right but I'm sure they will be. After we had finished firing we went back to the men's company and cleaned all the weapons. We got home at 1730. Then last night we had to clean up our rooms for a general to walk through today. We were sure tired last night. We had wieners and sauerkraut for supper.

After supper we started to play Parcheesi and at 2130 we heard what sounded to us like incoming rounds. We went out the door and listened and didn't hear any more so we went back in. A few minutes later the sirens went off and we hit the bunkers. One girl fell down the stairs and they had to get an ambulance to take her to the hospital. I guess she is one of the new ones because I don't know her. The last thing we heard last night was that she was on the x-ray table. Other than that there was nothing exciting. We sat in there about an hour and went back to our Parcheesi game. Today the report says we got 2 rounds (107mm rockets). This is getting ridiculous. Practically every other night we get hit with something. Mari and I use the walkie-talkies in the bunkers now. She's in a different one from me and we talk back and forth. 1SG Herney wants to get them for all the bunkers so nobody has to get out and walk around.

I guess I just had to catch one more cold before I left because I sure did. Everybody in the office has been coughing and sneezing and I couldn't resist it any longer. I wish this would make me immune to getting one when I get back to the states.

Boy I'm really getting short now, twenty six days and next week I go under 20. I think these last days are going to fly because I'm going to be doing last things that I want to do. Just packing my hold baggage will be a project by itself.

I have training tomorrow morning and I'm off this afternoon so I'm not doing too bad. I don't really want to leave the company because I have so many good friends here that I don't think I'll ever be able to replace. Here I know they like to be with me for me and not what I have. In the states my cars always attracted people and the Roadrunner will be worse than ever. Say, while I'm thinking about it, I got an answer from the NCOA about financing it. They had approved it temporarily pending credit investigation and it would be $145 for 24 months at 5%. The payments would be $66 per month. That sounds great to me and I intend to get it through them. They'll send me a check there to pay cash for the car and then I'll be paying off the loan. That would be great to have the car paid for. It looks like I can easily get it all done before I leave here and have the check waiting for me there. Then all I'll have to mess with is the insurance. I wonder if I could get it going while I'm here too. I'm hurrying because I have to catch my bus so I'll close now.

Lots of love,
Susie

20 April 1969

Dear Ruby,

I hope I can have time to write a good letter today. The last one I sent was rather rushed. Boy have I been getting mail lately—6 letters in 2 days. Everybody writes at once and then nobody for days. Ruthie is writing and sending packages to both Marni and me. Ruthie wants to come back.

In the morning here when it's cool I can imagine that it's like a spring morning at home even with the dry grass and brown leaves. I just can't wait to see everything clean and green again. You may think everything around there is dirty but I know I won't. A month from today I should have my Roadrunner. I want to pick it up on my first whole day at home. The way I plan it now is to stay at Oakland till Monday morning (19 May) and get home as soon as possible then. It sure won't take long if I can get the flights connected. I may be ready to leave before then but I think I'd better wait till the weekend is over. I don't want to get stuck someplace, that would be a lot worse than being in Oakland. Also, let me start telling you now that when I get my port call it will have a flight number and time on it. I'll tell you that time when I'm supposed to leave here and you can estimate the arrival in the US 15-22 hours later. You may never get it figured out since the time is so different between here and Travis and you but anyway, these flights are quite often delayed for as much as nine hours in Japan so you won't be able to expect a phone call from me till you get it. I might get a flight that goes through Hawaii but I may not. I'd like to land in Japan and Alaska but I don't want to be there long. Some of the flights get to Travis in 14 hours going back because of the tail wind. What a glorious feeling it will be to hear the engines on that freedom bird warm up and leave the ground at Bein Hoa.

Yes, I can send a pair of binoculars for Jim and Flossie. All I have to do is order them from PACEX and have them sent to their house. I should get a commission on all the pairs I sell for PACEX because almost everybody that uses mine wants some like them. I can't remember what the 10x50 means either.

I'm glad you think we're going to have to live out in the country while I'm there because I'm sure that's what I'll want to do. It's just going to be like coming back to a new world for me.

I got the address to Criterian. Mr. Sears got a bill from them and he gave me the address so I sent the card to them today asking for the price of my insurance. I'd like to get a little more coverage on this car than the other one but it will cost a lot more anyway being bigger and in the sports class. I'd like to pay cash if I can at all and not have that bill.

I will be home for Jim's graduation unless something would happen to get everybody stuck over here. You never know about that but it seems very unlikely now. Even though we're still getting hit now and then I don't think Charlie has enough troops down here to do much after us killing so many. I guess I hadn't told you that supposedly some VC cut an MPs throat at one of the gates to LBP and got on post Wednesday night I think. Anyway there were 7 on post and they burned some more of the jungle trying to find them. The last word was that they killed 5 but we never did hear what happened to the other two. They're probably sitting down in a tunnel in the "Monkey Jungle". Personally I can't see why in the world anybody would want to get on LBP, we all want to get off.

Well, I sure am under 30 today—24. You know a week from now I'll even be out of the 20's. It's really beginning to roll. Last night was the DEROS party for 8 of us, only 3 going to another post. The other 5 are getting out. I got my plaque and Vietnam Service Certificate. It's real pretty. Of course we had our champaign and I took some pictures. When I went up front to get my things, CPT J announced where I'm going and said she should give me a Roadrunner because that's roadrunner country. I don't think she knows about the car. I never thought the night would come when I'd be carrying champaign around giving everybody a drink. That's the tradition in the company. They all said they wouldn't catch my cold because the champaign would kill the germs. I believe it.

I don't really like champaign at all. It's just good for special occasions. We're going to have a bigger party for 1SG Herney next week.

I'm sending you the picture of me with the .45. The post behind me kind of ruined it but you can see me and the gun. You can see one of the maids in the background and the revetments. The building is the one I live in. This was taken on our patio.

I hope I explained the NCOA financing good enough the other time. I was in such a hurry I doubt if I did get through to you. Before I forget to tell you, the other night Cathy and I were listening to the short wave on her radio and we picked up Radio Peking and a woman was really going on about how great the communists are doing here in Vietnam and how the riots are getting so bad in the states and the Americans here can't go home to peace so of course they should go to North Vietnam or communist China. It was unbelievable that we were sitting there hearing a communist broadcast. I'd love to record it but it wasn't coming in that clear.

Well I'm going to close now and write to somebody else. I didn't get interrupted once during this and got everything covered. It won't be long now till we don't have to write at all for awhile.

Lots of love,
Susie

24 April 1969

Dear Ruby,

I guess I'll start typing you a letter. I got yours with the flowers in it today. They still smell a little and the pink ones look good. Our trees are beginning to leaf out again so maybe this time they will keep their leaves.

LTC L. came back from Hong Kong Tuesday and brought me my lenses. They cost $18 instead of $22. They fit perfectly so I'm sure they'll work. I won't know till I can take pictures and get them developed and I don't think I'd better take a chance on getting film back before I leave here. Sometimes it takes forever.

Nothing at all happened when I was on DNCO the other night. It was the most quiet night we've had for a long time. I told everybody it would be because it was my last night on duty. We have to make rounds of the clubs when we're on and we usually pick up some food. I was waiting for the food and who should walk up but Tom. He talked until my food was ready. He wants me to call him before I leave.

Every day at noon I'm lying out in the sun. I come home and get in my bathing suit as fast as I can and get outside. I can stay for about 35 minutes then go in and get back in my uniform. It's not the most pleasant noon hour in the world because I get too hot to have to put my fatigues back on but I'm determined to have a beautiful tan when I leave and I need sun everyday not just when I'm off. I've been doing pretty good getting off this week, 2 afternoons and 1 whole day. I'm going to take every minute I can get and that better be quite a few.

I'm glad Mom got her flowers all right. They sure travel fast. I don't know how I remember birthdays and everything else but I think of them and then write on my calendar to remind myself of them again.

I hope too you don't have cold weather when I'm home because I don't want to have to keep my tan covered up all the time. I got the package with the jacket and bras in it Tuesday. The other one never came yet. If it doesn't come before I leave I don't know what instructions to leave behind. I would tell the company to give it to my roommates and let them salvage what they could of the gum, etc., and send the other things back to me but by that time it probably wouldn't be in one piece. It sure makes me mad that I never got it yet. I especially hate it now that I know one thing that is in it. I have wanted an electric shaver for ages and was going to get one when I get back. I just have to find that darn package someway. Was it insured? I suppose it was.

I hate to tell you this but I don't know if I'm going to Fort Sam or not now. I still didn't have orders this week so we checked personnel and they have sent for a new assignment as an E-6. They never even asked me if I wanted to accept the E-5 assignment. They won't get anything back for 3 or 4 days but there is only a chance in a million that it will be the same. This one woman in my office that came here from the Pentagon a month ago is trying to get a call through to a LTC friend of hers there and we wrote him a letter so maybe she can get it for me. If not I could try to get it changed at Oakland, go to Fort Sam and ask them to change it or go to the Pentagon myself. I want to get it while I'm here so I don't have to use any of my leave trying to get it. AG wouldn't have changed it but somebody in personnel sent it back in. I know as big as 4th Army Headquarters is that they would almost have to have a place for me but DA might not think so. I may not get orders till a couple of days before I leave now so I sure can't ship my hold baggage. Even if my car wasn't ordered I wouldn't want to extend because I want out of here. I hope with all the people I have on my side I can get it straightened out.

The Roadrunner should be pretty well under construction now don't you think? A month from now I'll be behind the wheel. Boy is the time ever getting short—20 days today and when you get this about 16. That means not very many more letters to APO 96384. Heaven only knows where the next ones will be going, maybe Ft. Leonard Wood. Anyway, no matter where I get assigned, don't worry about the car or me extending, I won't.

We're having another DEROS party for 1SG Herney tonight. I bet our last week here is going to be full of parties. Bunnie said Doug (LTC Smith) will be up here from the Delta my last weekend and she thinks they should take me out. The party at Phu Loi on 4 May is getting pretty close. I'm still trying to go to Saigon. Major Cratty is going tomorrow so I'm going to see if I can. He said I could go as far as he's concerned but it depends on whether or not the driver can stay down there.

I'll start giving you your final warning now that you are all probably going to think I have shell shock or something when I first get home because I'm going to jump and do a lot of crazy things, at least they will look crazy there. Last night Nancy and I were playing Yahtzee and heard a siren. We both took off out the door and it was only on the movie. My natural instinct is to take off when I hear a siren and to look outside when I hear a noise. I don't know how long it will take to get over it so just be prepared. When I go looking for the bunker just ignore it. We all become very alert to any sound around us and the slightest noise makes us look to see what it is. I know now why those girls that came back from here when I was at Oakland jumped when a door slammed.

I'm going to quit for now. This is long and I don't think I really said much. What would you say if I brought a 4 legged friend home?

Lots of love,
Susie

27 April 1969

Dear Ruby,

I got your letter at noon today and needless to say I'm about to go out of my mind now. I can't believe that car got there so fast but I'm so happy that it is there and is perfect. How I wish you had a Polaroid camera so you could send me a picture of it. I bet it's a good looking car. It will be the best in Danville. Here I am sitting in Vietnam and I have that beautiful car sitting there just waiting to GO!! If you think you're thrilled over it wait till you see me. It still seems like a dream that in 2 ½ weeks I'm going to be back in "the world". It's such a short time and I think it's going to go fast. The only trouble is that I can't ship my hold baggage without orders and I don't foresee getting any for at least another week. Tiny, the civilian with the friend in DA, got her call through last night but of course the guy wasn't there so she talked to another LTC and told him the same thing and he seemed to agree to do what he could. I'm going to fight to the end for Fort Sam if I have to. My orders just might come for there and I wouldn't have to do anything but you'd better believe I'm not going to accept whatever they give me and let it go at that. How I envy you going to see that car. I bet you'll feel kind of funny knowing that it is mine and you will be riding in it but I'm still way over here.

I got another letter from the NCOA yesterday. The people I had credit with didn't have any record of my account—Mack Massey and SIC so NCOA wants a letter from my 1SG and CO as character references. 1SG Herney was going to Hong Kong today so I asked her about it last night and she wrote it and went to the orderly room and typed it herself. The CO doesn't get back from R&R till tomorrow then I'll get one from her and send them. I can't imagine those stupid places not having a record of my account when it's barely been a year but evidently they don't keep records long. Anyway, I should have this all straightened out soon. It seems like I get answers from NCOA so fast when I write to them. That insurance company may not be so cooperative. At least having the financing taken care of will help a whole lot. I know by the time you get this letter you will have seen my Roadrunner. I can't wait to hear your comments.

I can only figure out one way to get this money from the Bank of America to there. There is no way I can know exactly how much I have in there because it is not kept here—it is kept in San Francisco. These people don't even know the balance. My next statement probably won't come before I'm gone so the best thing I can think of is to either send you a check for most of it or I can write the check myself when I get home then wait till I get my next statement to write the final check. We have something like 60 or 90 days to get our money out of the country. I wouldn't leave much here. Next week is payday so I'll send you another couple of money orders then.

I know that the days our letters are in-transit really cut in on the countdown now. I guess the last letter you mail to me should be on Friday the 9th to make sure it gets here. That won't be very far away when you get this one. I won't hear from you for a long time but I'll keep writing at least as long as I'm working and you'll sure hear from me when I get to San Francisco.

Tiny has a sister in Lafayette, California which is right outside Oakland. I've been there several times and Tiny would like for me to either go see her sister or call her when I get there. This morning she gave me her address and phone number and we were talking about Oakland. It made me feel like I'm getting so close to going home. I really would like to see her. There's a girl (SP6) at Presidio who is there that I'd like to see if I can get her off post phone number before I leave or find her when I get there. I should have plenty to keep me busy for 3 days there. 1SG Herney got her port call for 15 May at 1115 hours. That means her flight should get into Travis on the afternoon of the 15th. I hope I get the same flight. I sure am beginning to feel like I've been away from home for a year. I don't know what I'm going to do when I get back. I'll be so happy there won't be any way to express it. I bet everybody that comes back from over here gives the appearance of being completely crazy to someone who doesn't know where the person has just come from. It's going to be so wonderful. I hope I can get you all as excited about me being back as I am.

I guess I haven't written to you since Thursday. I did go to Saigon with Major Cratty and Major Kennedy Friday morning. We went to the places where they wanted to stay then the driver and me took off to go downtown. He has been in-country since 5 April so he didn't know much about Saigon. I remembered enough to guide him to the general area where I wanted to go. I took a bunch of pictures and bought a bunch of bananas for Bunnie. I really saw Saigon for I guess the last time. I just thought, three weeks from that day I'd be in the states and Saigon would be history. It makes me so sleepy and tired to go down there and back. I don't know if it's the heat or riding or what but I'm always half asleep the rest of the day after I get back. I finally saw the John F. Kennedy Memorial. As far as I know, we'll still get to go to Phu Loi next Sunday so I should only have one more Sunday to work. Ruthie should be back at the end of next week if not before. Her port call was for 1 May if she didn't get it changed so she should get here on 3 May.

We haven't been in the bunkers anymore. Maybe the malaria is killing off all the VC. Oh, if it doesn't get there first, tell Aggie her bowl of fruit is on its way from Bangkok and that one cat and 2 elephants are hers and I want one cat out of it. Major Warren mailed them from Bangkok. The bowl of fruit cost $6. Did you get my speakers yet? I think you should have by now. Yesterday afternoon I was off and got some more sun. Boy I'm getting so dark. I don't look so extremely dark here with all these tanned people but I know I will there. After that I got back in uniform and Cathy and I went to the Long Binh PX and each carried a case of Coke back. We didn't think we'd ever make it. It's a long hot walk with a case of 24 cans of Coke.

I'm glad you sent the picture. The corsage must have been pretty. You look like you were startled and I think it must have been the flash bulb going off that made you look like that. I'll have to hand carry all my camera equipment back and I'm tempted to mail my binoculars. I've got to get started mailing this stuff soon. Well, I'm at the end of another page and I'm going to close. I hope you give me a full report on the Roadrunner.

Lots of love,
Susie

PS Today was Saturday last year and I left my "Junior" behind. It's a year since I've driven now.

30 April 1969

Dear Ruby,

I have quite a bit to say to you today so I'll start now about 30 minutes before time to go to lunch and finish this afternoon.

First of all I got my port call for 16 May, 1135 hours, flight T2B4 which is a TWA. This is a different day from 1SG Herney's and a day after my DEROS. It sure looks good to have that port call. I'm sending you a copy with other various things. I may have to use two envelopes.

Next, I got my package that has been on the road 40 days today. I couldn't believe it. When I picked it up at the PO it looked in perfect shape and there is no evidence that it has gone to other units so maybe the APO wasn't the reason for the delay. I opened it expecting to find everything in a mess and you would never believe how perfect it all is. You can't tell that it wasn't mailed last week. The cookies are all whole and none of the candy melted except the rabbit sunk in the middle. You really did a beautiful job of packing it, that's why it's so perfect now. Those cookies sure are good and if they are stale we don't know it. I'm going to leave part of them in the office and take the rest home. I eat more of them here in the daytime. I opened the shaver here and it is just exactly what I have wanted. I can't wait to try it now. Thanks so much for all of this, you really went all out. It's all so good because it's homemade and packed with tender loving care. I guess the box sure was too big for airmail. I think I'll keep the dog bone till 1SG Herney gets back and she can watch Otto chew it. I might give it to him when he's in my room some night, she would enjoy that. He's a little devil. When he smells us cooking something he's there right away and when it's gone so is he. The cats are in and out all the time.

Well I went through my last pay line this morning so as soon as I get my certificate from the orderly room, I'll go over and get the money orders for you. It's wonderful to know I only have half a month left. I'm sure going to hate to leave some of the girls here. The new NCOs that are coming in are all nice and I like a lot of them real well. We have a good group of career girls here. I hope I find the same thing somewhere else. Ruthie should be back any day now.

I'm so glad you saw my Roadrunner. I bet it's so beautiful and I'm in love with it already without ever seeing one. Did they honk the horn or what? I like the article about it especially that the air grabbers are called "coyote dusters". That car was just made for me. I bet I'll love looking under the hood. Oh, I'm going to have so much fun and it will have a lot of little things the Ramblers never had. I figured the seats would have a head rest because I think most new cars do now. I wish I could have asked you to look at the wheel covers. I hope they're real sporty too but I suppose they would be. I sure wanted the wide track tires. I have a feeling I'll think it will take off right out from under me the first time I drive it and I may not be far wrong.

If only you could know how it is to sit here today and know that 3 weeks from this day I'll be there with you driving that car. It's just impossible to describe the feeling no matter how much I try. Maybe you can get something from these two stories I'm sending. They aren't' real good and have too many personal things to be read by many people but they are just something I have written while sitting here. When I go to get my car I will most definitely go in uniform and I hope they do treat me like a VIP. As you know, I very much enjoy being the center of attention when I'm in uniform.

I don't have any word about my assignment yet. I almost wish I could go back to Oakland unassigned since I want to stay there awhile anyway. That way I should be able to get what I want. I'm not too worried about it. I'm too short to worry about anything now. Boy, two weeks from today or tomorrow, I'll be flying out of here. Have you heard the commercial "Up Up and Away with TWA"? That's for me now. I heard that in California before I left. At noon today I had the radio on and they played "San Francisco" and "I Left My Heart in San Francisco". Also this morning they played "Coming Home Soldier".

If you get anything there from San Antonio (NCOA) before I come home, open it and read it. They might start sending things to me there.

I should get the COs letter tonight and I can mail both letters to them tomorrow.

We are still all planning on going to Phu Loi Sunday. That will be great to stay off post a whole day. I hope most of the girls can get off for it. We all need a break now and then, a lot more often than they come. Write a lot of letters between now and 9 May so I don't feel like I lose contact with you for long. When you get this that date will be close.

Well I'm going to close for now. It's 1430 and everybody else in the office is in a meeting so I've had a nice peaceful time typing this.

Lots of love,
Susie

PS Bunnie got a green $5 from somebody and I bought it so now I have real money in my pocket. It sure is pretty.

CHAPTER XIV

MAY 1969

3 May 1969

Dear Ruby,

I have to get this letter in the mail to you as fast as I can. I got my orders at noon today, as you can see for BAMC. It's the same thing I had before except as a SSG. Boy talk about luck, just how much can you have? I couldn't believe my eyes. Once seemed a miracle but 2 assignments in a row to the same place is 10 times more of a miracle. I had myself convinced last night that Ft. McClellan wouldn't be too bad because I sure thought and so did everybody else that I would end up there. Now I can ship everything as soon as I finish packing. I started yesterday but didn't get all of it in the boxes. I don't know where to ship it to now that time is so short. I'm going to see if I can split it between home and Ft. Sam.

Ruthie got back this morning too. She's so happy to be back. The closer I get to leaving the more I realize just how much I am going to miss this place. Ruthie said she thought about us all the time she was home and I know I'll think about them for a long time too. This is so different from any other assignment. Eleven more days now—7 more to work. These orders I have don't allow a 30 day leave as you can see by the EDCSA to Ft Sam of 19 May so I'll have to have them amended. Usually they put the 30 days on the orders whether or not you ask for it but not this time.

The last time I wrote I hadn't tasted much of the cookies and candy from this box but I have now and they are all delicious. I'll never know how they could last so good but they sure did. I especially like the dropped cookies with the gum drops or whatever it is in them. The divinity is so soft and good too. I love the shaver. I have tried it out and it's just what I wanted and so convenient and easy to use.

I really feel like I'm coming home now with my orders and getting my stuff ready to ship. I sure feel a lot different now that I did on 3 May 1968. Everything was so new and I didn't know if I wanted to stay here or not. It's strange how a place gets to be "home" no matter what or where it is. I didn't get the money orders for you yet because there was such a long line in the bank I didn't want to wait through it.

For once the PX got in a big film supply so I'm all ready to go to Phu Loi tomorrow. About 40 of us have signed up to go. Marni has to work so she can't go. Ruthie will I suppose. I know Cathy will go. I wish I could bring my friends home with me. Cathy and I were talking about always leaving people behind as long as we're in the Army and we both agreed if we weren't in the Army we would never meet anybody worth not wanting to leave anyway.

I hope there's nothing else I wanted to tell you because I can't think of it now. I won't be thinking very straight the rest of my time here so don't expect it. I'm going to close for now.

Lots of love,
Susie

5 May 1969

Dear Ruby,

It's 1710 and I'm going to use this last hour to type a letter to you. I don't think I'm writing as much as I used to but I'm always preoccupied somehow. Of course I never write at home and I have been pretty busy at work. The last few days I'm here I won't be working (3 days) so I don't know if I'll write or not. I'm beginning to feel real good now I guess just the knowledge that I'm coming home does it. I'm not so tired anymore and we never go to bed at a decent hour, usually 1130 or later). I want to have every last minute I can with my roommates and Cathy. It's such a waste to sleep.

I got a letter from you today that was mailed 16 April. It's history now. I'm glad to know I got the package from Spencer gifts. Open it if you want to, you'll like it too. You can bet I'll want plenty of soup beans and onions. They sound good anytime and after a year they really will be good. I don't really eat much around here and the shorter I get the less I care about eating. I'm getting pretty nervous like everybody else does about a week before they leave. I guess it's just a combination of everything together. I'm sure once I'm gone from here I'll settle down. I feel like I have so much excess energy now and want to be on the move all the time. I've never felt like this since I left the states so I know it's because I'm excited.

I am getting a good tan. The party at Phu Loi yesterday was a lot of fun. Can you imagine me in a bathing suit with men all around? I just thought when I was sitting at that pool yesterday that a few years ago I wouldn't even wear short shorts and look at me now. Cathy and I were together most of the time. Ruthie went but she was in the pool more than us. The chopper ride was great as always but only 15 minutes and

389

that's too short. I'm sure going to miss them. Phu Loi is a nice place. The only excitement we had was at 1200 when their noon siren blew and we all just looked at each other like we were saying "What do we do now"? but the guys said it was the noon siren. In the afternoon some guy from another company walked by and threw a gas grenade over the fence. Everybody thought it was just a smoke grenade till the ones closest started running away. We all got out the two gates of the compound and walked around to get rid of it. I just got about one breath of it so it didn't bother me much but some of them really got a dose. We all said it's a good thing we were military so we knew what to do. We've had extra CBR training now in practical use. It sure makes everybody feel good to get off post for a day like that.

I'd just as soon sleep in the room where I always do because it's more like my room with all my junk on the walls (I guess it still is). I don't care what kind of bed I've got after sleeping on the ground, sidewalk, in chairs and bunkers. I'll just have to keep busy enough to be tired. I do intend to take the four footed friend with me but not immediately. His name is Murphy and he's a cat who was born in the WAC DET sometime in January. He's white with gray tiger and so sweet and loveable. He has a sister named Joanne but I couldn't take both of them. A major was supposed to take them but she hasn't yet and it looks doubtful if she will. I guess if she would say she still wanted them I wouldn't try to keep him but otherwise I want him. Of course I'll have to pay to ship him home but it won't cost too much since he's small. I'd like to have something live from this place with me. I'm sure you'd love him too. If I do bring him, I'll probably ship him a day or two before I come. He would come into the airport in a wire cage and you would be called to come and pick him up. My advice would be to leave him in the cage for awhile at least till you see how he reacts to strangers. Right now he's very friendly and calm but after 10,000 jet miles he might not be. He has been eating tuna and shrimp and horse meat dog food so I don't know if he would eat cat food or not. He's not very choosy about what he eats or when. He would have all his shots and a medical certificate. He is completely house trained, all he needs is a box of dirt or newspapers and he will use it once you put him in it so he knows where it is. I have talked to SFC Gold about it but I didn't want to say for sure that I wanted him till I got some kind of a comment from you. I couldn't take him in the car with me to San Antonio I don't think because I have to find a home first but I would want him then and in the meantime I'm sure we could work out something. You presumed I meant a cat or dog. Cathy said to tell you it's a horse I made friends with.

1SG Herney couldn't get my port call changed so I'll be leaving here at 1125 hours, 16 May (Friday) on flight T2B4, TWA through Hawaii. We all refer to the flight by its military name—Tango 2, Bravo 4. I should get into Travis at about 1300 the same day. I wouldn't mind being delayed in Hawaii for awhile. I wouldn't be charged leave. I'm going to try to sign in at Oakland, supposedly to get uniforms and maybe I can save a day or two of leave that way. I don't have to have my orders changed, the leave is automatic. I report to Fort Sam a month after I leave here or Oakland whichever is applicable.

I got a nice letter from Vic. He sounds anxious to see me when I get to Ft. Sam but to tell the truth I'm not sure I want to see him. I want to go there but not because he's there. A year in Vietnam sure does strange things to a person.

Well, I've gone on long enough for now. When you get this, you'll be just about mailing your last letter to me. Two weeks from today will be my first day at home.

Lots of love,
Susie

Tell Aggie thanks for the flag.

6 May 1969

Dear Ruby,

I'm sitting here daydreaming so I guess I'll write to you. I'm sure you would be happy to get an extra letter. I'll bet never again in my life will I write as much as I have this year unless I get in another combat zone someday.

I'm off this afternoon so I have to finish packing and throwing out junk. I've got to get organized while I'm still working so I won't have to do anything but clear post those last 3 days. I just can't believe that 2 weeks from today I'll have my Roadrunner. Also now I can say I leave next week. I can't wait to come home but I sure wish I could bring a few people with me. Cathy says she wants to come back in my duffle bag. I told her I could take her home in it and drive her to Ft. Monroe, Virginia where she wants to go. It's too bad that wouldn't work. She's only been here two months.

The violets you sent are so pretty pressed against that cardboard. They look almost like a picture. Marni says they don't have them in northern Illinois.

In your comments about the car you didn't say you rode in it, just about the seats, under the hood and the horn. If you did say you rode in it I sure can't find it. I should hear about my loan from NCOA next week. I'm sure I'll get it now. I used to use my name plain on everything but I don't anymore. SSG looks so good in front of it.

I don't know what I'll be doing in Oakland and San Francisco. Barb doesn't write much anymore and I guess it's because she has a boyfriend. Marty Contreras, a SP6 who was here is at Presidio now and lives off post so I'd like to look her up and I have to see Tiny's sister too. Since I'll only be there 2 days I won't get tired of it. I wish I could get to ORD in time for that 0900 flight Monday morning.

Boy these people around here keep telling me to extend and they sure don't make it any easier to leave. Of course most of them know I have a car waiting for me. It's a good thing I do too.

I'm going home now so I'll close.

Lots of love,
Susie

9 May 1969

Dear Ruby,

I'm finally back at work so I'll write to you. I've had a pretty good week, not in the office much. I was off Tuesday afternoon then Wednesday Major Warren took me to Saigon and did we ever have a time. He picked up a major friend of his down there and we toured the city. While Major Warren was with this other guy at his office I shopped up and down the street by the USO and stayed in there part of the time. All I bought the whole time was a few roses and a couple of little things, a Buddah and another stone. I felt right at home down there this time. A few more trips and I'd really know my way around, too bad there won't be any more. Well, there might be one more too but only to ship Murphy. That major was supposed to take him yesterday but didn't. Anyway the two majors and I walked all over the place and on Tu Do Street which is the most famous street in Saigon because of the bars. I had always wanted to see how the girls in those bars act so we went in and I got my first taste of Vietnamese beer (Ba-Mi-Ba) and watched the girls. It's really something. I'm so glad I got to do that because I have that much more to remember and tell people. We came back at 1600 so it was really a day.

Yesterday I was off all day shipping my hold baggage. I finally got it all packed and carried down to the supply room and the supply sergeant went through it and was going to ship it this morning. Everything is going to Ft. Sam if I didn't already tell you. I sure wanted to have my tape recorder at home but there was no way I could. I'm going to be mailing a lot of stuff now. I'm also going to leave a lot of junk behind. I guess my room-mates will have fun.

I should be off tomorrow afternoon because Bunnie and Doug are supposed to take me to the Chinese Restaurant for lunch and then to her trailer for a drink. Tomorrow night is the 27th WAC Anniversary party. I'll have to work Sunday and Monday I guess then I'm through with this office. I want out of here but I would like to have this whole last week just to be at home and have my friends there too. We should have some pretty good farewell parties next week. We want to stay up all night one time before I'm gone but I don't know if we'll get it done or not because the other 3 have to work all the time. Marni has DNCO the night I have to report to the 90th. Last year when I left OAB Barb was on CQ. If Murphy is still in the company next week he is going to be mine major or no major. She must not want him very bad because she hasn't taken him for weeks. I might get him shipped a few days before I leave or I may not at all but if you get a call from the airport to pick up something, go get him.

Well at the very most, I only have 3 more days to sit in this office. This typewriter needs a new ribbon but I doubt very much if it's going to get one. I can't believe that this time one week from today I'll be at Bein Hoa and almost getting on the plane. I want to go yet I don't. It's really a weird feeling. I'm so afraid I'll miss something by leaving. I know you think I'm crazy. I can't ask you any questions now because you can't answer them anyway. When you get this letter I'll have 2 or 3 days left. Where did this year go? It probably didn't go so fast for you and I know you aren't afraid of my missing anything by leaving.

I'm going to close at the end of this page. The time is so short-get ready for some excitement in your life!

Lots of love,
Susie

11 May 1969

Dear Ruby,

I think I'm going to have loads of time so I'll start writing a letter to you. It's 0745 Sunday morning, the last Sunday morning I'll spend in this office. I'm going to try not to stay all day tomorrow and then I'm through except to come back for my award and to get my efficiency rating on my clearance papers.

The way it looks now you should be honored with the presence of 1 Vietnamese cat sometime at the end of the week. SFC Gold said last night she wasn't going to fool with the major anymore and that I can take him. She tried to talk me into taking both, even said she would pay for one but I knew I wouldn't dare bring in two. I'd like to send him out Wednesday which should get him to Danville sometime Thursday your time but I may have the chance before. I'll sure be worried about him till I can call you and find out if he got there all right. I get all of his medical papers here but I have to get his customs papers in Saigon.

My baggage is on its way to Ft. Sam now. I have some boxes of stuff to mail and I have to get my tapes and slides in a box. I sure can't write many more letters and put "Free" on the envelope.

We've been staying up later all the time. Bunnie and Doug did take me to the restaurant yesterday and we had a nice time. He gave me a 9th Infantry Division crest. I went home at 1500 and slept for 2 ½ hours to get revived for last night. I went to bed at 0030. One of two real late nights are OK but with several in a row I can't keep my eyes open at work. Only one more morning to get up and then I don't have to worry about when I go to bed.

There is talk that there is going to be a new company policy of no fraternization between NCOs and lower graders. Tuesday the others are all having a meeting so if that's true, it will probably go into effect Wednesday. I sure hope it's not true because I want to be with Cathy my last few days and she has enjoyed being in our room. I don't know how they could separate us here but I guess they could. I hope it's just a rumor.

I'm so short now I don't even have to think about time passing-it is. I hope it's going as fast for you. I got a letter from Barb and she's still going with her guy and still has plans for all the things we can do. I can't wait to get there and call you. My calendar sure looks nice; all I have left to color is Illinois. I never thought I'd get that far.

Well, I'm going to quit for now till I have your letter with me to answer.

0915 Monday 12 May

I got off yesterday afternoon and needless to say I didn't write anymore. I got some more sun and just messed around. Marni decided we should go to the club since she didn't have school so the four of us did. We had a great time. I wish we had been doing that before. We were all feeling pretty good when we got home and we continued there. We sat on the steps below 1SG Herney's room most of the time and she had a drink with us. Cathy and I had gone to bed around 2400. At 0100 I was dead to the world and Ruthie woke me up yelling "incoming!" I didn't even hear the rounds and she scared me half to death. I hadn't heard them so I had no idea where they had hit. We stayed in the bunkers till 0315 and then went back to bed. It was so hot and stuffy in the bunker, much worse than usual. It started raining about ½ hour before we got out. Then we waded through mud back to our rooms. This morning's report says it was 12-15 107mm rockets and they hit in scattered areas—one killed, 16 wounded. I thought with everything together I'd feel terrible this morning but I don't at all. I guess I'm going to get my ARCOM (Army Commendation Medal) this afternoon and then I'll be through here except to get my clearance papers signed. I just can't believe this is really happening to me yet. I took my tape recorder out and recorded the band this morning, my last chance.

I'm sure glad the WAC record got there. Those slides sure got there fast and I still have some on the way here that should have come back long ago.

I have plenty of Vietnamese money both coin and paper for souvenirs. Their 20 dong pieces are real pretty.

Whatever letters I write after this you probably won't get till after I'm in the states. Just remember and especially now that action is increasing, I might not get out of here on schedule so don't worry. Just wait for the phone call to tell you I'm there.

I really want to come home but the closer it gets the more I wish I was coming back here. I hope my feelings change after I get home because I have everything there that I wanted and I have to be willing to give up this life.

I can't say for sure that I'll write again because I won't be at the office. If I don't this is the end of our trans-world correspondence. I'll be there soon and your dull routine life will be no longer.

I love you,
Susie

Long Binh, RVN

14 May 1969

Dear Ruby,

I know by the time this gets to you I'll be in the states and possibly home but I'll write it anyway and send this check. I've been busy yesterday and today processing and mailing things. All I have left to clear is the orderly room and personnel.

I got my ARCOM Monday and it was a real nice ceremony with all my favorite people there. Major Warren presented my plaque in our office later. I'm going back this afternoon to take some pictures and say good-bye because I may not have time tomorrow. I'm having quite a time getting Murphy out of this country but I hope when you read this you are looking at him.

1SG Herney leaves tomorrow morning and the next day it's my turn.

Well, that's all from your girl in Vietnam.

Lots of love,
Susie

CHAPTER XV

Returning Home

So ends the "Vietnam Letters". My flight back landed in Hawaii where we deplaned and walked around the airport before boarding for the final leg into Travis Air Force Base California. There are no words to describe how it felt to land on US soil again. I was at Oakland Army Base for a few days while I was issued new uniforms and such. I saw my friends who were still there and just enjoyed being back in the states. I flew from San Francisco to Chicago on a small commuter plane to my home town, Danville, IL. I remember that at O'Hare in Chicago we were taken out to the tiny plane on a bus. As we were taking off a huge jet was landing and I had the thought that I survived a year in Vietnam, I didn't want to be run over at O'Hare Airport. My mother met me at the Danville airport. I was so very, very happy to be home and I'm sure she was just as happy to see me. I had a 30 day leave to look forward to and my new Roadrunner. It was everything I hoped it would be. My mother and I went to the dealership in Danville and I remember my first drive in it. "Eddie", the salesman who had ordered it went with us for a few miles out of town. While I was on leave my mother and I attended Memorial Day services at Eugene, IN where I had always wanted to go in uniform. The grass was green and flowers were in bloom just as I had thought about for so long during the year. I had a wonderful 30 days then reported to Fort Sam Houston, Texas where I spent 2 years as a platoon sergeant in the WAC Company. I volunteered to go to Fort McClellan, Alabama to be a platoon sergeant with basic trainees and spent 3 years in that assignment. My career went on and I was assigned to many more posts stateside and in Germany. My dream of being a platoon sergeant and first sergeant both came true. I served 24 wonderful years and retired in December 1988 as a First Sergeant.

The cat, Murphy, made it back just fine and lived to be 18 years old. He spent a large part of that time with my mother since I wasn't always living where I could have a pet. His sister, Joanne also came back to the states as did most of the pets we had in the WAC Company.

For most of my career I didn't think much about being a Vietnam Veteran. I never received any of the negative comments or treatment that many speak of but I just went on with my career. I was proud of the ribbons on my uniform and felt very "special" as I expected to for having served in a combat zone. I have always been proud of my service and would gladly do it all again.

THE LAST DAYS

The last few days a person spends in Vietnam are filled with many conflicting feelings and thoughts. As I write this my days left here are few and I'm going to try to express some of my thoughts.

First and most of all there is the great anticipation of going home which grows with every day. The sound or sight of a Freedom Bird is exciting in itself now because I know before long I'll be up in the sky in that jet on my way to "the world". The glory of my homecoming will be when I step off the plane at Vermilion County Airport in Danville. I'll be so proud and happy; proud of my decorated uniform and happy to be back home. I have so much waiting for me there.

Second, there are thoughts of what will be left behind. Life in Vietnam is anything but dull and after living this life for a year, it must be taken into consideration that stateside life may be a little boring after awhile. Most of all, I'll be leaving behind many friends. Leaving them in Vietnam is a little different from leaving stateside posts. You just don't walk away from anybody in a combat zone and forget the danger that is constantly around them.

The life we lead here is very informal and casual and it will take some time to adjust back to a normal society. One of the biggest adjustments will be getting used to the fact that sirens don't mean "incoming rounds" and a loud noise is not going to mean to go to the bunker. I'll have to remember also when I go in a store the clerks do speak English and I can ask for something using whole sentences. I will miss seeing the many bugs holding their morning formation in my dresser drawers and the ants carrying some unfortunate bug out the door. There will be no more midnight conferences standing or sitting beside the revetments and watching the flares and tracers. All these things have made my life here in Vietnam for a year and they won't be soon or easily forgotten. My 365 days have gone by fast. It seems almost impossible that I will be going home so soon. At times and in many ways this has been a disgusting and difficult year but it has also had many good points. It has made me appreciate my home and my heritage as never before. It has advanced my career and shown me that I can live and work through tense and trying situations. I have had experiences and gained knowledge that could come only from life in a combat zone.

As I prepare to depart Vietnam I can honestly say that I have never regretted volunteering to come here. It is 365 long days of hard work and trying situations but to me it is worth every minute of it. I leave with a feeling of accomplishment and satisfaction knowing I have been here and put forth my effort toward peace.

Written By:

SSG Linda S. Earls
Long Binh Vietnam
APO San Francisco 96384
29 April 1969

Military Terms and Abbreviations

AFVN	Armed Forces Vietnam (Radio)
APO	Army Post Office
ARVN	Army of the Republic of Vietnam
CBR	Chemical, Biological, Radiological
Charlie	Vietcong
CID	Criminal Investigative Department
CO	Commanding Officer
CQ	Charge of Quarters
DEROS	Date Estimated Return from Overseas
DET	Detachment
DF	Disposition Form
DNCO	Duty Non-commissioned Officer
ETS	End Term of Service
LN	Local National
MACV	Military Assistance Command Vietnam
MARS	Short Wave Telephone Service
MPC	Military Payment Certificate
NCOIC	Non-commissioned Officer in Charge
OAB	Oakland Army Base
PACEX	Pacific Exchange
PAL	Parcel Airlift
Piasters	Vietnamese Money
PX	Post Exchange
R&R	Rest and Recuperation
RMS	Recruiting Main Station
RVN	Republic of Vietnam
SAM	Space Available Mail
SP	Trps Special Troops
TSN	Tan Son Nhut (Air Base)
USARV	United States Army Vietnam
VC	Vietcong
VN	Vietnam
WAC	Women's Army Corps

US Army Rank Chart (1960's)

<u>Enlisted Rank</u>
Private
Private First Class
Specialist Four
Specialist Five
Staff Sergeant
Sergeant First Class
Master Sergeant
First Sergeant
Sergeant Major

<u>Officer Rank</u>
2nd Lieutenant
1st Lieutenant
Captain
Major
Lieutenant Colonel
Colonel
Brigadier General
Major General
Lieutenant General
General

MILITARY TIME

0100	1:00 AM
0200	2:00 AM
0300	3:00 AM
0400	4:00 AM
0500	5:00 AM
0600	6:00 AM
0700	7:00 AM
0800	8:00 AM
0900	9:00 AM
1000	10:00 AM
1100	11:00 AM
1200	12:00 Noon
1300	1:00 PM
1400	2:00 PM
1500	3:00 PM
1600	4:00 PM
1700	5:00 PM
1800	6:00 PM
1900	7:00 PM
2000	8:00 PM
2100	9:00 PM
2200	10:00 PM
2300	11:00 PM
2400	12:00 Midnight